WASHINGTON AREA
PRIVATE SCHOOLS

A complete guide to independent schools in and
around Washington, D.C. including a directory of
local Educational Specialists and Counselors.

INDEPENDENT SCHOOL GUIDES   CHEVY CHASE, MARYLAND

All rights reserved.

Copyright c   1971, 1973, 1977, 1980, 1983, 1987, 1989, 1991, 1993, 1995

Lois H. Coerper   Shirley W. Mersereau

Additional copies may be obtained @ $14.95 (add $2.00 for mailing) from
Independent School Guides
7315 Brookville Road
Chevy Chase, Maryland 20815

(301) 986-5370
or
652-8635, 986-0698

Published in the United States of America

FOREWORD

With the growing pressures for quality education, independent schools in the Washington area have become of vital interest to an increasing number of parents. Prior to the publication of our first edition of The Independent School Guide in 1971, there was no single source of information about the more than 300 elementary and secondary schools in the area. We were encouraged in this project by several school administrators and secured the cooperation and approval of the Association of Independent Schools of Greater Washington . Now in our tenth printing, we are even more aware of the variety of school choices available to parents at all levels of education.

This guide sets forth a concise, factual and comprehensive listing of non-public schools serving the normal child in grades 1 through 12. It does not include pre-schools with no primary grades nor schools with curriculum directed exclusively towards children with severe handicaps: for assistance in this area contact IPACHI:

    Information, Protection & Advocacy Center for Handicapped Individuals
    300 I street N. E. #202, Washington, D. C. 20007;   phone (202)-547-8081.

In addition to a variety of religious affiliated schools, this Guide also includes some Catholic Parochial elementary schools which generally welcome non-parish and non-Catholic students; a more complete list of these schools is available from the local Catholic Dioceses Offices (see following page).

The Independent School Guide includes as much information on the student body, faculty, and special programs offered by the various schools as it was possible to secure from interviews, brochures, and our own questionnaire. The facts reported are, of course, subject to yearly change although provision was made for schools to announce planned changes in plant or programs. Also included is useful information on summer programs (recreational and academic), as well as Day Care (Extended Day).

We are most grateful for the enthusiastic support of the school community, including teachers, administrators, and counselors; we also would like to express a special thank you to The Association of Independent Schools of Greater Washington for their continuing cooperation. We hope that this directory will continue to be a valuable aid to them as well as to parents seeking the best placement for their individual child.

For those parents who are seeking professional advice and counseling, a brief description of some Washington area Educational Specialists can be found immediately following the last school in the back of this book.

Lois H. Coerper

Shirley W. Mersereau

ABBREVIATIONS

ACE...............................Accelerated Christian Education Program
AP.................................Advanced Placement
ESL...............................English as a Second Language
K...................................Kindergarten
N...................................Nursery
PG.................................Post Graduate
Req................................Required
SAT...............................Scholastic Aptitude Test
SSAT.............................Secondary School Admission Test
LD/ED...........................Learning Disability/Emotionally Disturbed

Information and Resources

Association of Independent Schools of Greater Washington (AISGW): Executive Director, Ritalou Harris, P.O. Box 9956, Washington, D. C. 20016; (202) 537-1114

Association of Independent Schools of Maryland (AIMS): Box 813, Millersville, MD 21108 (includes Washington Schools)   (410) 987-7182

Catholic Archdiocese Office of Education for D.C. and Maryland: 5001 Eastern Avenue, Hyattsville, MD.; P.O. Box 29260, Washington, D.C. 20017. (301-853-3800).   Diocese Office of Education for Northern Virginia: (703-841-2519)

Council for American Private Education (CAPE): 1726 M Street, N.W., Suite 703, Washington, D.C. 20036 Director: Joyce G. McCray   (202) 659-0016

Montessori Institute: 2119 S Street, N.W., Washington, D.C. 20008 (202)-387-8020.

National Association of Independent Schools (NAIS): 1620 L Street, N.W., Washington, D.C. 20036. (202)973-9700.   Boarding Schools and Summer Program Directories: 1-800-541-5908

National Association of Private Non-traditional Schools and Colleges: 182 Thompson Road, Grand Junction, CO 81503   (303) 243-5441

National Coalition of Alternative Community Schools: RD 1, Box 378, Glenmoore, PA 19343 (610)-458-5138

Washington Small Schools, 4894 16th Street N.W., Washington, D. C. 20011; Ron McClain (202)-762-0740.

Washington Independent Services for Educational Resources (WISER): 1140 Rockville Pike, Rockville, MD 20852 (301) 816-0432

WHY SHOULD I CONSIDER AN INDEPENDENT SCHOOL ?

Far more than public schools, *private schools are designed to meet the individual needs of each student.* Smaller classes and personal attention assure a better learning enviornment and greater academic and social growth. Close student/teacher relationships are developed not only in the classroom but also on the playing fields, on the stage, and in a variety of extra-curricular settings.

These schools emphasize values, self-confidence and responsible citizenship; foundations for critical thinking and future achievement. Studies have shown that independent school students are far more likely to participate in varsity and intramural sports, and generally assume an active role in the school community.

Due to the private school selection process, teachers are relieved from the burden of unruly, disruptive students and are thus free to devote their energy to communicating knowledge and ideas. *Individual academic problems and potentials are more easily identified and addressed* as all students are helped and encouraged to work to their highest potential. Likewise, guidance counselors have time to spend with each student so that their course selection and college applications are carefully reviewed.

Private schools also allow parents to make clear choices about the basic direction of their child's education. Therefore, be sure to determine what's important : Is a specific religious emphasis desired? Do you seek greater opportunities in art, music, theater, dance or want a particular second language? Does your child need the expertise of trained LD/ED teachers? Will you and your child be happier in a completely free atmosphere or is a more highly structured, firmly disciplined daily routine, more compatible with your home life-style?

You do have a choice! Examine a school's philosophy and objectives to understand what is expected not only of each student but of each parent. Today, *the single largest financial commitment you may ever make will be to the education of your children.* Make the choice carefully and analyze at which level in school the expenditure will be the most valuable. Many educators believe that the excitement for learning and the development of good study habits must happen in elementary and secondary school if students are to achieve at the college level and in later life.

THINGS TO CONSIDER WHEN LOOKING FOR A SCHOOL FOR YOUR CHILD

First, *Know your child*: If he/she is presently enrolled in school, is it a happy and challenging situation? Are his work habits good ? Are her extra-curricular activities and friends constructive and satisfying? Confer with the teacher to determine if your child is progressing at an appropriate rate. For the younger child, an excellent analysis of school readiness is contained in the Pre-school and Day Care Guidebook for the Washington Area, by Merry Cavanaugh.

Second, *Decide on your basic requirements*: i.e., religious, single-sex, boarding, special programs, extended day-care, etc. Then, with the aid of our geographically keyed index, identify some appropriate schools. Request catalogues and other pertinent information from the schools, and determine then which philosophy and program seems to meet your needs.

Plan to visit several schools and talk to the admission directors. Each school is a unique community: to find the right match between your child and a school is not an easy task but is the most important goal in the admission process.

If you feel in need of additional advice, some one who can realistically evaluate your child's potential and give an objective opinion, there are many Educational Counselors trained to do this very thing. These Counselors will also have broad knowledge of the local school market and be able to guide you towards an appropriate school choice as well as identify ways of obtaining financial assistance should that be needed. (Several of these counselors are listed in the back of this book under Educational Specialists).

Perhaps you have other concerns......................

Will your child be insulated from the "real" world ?

Today's private schools are committed to diversity as well as the community. Indeed, many private schools have a much broader ethnic, cultural, and international mix than the "neighborhood" public school; also, each student in the independent school is valued as an individual for his or her unique contribution to the group. Through school community service programs and other involvement the students are made aware of the needs of others not only on the local level but nationally and internationally as well.

How do Independent Schools assist working parents?

Most schools today offer Extended-Day or After-School programs to allow parents flexibility with their work schedules.(This information is carried in the Index of The Independent School Guide). Some schools offer transportation or help with arranging car pools. Conference and meeting times are individually set to give parents the opportunity to be involved with their child's education. Many of the schools offer summer programs designed specifically to cover the same hours as the school year.

What is involved in the actual application process?

Call or write the schools you wish to know more about and ask for their literature to be sent to you. Arrange to visit the school and meet with the admissions director. At that time review with the director the admissions procedure, ask questions about financial arrangements and school programs. Quite often the school policy will require: (1) an interview with your child; (2) a transcript of grades (3) some standardized testing (4) personal and/or teacher recommendations. If you are applying to more than one school, inquire about the testing procedure because many of the local independent schools have agreed to share the test results to keep the child from having to take the same intelligence, aptitude, and achievement tests more than once.

Application dates vary from school to school, but generally application is made between September and January for the following fall; acceptances are usually made in mid- March/April. However, many schools have "rolling admission" which means a child may apply and be accepted at any time during the year, space permitting.

What if you need Financial Aid?

Most independent schools seek a broad economic and ethnic student body today and have established ways of providing tuition assistance. Some schools have funds specifically designed for scholarships; they may be need-based or awarded to students with outstanding talents and accomplishments. Many religious affiliated schools offer reduced tuition for parish or denomination members. Some schools allow discounts for more than one child enrolled.

Budget plans, loan programs and other finance options also exist.(See list at end of this section)

In certain instances, when a child has not been able to perform in the public school setting state and/or local jurisdictions may fund part or all of the private school costs.

An excellent resource for general information is: <u>Applying for Financial Aid at a Nonpublic School.</u> This can be obtained from the Educational Testing Service, P. O. Box 6657, Princeton, N.J. 08541.

"A Better Chance" (ABC) at 419 Boylson Street, Boston, MA 02116 offers placement and scholarship information for minority students seeking private school education.

In the Washington area, The Black Student Fund, 3636 16th Street N. W., Suite AG 19, Washington, D.C. 20017 (202-387-1414) provides extensive counseling and also offers some funding for scholarships.

It is always appropriate to inquire about financial assistance when contacting and independent school The admission office will generally ask parents to complete a financial statement and may also ask for their IRS 1040 form. At most schools a request for aid does not affect a student's chances of being accepted.

Budget plans
(generally interest free but carry a small processing fee; some may require the school to participate)

Academic Management Services, 50 Vision Blvd., East Providence, RI 02194 (800-635-0120)

F.A.C.T.S. Tuition Management, P.O.Box 67037, Lincoln NB 68506 (800-624-7092)

School Financial Management Services, Inc., 95 Wall Street, New York, NY 10005 (800-SMART-08)

TADS Tuition Aid Data Services, 2305 Ford Parkway, St. Paul MN 55116 (800-477-TADS)

Tuition Loan Programs
(charge interest and other fees; repayment time varies from 6 months to 10 years)

Consern: Loans for Education, 205 Van Buren St., Suite 200, Herndon VA 22070 (703-709-8100)

Knight Tuition Payment Plan, 855 Boylston St., Boston, MA 92116 (800-255-6783)

TERI The Education Resources Institute, 330 Stuart St., Suite 500, Boston, MA 02116 (800-255-TERI)

The Tuition Plan, 57 Regional Dr., Concord, NH 03301 (800-258-3640)

HOME SCHOOLING- Another Choice

While disillusionment with the public school system has lead many parents to seek alternative schooling in a variety of independent schools, some parents are turning to another educational solution, that of Home Schooling.

According to Sue Welch and Cindy Short, Editors of The Teaching Home magazine, there are many reasons why families choose to home school. "Each child receives individual attention and has his/her unique needs met. Parents can control destructive influences and negative peer pressure. Home schooling makes quality time available to train and influence children in all areas of their lives in an integrated way. The family experiences unity, closeness, and mutual enjoyment and respect. Children develop confidence and independent thinking and have more time to explore new interests. Tutorial-style education helps each child achieve his full educational potential. Flexible scheduling can accommodate variable work and vacation times and allow for many outside activities."

Although home schooling is inexpensive (compared to private school costs) it does demand some sacrifices on the part of the family. One parent usually must give up outside work and income. The job of teaching itself requires a great deal of time and energy and may even seem intimidating to the non-professional. However, the boom in information technology and curriculum supplies now readily available have made the job much less daunting to most parents. In fact, studies show that home-schoolers generally achieve considerably higher test scores than the national average and that they are actively recruited by many of the leading colleges and universities.

To help parents and students, there is a large and well organized net-work of services and organizations devoted to the needs of home-schoolers. This is a fast growing segment of the school age population and for some families has proven to be the "right choice."

The following resources may be of interest to families considering home-schooling as their educational choice:

The Home School Legal Defense Association..............(703) 338-5600
    Box 159, Paeonian Springs, VA 22129

Distance Education and Training Council
    1601 18th Street, N. W., Washington, D. C. 20009-2529
    (An accrediting information service for home schooling/correspondence study)

Christian Home Educators Association
    P.O. Box 2009, Norwalk, CA 90651-2009

Local Organizations

Home Educators Association of Virginia...................(703) 635-9322
    P.O. Box 1810, Front Royal, VA 22630

Maryland Association of Christian Home Education....(301) 663-3999
    Box 1041, Emmitsburg, MD 21727

Christian Home Educators Network............................(410-744-8919)
   304 N. Beechwood Ave., Catonsville, MD 21228

Bolling Area Home Schoolers of D.C.
   1516 Carswell Circle, Washington, D. C. 20336

Publications

The Big Book of Home Learning (4 Volumes) by Mary Pride, Crossway Books, 1300 Crescent Street, Wheaton, IL. 60187. An excellent and extensive bibliography on all related subjects including lists of curriculum and on supplies; includes a chapter on "How to Start Your Own Private School".

Home Education Resource Guide. Bluebird Publishing, 1713 East Broadway, #306, Tempe, AZ. 85282

Home Grown Kids, Raymond and Dorothy Moore

Home Spun Schools, Raymond and Dorothy Moore

The Teaching Home Box 20219, Portland, OR 97220-0219 (a magazine for and about Home Schooling)

Local Home School Programs:

CALVERT SCHOOL......................(410) 243-6030

   Tuscany Road, Baltimore, MD 21210
   Founded 1897 **Grades**: K-8

   The oldest and probably best known correspondence school in America serving students both here and abroad. The program is traditional, structured and textbook oriented. Tests are administered and parent/student assistance is available from the professional staff.

CAMBRIDGE ACADEMY..904-620-2717 or 800-252-3777

   1111 S.W. 17th Street, Ocala, FL 34474
   Head: Ray Silver

   Grades : 6-12 **Enrollment** 1,483 All Home taught.

   Special Programs: Beginning students are sent an evaluation and placement package including proficiency tests for Math and English. Student's skills are identified and previous grade levels and credits are verified. Students are then assigned a course of study to meet individual needs. Study guides accompany each text or workbook. Students can call for tutoring or clarification at any time. Students must pass periodic tests.

   Tuition: (1995-96) $495 plus $25 Registration fee.

HOME STUDY INTERNATIONAL......................................(301) 680-6579

12501 Old Columbia Pike, Silver Spring, MD 20904
Head: Dr. Alayne Thorpe   **Grades**: Pre-school through College

Special Programs: Courses include all supplies, i.e. textbooks, cassettes, lab equipment, reading supplements, etc. Students progress at their own speed but generally 2 exams are required each semester. Students may call teachers for additional help or information.

Tuition: $1,405. Books and supplies: $300-$400.

RICHARD M. MILBURN HIGH SCHOOL...................(703) 494-0147

14416 Jefferson Davis Highway, Suite #12, Woodbridge, VA 22191

Grades: 9-12   **Program**: Courses in full 4 year high school diploma program.

SETON HOME STUDY SCHOOL....................................(703) 636-9990

One Kidd Lane, Front Royal, VA 22630

Catholic Correspondence Program which is strongly individualized with special attention to both accelerated and slow students. Early grades have lots of parents helps; later grades are increasingly self-taught.

WALKERSVILLE CHRISTIAN FAMILY SCHOOLS............(301) 663-0022

1 West 2nd Street, Frederick, MD 21701
Head: Gary Cox   **Grades**: K-12

Special Programs: A fully accredited Bible based Christian education based on child's test results, discernment of the child's nature, talents, and needs. Individual testing done at regular intervals. Six different high school diploma programs are available: Basic, College Preparatory, Vocational Tech, Christian Service, Business, Home Maker.

Tuition: $750 plus $75. Application fee (reduction for siblings).

ACADEMIC ENRICHMENT CENTER PREPARATORY SCHOOL.........(202) 829-2429

6119 Georgia Avenue N.W., Washington, D.C. 20011
Founded 1977   **Head**: Ms. C. Lillette Green-Campbell B.A., M.Ed.

Grades: N-8 **Enrollment**: 170 Co-ed   **Faculty**: 13 full-, 5 part-time.
Average Class Size: 15.

Special Courses: Spanish Pre K-7. Sign Language PreK-7. Pre-Algebra, Computer. General Science. **History Studies** include American, European, African, and African American Heritage. Remedial Reading and Math. Art, Music, Chorus, Drum Corps, Majorettes, African Dance Troupe. **Extended Day**: 6:30 a.m.-6:30 p.m.

Athletics: P.E. req. Intramural Soccer; Tennis, Basketball. **Clubs**: Cooking, Sewing, Drama, Crafts, Computer. **Publications**: Yearbook, Newspaper. **Community Involvement**: Inter-generational interaction, students grade 5 and above must perform 6 hours per tri-mester of community service.

Plant: Library 3,500 vol., Language Lab, Science Labs, Art Studio, Playing Fields.

Admission: Testing, Interview, School Visit by child for a day.

Tuition: (1995-96) Call for information

ACADEMY OF THE HOLY CROSS............ (301) 942-2100   FAX (301) 929-6440

4920 Strathmore Avenue, Kensington, MD. 20895.
Catholic 1868. **Head**: Sister Katherine Kase, CSC.

Grades: 9-12. **Enrollment**: 400 Girls. **Faculty**: 40 full-, 2 part-time.
Average Class Size: 18.

Special Courses: Languages: Latin I-IV, French I-V, Spanish I-IV, Math through Calculus. Science Physical Science, Biology, Chemistry, Physics, Physiology, Environmental Science, Independent Study. Social Science: World Studies, Latin American Studies, Asian Studies, African and Middle Eastern Studies, U.S. History, U. S Gov't, Democratic Thought. English: English I-IV, Espository Writing, Speech. Religious Studies, Art, Performing Arts. Honors Program. AP.: English, French, Spanish, Calculus, Biology, Chemistry, and U.S. History.

Athletics: P.E..; . Field Hockey, Soccer, Tennis, Cross Country, Cheerleading, Basketball, Volleyball, Track, Softball, Swimming and Diving. **Clubs**: French, Spanish, Amnesty International, Black Student Union, Equestrian, Drama. International Thespian Society, Model U.N., Math, Science, French, Spanish, National Honor Society, Peer Support, Photography, Pro-Life, SADD, SAFE, Speech and Debate. **Publications**: Literary Magazine, Newspaper, Yearbook. **Community Involvement**: Students are involved in ongoing Service   Projects. through Christian Service Commitment.

1

Plant: Library 10,000 vol.; Science Labs, Art Studio, Auditorium, Gym, Playing Fields, Computer Lab, Chapel, Cafeteria.

Admission: Interview, Washington Archdiocese Entrance Exam, Transcript, Recommendations;

Tuition: (1995-96) $6,700. <u>Books</u>: $200   <u>Activities Fee</u>: $100   *Dress Code* Uniform Req. **Financial Aid** . Some available.

Summer Program: Basketball camp.

ACCOTINK ACADEMY.........(703) 451-8041   FAX (703) 569-5365

8519 Tuttle Road, Springfield, VA. 22152.
Founded 1963. **Head**: Mrs. Elaine McConnell.

Ungraded: Ages 5-21 for LD/ED students. **Enrollment**: 114 Co-ed. **Faculty**: 65 full-time: 5 psychologists, 7 speech pathologists, 2 art therapists, 1 occupational therapist, physical education director, 4 job coaches. **Average Class Size**: 9 (3:1 student/teacher ratio).

Special Courses: One of the primary goals is the re-establishment of a good self-image. Program is structured but ungraded so each child may progress at own rate without undue pressure. Reading, Math, and Perceptual Skills are developed through individualized programs, while language arts provide group work experience. A multi-sesnsory approach is used in all classroom instruction. Science, Social Studies & History are part of the classroom instruction. In addition to regular classroom, school offers intensive services: psychological services which include individual and group psychotherapy and art therapy, intensive language therapy and occupational therapy and a socialization program. A strong behavior management program is an integral part of the student's daily educational plan. Pre-vocational training and on-the-job training is available for the older student.

Athletics: Full-time program with special emphasis placed on perceptual motor activities. Consultation with occupational therapist is included.

Plant: Library, Computer Lab, Offices for individual psychological, speech, art, and occupational therapy services; Curriculum Room, and Testing Facilities.

Admission: Referral through local area school systems. Generally referred by local agencies.

Tuition: County-funded; call for information. **Lunch**: Bring. **Transportation** : Provided and funded by the counties.

AIDAN MONTESSORI SCHOOL.........(202) 966-0360   FAX (202) 966-1878

3100 Military Road, N.W., Washington, D.C. 20015
Founded 1961. **Administrator**: Marsha Donnelly

Ungraded: N-age 12. Enrollment: 140 Co-ed. Faculty: 11 Montessori trained Faculty and staff; 13 support Faculty/Staff. Average Class Size: 25.

Special Courses: Association of Montessori Internationale ; Montessori program with integrated curriculum. Mixed aged classes, 18-30 months, 3-6 yrs., 6-12yrs.
Extended Day: 7:30 a.m.-6 p.m.

Athletics: P.E. Program offered for ages 5 and older. Community Service: Projects in cooperation with the Parents Association.

Plant: Library, Playground, Art Room. Montessori designed environment.

Admission: Rolling admissions; follow AISGW guidelines. Interview parent and child required. Class Observation and attendance at Open House recommended.

Tuition: (1995-96) $2,380- $7,703 ; reduced rates for siblings.Financial Aid: Some available after first year of enrollment.

Future Plans: To move in September, 1995 to: 2700 27th Street, N.W.
Washington, D.C. 20008

Summer Programs: Art Summer- ages 3-10; includes studio art, music, creative dramatics, dance.

ALEPH-BET JEWISH DAY SCHOOL..........(410) 263-9044

1125 Spa Road, Annapolis, MD 21403
1989 Jewish-Community   Head : Leslie Smith Rosen, M.A.

Grades: K(full day)- grade 5. Enrollment: 50 Co-ed Faculty: 4 full-, 3 part-time.
Average Class Size: 10

Special Courses: Traditional, rigorous elementary school curriculum enriched by daily prayer, Hebrew and Judaic studies; Students participate in Community Service.
Extended Day: 7-8:30 a.m.; 3-5 p.m.

Athletics: Various sports, Israeli Folk Dancing.

Plant: in Kenneth Israel Congregation

Admission: Rolling admission; call school for further information.

Tuition: (1995-96) $4,800 Financial Aid: Available

Future Plans: 1995 begin building

Summer Programs: Summer camp on premises.

ALEXANDRIA COUNTRY DAY SCHOOL ....(703) 548-4804   FAX (703) 549-9022

2400 Russell Rd., Alexandria, VA. 22301
Founded 1983   **Head**: Dr. Joan Barton

Grades: K-8   **Enrollment**: 228 Co-ed **Faculty**: 27 full-, 5 part- time.
Average Class Size: 12-20

Special Programs: Spanish K-8. Algebra, Geometry, Computer. General Science, Biology, Earth and Space. History- U.S., Ancient, Medieval, Virginia. Note: tutor for special needs students. Art, Music, Drama & Public Speaking; Band, Chorus, Handbells. After-school Enrichment Program. **Extended Day**: 7 - 8 a.m; 3:15- 6 p.m.

Athletics: grades 5-8; Soccer, Basketball, Softball, Field Hockey. **Clubs**: Art, Drama, Student Council. **Publications**: Yearbook, Newspaper. **Community Involvement:** Students participate in fund raising for local charities.

Plant: Library, Computer Lab, Science Lab, Art Studio, Gym, Auditorium. Playing Field.

Admission: School Visit, Interview, Testing.

Tuition: (1995-96) $6,150- $7, 820. Lunch: Extra   Books: $185   *Dress Code*: Neat, Clean, Grades 2-8: Kahki pants, skirts, shorts, hunter green shirts.   **Financial Aid**: Some available.

Future Plans: Possible expansion to 250 students.

Summer Program: Facility is used for sports camp.

ANNAPOLIS AREA CHRISTIAN SCHOOL............(410) 266-8251 FAX (410) 573-6866

716 Bestgate Road, Annapolis, MD. 21401 (Main campus, administrative offices)
Non-denominational Christian 1971. **Head**: Ron Whipple

Grades: K-12. **Enrollment**: 800 Co-ed. **Faculty**: 54 full-, 3 part time.
Average Class Size: 25.

Special Courses: Primarily College Preparatory Curriculum. French and Spanish 8-12. Math through Calculus. Science Gen'l Science, Biology, Chemistry, Physics, Anatomy, Physiology. History-Ancient, World, U.S., Gov't, Maryland, World Geography.   Religious Studies req. Typing, Band, Art, Music, Drama. LD program..   **Extended Day** 8 a.m.- 6 p.m.

Athletics: Req.; Intramural & Interscholastic: Soccer, Softball, Baseball, Basketball, Cheerleading, Wrestling, Lacrosse. Publications: Yearbook, Newspaper. Clubs Various ones; Drama Productions.

Plant: Library 14,000 vol., Gym, Use of nearby Playing Fields.

Admission: Interview; Testing and/or Transcripts.

Tuition: (1995-96) Half-day K, $2,300; K-12, $2,400- $4,500. **Transportation**:
Available from select areas, $60/mo.. *Dress Code*: Uniform req. **Financial Aid**: Available.

Future Plans: To expnd High School plant, add Middle School wing, establish sattelite campus
for lower school

Summer Program: Summer academy for remediation in varied subject areas.

ANNUNCIATION SCHOOL...........(202) 362-1408

3825 Klingle Place, N.W., Washington, D.C. 20016
(Corner of 39th and Massachusetts Avenue, N.W.)
Catholic 1954. **Head**: Sister Joan Rigney, SHCJ

Grades: K-8. **Enrollment**: 200 Co-ed. **Faculty**: 12 full-6 part-time: Aides in Primary
Department 2 full-time, 1 part-time. **Average Class Size**: 25

Special Courses: Spanish 7-8. Enrichment Math courses, 4-8; Algebra 8, Computer. English
Language Center. Art, Music. Religious Studies req. Science Fair grades 4-8.
Extended Day: 3 p.m.- 6 p.m.

Tuition: (1995 -1996) Call for information. Discount for siblings. *Dress Code*: Uniform req.

ANTIOCH CHRISTIAN SCHOOL......(410) 757-5000

1535 Ritchie Highway, Arnold, MD. 21012
Head: David Wright, Principal

Grades: age 2 - grade 12 **Enrollment**: 130 Co-ed

Special Programs: **Extended Day**: 7:30 a.m.-5 p.m.

Tuition: (1995-96) $1,880 grade 1-12.

APPLE TREE SCHOOL...........(703) 281-2626 in Vienna; (703) 281-7747 in Fairfax

712 Tapawingo Road, S.E., Vienna, VA 22180 (N & K only)
9655 Blake Lane, Fairfax, VA 22031 (N-3)
Head: Mrs. Klaasen

Grades: N3-grade 3. **Enrollment**: 165 Co-ed

Special Programs: **Extended Day**: 7 a.m.-6 p.m.

Tuition: (1995-96) Half-day, $75/wk.;　Full day $118/wk.

AQUINAS MONTESSORI SCHOOL ....(703) 780-8484

8334 Mount Vernon Highway, Alexandria, VA. 22309
Founded 1966. **Head**: Mrs. Kathleen Futrell.

Grades: Ungraded age 2 1/2 to 12. **Enrollment**: 175 Co-ed. **Average Class Size**: 25
Faculty : 7 full, 9 part-time.

Special Courses: French K-6, German 1-6, Art, Music. Science, Geography. Great Books
Discussion Program. Drama. **Extended Day**: Call for information.

Admission: Evaluation Test for elementary; Interview; $45 Application fee.

Tuition: (1995-1996) Call for information　**Lunch**: Bring **Extended Day**: Extra　*Dress Code:*
Uniform req.

ARCHBISHOP CARROLL HIGH SCHOOL..........(202) 529-0900　FAX　(202) 529-5989

4300 Harewood Road, N.E., Washington, D.C. 20017.
Catholic 1951. **Head**: Mrs. Wilma Durham

Grades: 9-12. **Enrollment**: 700 Co-ed. **Faculty**: 58 full-, 28 part-time.
Average Class Size: 20.

Special Courses: Foreign Language: Latin 9-10, French 10-12, Spanish 10-12; Science General
Science, Biology, Chemistry, Physics, Environmental Science, Ecology, Lab Ass'ts; Math through
Calculus; Economics, Accounting; Computer Science. History: U.S. and World, U.S.
Government, World Cultures;　Other-Psychology; Remedial Reading; Religion (req.); Art,
Architectural Drafting,　Engineering Graphics; Music, Concert Band, Orchestra, Gospel Choir,
Keyboarding. Note: Concurrent enrollment with colleges and universities Hi-Skip; work study
with government agencies. AP.: English, History, Physics, and Calculus.

Athletics : P.E.(req.); Interscholastic Sports: Football, Basketball, Soccer, Baseball, Wrestling,
Track, Softball, Rugby, Tennis. **Clubs**: Swimming, Drama, Cycling, History, Science, Chess,
Guitar, Bowling, Film-making, Cheerleaders, Pan-African Society, Cultural Passport with
Kennedy Center, Spanish Honor Society, Future Business Leaders of America, Jazz Band, Mock
Trial. **Publications**: Newspaper, Yearbook **Community Involvement**: Service at Zacchaeus
Community Kitchen, Thanksgiving Food Drive.

Plant: Library 18,000 vol., Learning Center, Science Labs, Art Classroom, Gym, Auditorium,
Playing Fields, Computer Labs- IBM and MacIntosh.

Admission: Non-Catholic elementary school students must register for exams.　Interviews and
Recommendation Letter advised.

Tuition: (1995-96) Catholic $3,750; Non-Catholic $4,000. **Lunch**: Extra **Books**: Averages $375. **Transportation**: Metro-CUA Station. *Dress Code*:Uniform- Boys: slacks, shirt, tie, blazer; Girls: skirt, blouse, blazer (for fall and spring). **Financial Aid** : Available

Summer Program:. Academic Enrichment and repeat courses offered. Summer Camp: Band, Football.

ARCHBISHOP SPALDING HIGH SCHOOL..........(410) 969-9105 or (301) 261-2170

8080 New Cut Road, Severn, MD. 21144
Catholic, 1966   **Head**: Mrs. Barbara Schwitzer

Grades 9-12 **Enrollment**: 750 Co-ed **Faculty**: 31 full-, 2 part- time.
Average Class Size: 24

Special Courses: French, Spanish, 9-12, Russian. **Math** includes Calculus, Computer-Basic Programming, and Programming in Micro-Application and in Micro-Spreadsheets Lotus. Science Biology, Chemistry,Physics, Psychology, Introd. to Life Science, Physical Science, Botany, Zoology, Human Anatomy, & Physiology, Earth Science, Marine Science, and Introd. to Research. History- World, U..S., Introduction to World Geography, Amer. Gov't & Current Issues. Religious Studies required. Remedial Reading & Math, 9-10. Skills courses 9-12. Art- Drawing, Print Making, Ceramics, Art History & Aprreciation, Painting, General Fine Arts. Music- Band, Chorus, Guitar, Music Theory I & II. Home Economics, Childhood Develop. AP: English, Calculus, Biology, U.S.History, Current Events & Gov't., European History. Various Honors Courses; some students may enroll for a course at Anne Arundel Community College.

Athletics: P.E. req.; Interscholastic: Field Hockey, Lacrosse, Ice Hockey, Basketball, Baseball, Softball, Volleyball, Wrestling, Swimming, Golf, Soccer, Football. **Clubs**: Drama, Spanish, French, Health Careers, Black Student Union, Chess, SADD, "Help Our Planet Earth". **Publications**: Yearbook, Literary Magazine. **Community Involvement**: 30 hours of Community Service required during Jr. & Sr. years.

Plant: Library, 11,000 vol.; Science Labs, Art Studio, Gym, Auditorium, Playing Fields, Chapel, Cafeteria, Computer Lab, Home Ec.Labs for Sewing & Cooking.

Admission: Archdiocese Test, Transcript, Teacher Recommendation. $100 Registration fee.

Tuition: (1995-96) $4,300. **Lunch, Books, & Transportation**: All Extra. *Dress Code*: Uniform req. **Financial Aid**: Available.

Future Plans: Renovation of Outdoor Athletic Facility

Summer Programs: Remedial and Developmental in all disciplines for students grades 10-12; For entering 9th grade students, offerings available in English and Math only.

ARNOLD CHRISTIAN ACADEMY..........(410) 544-1882

804 Windsor Road, Arnold, MD. 21012
Head: Mrs. Joan Harris

Grades: K4-grade 6. **Enrollment**: 55 Co-ed.

Special Courses: ABEKA program. Students work independently at their own pace with a supervisor/teacher in each class to assist as needed. Note: K classes meet only in afternoon; Care provided from 9 a.m.-12:30 p.m. for those K students (if needed). School day ends at 2:30 p.m. on Mondays, 3:30 p.m. other days. **Extended Day**: 7:30 a.m.-6 p.m.

Plant: Library, Math room, Auditorium.

Admission: Interview with Administrator

Tuition: (1995-96) Call for information. *Dress Code*: Uniform req. **Extended Care**: Extra

ASCENSION LUTHERAN SCHOOL..........(301) 577-0500

7420 Ardmore Road, Landover Hills, MD. 20784
Lutheran 1952   **Head**: Jack Bartels

Grades: N-8   **Enrollment**: 200 Co-ed

Special Courses: Music & Art; Religious Studies, req.; P.E. req.;   After school programs: Choir, Computer, Drama. **Extended Day Care**: 7 a.m.-6 p.m. (Extra)

Plant: Library, All- Purpose Room, Playing Fields.

Admission: Interview, Transcript.

Tuition: (1995-96) Call for information.

ASSUMPTION SCHOOL..........(202) 562-7070   FAX (202) 574- 5829

220 High View Place, S. E., Washington, D. C. 20032
Catholic **Head**: Christopher Kelley

Grades: N-8 **Enrollment**: Co-ed

Special Programs: Extended Day: 6 a.m.-6 p.m.

Tuition (1995-96) $1,680 **Extended Day**: Extra

ATHOLTON ADVENTIST SCHOOL..........(301) 596-5593

6520 Martin Road, Columbia, MD. 21044
Head: Linda Bates

Grades: PreK-8   **Enrollment**: 80 Co-ed   **Extended Day** 7 a.m.-6 p.m.

Tuition: (1995-96) Call for information

THE BANNER SCHOOL..........(301) 695-9320   FAX (301) 695-9336

1730 N. Market Street, Frederick, MD. 21701
Founded 1982. **Head**: Mr. Michael Mullin

Grades: K-8. **Enrollment**: 150 Co-ed. **Faculty**: 15 full-, 6 part-time.
Average Class Size: Limited to 15

Special Courses: Spanish K-8, General Science. Music Appreciation, Drama, Art, Computers.
Extended Day: 7:30 a.m.-6 p.m.

Athletics: Req . Basketball, Soccer, Softball, Field Hockey. **Clubs**: After school activities-
according to interest. **Community Involvement**: Annual winter drama based on Frederick 100
years ago as published in newspapers, etc. presented to public. Support local Historical events,
local and national charities..

Plant: Library 1,500 vol., Science Labs, Auditorium, Playing Field.

Admission: Application fee; Student and Parent Visit; Transcripts and Test Scores.

Tuition: (1995-96) Half-day K, $2,324; Full day K, $4,270;   1-3, $4,607;   4-8, $4,847;
Note: Includes books and most Activity fees.   **Extended Day**: Extra   Lunch: Bring.
Financial Aid: Available.

Summer Programs: (Age 4-14) Summer Discovery Camp.

BARNESVILLE SCHOOL..........(301) 972-0341   FAX (301) 972-4076

21830 Peach Tree Rd.,(P.O. Box 404) Barnesville, MD. 20838.
Founded 1969. **Head**: Jaralyn L. Hough

Grades: N-7. **Enrollment**: 185 Co-ed. **Faculty** : 18 full-, 5 part-time.
Average Class Size: 15

Special Courses: Strong Basic Skills program, Computers, hands-on Science. Involvement with
community service. **Extended Day**: 7:15 - 8:30 a.m.; 3 - 6 p.m.

9

Athletics: Developmental skills program, all grades; Soccer teams grades 1-7, Basketball grades 5-6, Baseball. **Publications**: Literary magazine.

Plant: Library 6,000 vol., 2 Buildings, 11 acre campus. Science Lab, Art Room, Music Center Playground, Soccer Field.

Admission: $50 Application fee. Transcript; student visits school for one or two days. Preference given to siblings

Tuition: (1995-96) K-5, $5,985 includes Books; 6-7, $6,465 plus Books. **Transportation**: $1,125 round trip to designated stops. *Dress Code*: Good taste **Financial Aid**: Some available.

Future Plans: Additional of 8th grade 1996-1997.

Summer Program: Ages 4-12 - Computers, horseback riding, sports, crafts. 9 a.m.- 4 p.m..

BARRIE SCHOOL..........(301) 871-6200

13500 Layhill Road, Silver Spring, MD 20906
Founded 1932. **Head**: M. Jeffrey Moredock

Grades: N-12. **Enrollment**: 485 Co-ed. **Faculty**: 45 full-, 11 part-time.
Average Class Size: 16.

Special Courses: Montessori curriculum in pre-school through 6th grade- emphasis on hands-on learning, cooperation, respect and independence. Spanish, Arts. Drama, Music included.
Upper School program is college preparatory and challenging, innovative academic program in a warm, supportive atmosphere. Integrated humanities program; Math includes Calculus; Science: Biology, Chemistry, Physics. Study Skills, Creative Writing, Journalism, Human Relations, International Affairs. Fitness and Fine Arts Curriculum includes Music, Arts, Drama, Yoga..
Note: Extension Day Program Grades 7-12 once a week, Science/Cultural/Envionmental Activities outside classroom that extend the curriculum out into the community. AP: Biology, French, and Spanish. **Extended day**: 7 a.m.-6 p.m.

Athletics: (P.E. req.) Intramural and Interscholastic. Basketball, Softball, Movement, Soccer, Track, Horseback Riding, Camping\Outdoor Exploration, Hiking, Canoeing, Rock Climbing and Biking, Tennis, Racquet Ball, **Clubs**: Drama, Keyette, Student Gov't, SADD, Choral Group, Clown Club, Math, and Chess.. **Publications**: Student Newspaper, Yearbook **Community Involvement**: Grades 9-10 includes Community Service Project, and in Grades 11-12, Internship Program for one trimester.

Plant: 3 Libraries 16,500 vol., 2 Art Studios, Gym,, Playing Field, 2 Swimming Pools, Stables.

Admission: Open House twice weekly. Application Fee $50. Interview, Classroom Visit, Testing. Recommendations and Transcript.

Tuition: (1995-96)) N half-day $5,293; N full day $7,135; K, $7,869; 1-12, $8,173--$10,078.
Transportation: Available, $1,795 both ways. **Extended Day**: $750-$1,125. Books: $250
Other Fees Building & Grounds Assessment $400 per family. **Financial Aid**: Some partial Aid

Summer Program: Day camp: for age 3 1/2- 14, swimming, riding, camping, canoeing, arts
and crafts, nature study, sports, etc. computer camp & drama camp,

BEAUVOIR.........(202) 537-6492

3500 Woodley Road, N.W., Washington, D.C. 20016
(On the grounds of the National Cathedral.)
Episcopal, 1933 **Head** : Paula J. Carreiro

Grades : PreK- grade 3 **Enrollment** : 364 Co-ed **Faculty** : 40 full-time
Average Class Size : K & 1,-19; 2 & 3, 18.

Special Courses: General Science, Art Workshop, Music, Media, Sports, Computers;
Learning alternatives provides academic support. Chapel Service in the Cathedral.
Extended Day : Available

Plant : Library 9,000 vol. computerized with on-line catalogue. Computer Lab. Science Lab, Art
Workshop, Gym, Auditorium, Playing Fields, Swimming Pool; Access to 60 acres of Cathedral
Close.

Admission : Applications accepted Oct. - Jan. for following year; Children applying are
evaluated on an individual and group basis. Application and Testing

Tuition: (1995-96) $9,331 includes Lunch and Books.   **Transportation** : Available.
Financial Aid : Available

Summer Program: Recreational Junior Program, Half day, Mid June thru July, Ages 3-4.
Summer Adventure; ages 4-7; arts & crafts, drama, music movement, science, P.E., and field
trips; Academic: for ages 6-10, Enrichment program concentrating on regular skills and
learning alternative program; " Computers of Course" Logo, graphics, Bank Street Writer and
Problem solving challenges. Note:: all programs offer daily swim instruction in Olympic-size
outdoor pool. **Extended Day** : 3 p.m.-6 p.m.

BEDDOW SCHOOL....(301) 567-0330

8600 Loughran Road, Ft. Washington, MD. 20744
Founded 1972. **Head**: Trudy Beddow.

Grades: Ungraded ages 2-1/2-14.(PreK- grade 8) **Enrollment**: 150 Co-ed

Program: Montessori; French.. **Extended Day Care**: 7:30 a.m.-6:00 p.m.

Tuition: (1995-96) $3,146, Half-day PreK; $4,118 Primary. **Extended Day** : Extra

Summer Program: Day Camp, ages 2 1/2-14; Nature study, field trips, swimming lessons, crafts; some academic review. **Extended Day**

BELTSVILLE SEVENTH DAY ADVENTIST SCHOOL..........(301) 937-2933

4200 Ammendale Road, Beltsville, MD. 20705.
Adventist 1956. **Head**: Wendy Pega

Grades: K-8. **Enrollment**: 215 Co-ed. **Faculty**: 10 full-, 1 part-time.
Average Class Size: 25

Special Courses: Music, Religious Studies req., Gymnastics; 2 Bell Choirs, Treble Choir.
Extended Day: 7:30 a.m.- 6 p.m.

Athletics: Req. 1-8. **Publications**: "Small Talk."

Plant: Library, Playing Fields, Auditorium/Gym.

Admission: Application, Interview. Registration fee $60.

Tuition: (1995-96) $355/mo. (reduction for church members)   **Limited Transportation**:
$45- $80/mo., depending on distance *Dress Code*: Neat, modest attire.

BERWYN BAPTIST SCHOOL..........(301) 474-1561

4720 Cherokee Street., College Park, MD. 20740
Baptist, 1967. **Head**: Ann Elizabeth Zibrat

Grades: N3-grade 6. **Enrollment**: 150 Co-ed **Faculty** : 12 full-, 2 part-time.
Average Class Size : 20.

Special Program: Computer in each class; Self-contained classes for each grade.
Separate instructors for Library, Music, & P.E.

Athletics: P.E. **Clubs** : Gymnastics, Handbell Choir   **Publications** :Yearbook .

Admission: Open Enrollment begins March 1

Tuition: (1995-96) N3, $770; N4, $1,177; K, $1,562;   grades 1-6, $2,750.

BETHEL BIBLE CHRISTIAN SCHOOL..........(301) 449-3000

5406 Brinkley Road, Camp Springs, MD. 20748
Founded 1981 I.F.C.A. **Head**: Dr. Dick Schimkus

Grades: N3-grade 9. **Enrollment**: 320 Co-ed **Faculty**: 17 full-time, 5 aides. **Average Class Size**: 18

Special Programs: Religious Studies required. Chosen Generation, Discovery, and J & C. Music. **Extended Day** : 6 -8:30 a.m.; 3:30.- 6 p.m.

Athletics: Not required Complete Sports Program: B & C Basketball, Soccer, Volleyball, Softball, Baseball , Track.. **Clubs**: Chess, Yearbook. **Publications**: Yearbook.

Plant: Library 4,000 vol.; Gym, 3 Playing Fields

Admission: Pre-Registration Feb.-April: N3-K5, $100; grades 1-8, $125. Regular Registration, May 1: N3-K5 $100; grades 1-8, $100. Testing, Interview required.

Tuition: (1995-96) N3-K5 $2,750; 1-8 $2,750. **Extended Day**: $1,000/yr. **Transportation**: Limited, $1,000/yr. *Dress Code*: Uniform required. **Financial Aid**: Available

Future Plans: Complete a High School Program

Summer Programs: Academic for ages 3-12: Remedial Reading and Math. Non-Academic: one week of Basketball camp; Arts & Crafts, Swimming, Field Trips for ages 3-12.

BETHEL CHRISTIAN ACADEMY.......(301) 725-4673   FAX (301) 490-0153

8455 Savage-Guilford Road, Savage, P.O. Box 406, MD. 20763
Head: Mrs. Rose Marie Cox

Grades: PreK - 8 **Enrollment**: 200+ Co-ed **Faculty** : 15 full-, 5 part-time
Average Class Size 20-22

Special Programs: Spanish, Algebra, Computer, Art, Music, Choir.**Extended Day**:7:15 a.m.-6 p.

Athletics : Girls: Softball, Soccer, Basketball; Boys: Softball, Soccer, Basketball.

Plant: Large Multi-purpose room, Media Center, Large Playing Field

Admission: Registration; $175 fee for new students.

Tuition: (1995-96) Call for brochure.

Future Plans Expand to High School

BETHLEHEM BAPTIST CHRISTIAN ACADEMY..........(703) 631-1467   FAX (703) 378-8139

4601 W. Ox Road, Fairfax, VA. 22030.
Independent Fundamental Baptist 1973. **Head**: Mr. Gene Spurrier

Grades: K3-12   **Enrollment**: 500 Co-ed   **Faculty**: 33 full-, 5 part-time
Average Class Size: 20.

Special Courses :   Spanish I-IV, Math: Algebra-Calculus; Business Math, Computer. Science
Physical Science, Biology, Chemistry, Physics. History- World Geography, World History,
US/VA History, US./VA Gov't, Political Science/Economics. Religious studies req.; Remedial
Reading & Math. Note: Limited LD enrollment. Art, Music, Speech, Typing, Accounting,
Choir, Band. **Extended Day:** 7 a.m.-5:30 p.m.

Athletics: Req. to grade 10. Interscholastic: Soccer, Baseball, Basketball, Cheerleading,
Volleyball, Softball. Clubs: American Christian Honor Society. **Publications:** Yearbook,
Newspaper.

Plant: Library, Science Labs, Art Studio, Gym, Auditorium, Playing Fields

Admission : Parent/child Interview, $150 Registration Fee. Nine-week probationary period;
satisfactory academics.

Tuition: (1995-96)) $2,596-3,543   Lunch Program Books: $250. **Transportation**: Limited
Dress Code: Conservative.

Summer Program: Recreational camp, K4-grade 8

BISHOP DENIS J. O'CONNEL HIGH SCHOOL..........(703) 237-1400

6600 Little Falls Road, Arlington, VA. 22213
Catholic, 1957. **Head:** Alward V. Burch.

Grades: 9-12. **Enrollment**: 1300 Co-ed. **Faculty**: 70 lay, 15 religious.
Average Class Size: 19.

Special Courses: Religion; Latin, French, Spanish, German, Russian; Science Biology,
Chemistry, Physics; History: World Culture, Mod. European History, U.S. & Va. History,
U.S. & Va. Gov't.; Math includes Trig, Functions & Finite Math, Analysis, Calculus; Economics,
Practical Law, Accounting, Business & Law Management, Computer Programming; Studio Art,
Technical Drawing, Public Speaking, Journalism, Theater Arts, Creative Writing; Music, Typing
AP: English, Spanish, Biology, Chemistry, History, Calculus, French, German, Art, Economics,
U.S. Government.

Athletics: Intramural & Interscholastic: Football, Basketball, Soccer, Swimming, Tennis, Golf,
Wrestling, Cheerleading, Bowling, Track, Cross Country, Softball. **Clubs**: 30, all varieties.
Publications: Newspaper, Literary Magazine, Yearbook. **Community Involvement**: Key &
Keyette Clubs, Red Cross. Parish Activities, Junior Achievement, Charity Drives.

Plant: Library, Science Labs, Art Studio, Gym, Auditorium, Cafeteria,
Playing Fields, Computer Lab; Use of Tennis Courts and Swimming Pool.

14

Admission: Grade 9-High school Entrance Exam; All grades: Transcripts, Interview, References; Application fee, $100.

Tuition: (1995-96) Parish member $4,150; Non-Parish member $4,600 (note: reduced tuition for siblings). Non-Catholic: $5,400. Lunch: Cafeteria. Books: Extra. *Dress Code*: Uniform req. **Transportation**: Limited-from E. Falls Church Metro, and some areas. **Financial Aid**: Available

Summary Program: Sports Camp - basketball for boys. Academic- enrichment program for incoming 9th graders, Study Skills, Typing. Computer Programming. Credit courses in Math and Languages.

BISHOP IRETON HIGH SCHOOL..........(703) 751-7606

201 Cambridge Road, Alexandria, VA. 22314
Catholic 1964. **Head**: Rev. William J. Metzger, OSFS

Grades: 9-12. **Enrollment**: 750 Co-ed. **Faculty**: 40 full-, 6 part-time.
Average Class Size: 20-25.

Special Courses: French, Spanish, German, Latin, all 9-12; Japanese, Chinese, Russian. Math includes Calculus; Computer-Introd., Pascal, Applications, Programming, Keyboarding; Science: Biology, Chemistry, Physics, Astronomy, Organic Chemistry, Introd. to Psychology. History- World Cultures, Modern European, U.S.& Virginia Government and History. Economics. Religious Studies req. Remedial Reading & Math, Creative Writing, Public Speaking, Journalism, Publishing, Art, Wind Ensemble, Concert Band, Drama, Theatre, Stage Crafts. Honors and AP Program: English, U.S. History, Gov't., Chemistry, Art I & II, Computers, Biology, Calculus, AB, BC. Note: Academic Enrichment, Study Skills.

Athletics: Req. 9-10. Intramural Basketball. Interscholastic: Football, Basketball, Baseball, Tennis, Swimming & Diving, Lacrosse, Soccer, Golf, Cross-Country, Wrestling, Track & Field, Softball, Volleyballl, Cheerleading. **Clubs**: Chorus, Competition Math, Drama, French, German, Spanish, Latin, "It's Academic", Key, Model U.N., National Honor Society, Stage Crew, Student Government. **Publications**: Newspaper, Yearbook. **Community Involvement**: Key Club, Blood Bank, Social Concern, Tutoring in grade schools, Volunteers.

Plant: Library, 12,000 vol., Computer Lab, Science Labs, Art Room, Gym, Fields, Use of Tennis Courts & Pool.

Admission: Placement exam for incoming 9th grade; Interviews upper grades. Transcripts and Recommendation

Tuition: (1995-96) $4,600-$6,600. Books: Extra Lunch: May be purchased. **Transportation**: $800-$1,000 both ways. *Dress Code*: School uniform req. **Financial Aid**: Available.

Future Plans; New Auditorium & Classroom Wing scheduled for completion for 1996-97 school year.

Summer Program: Academic- Remedial and study skills.

BISHOP McNAMARA HIGH SCHOOL...........(301) 735-8401; FAX (301) 735-0934

6800 Marlboro Pike, Forestville, MD. 20747
Catholic 1963. **Head**: Brother John Paige, CSC

Grades: 9-12. **Enrollment**: 625 Co-ed. **Faculty**: 47 full-, 2 part-time
Average Class Size: 22.

Special Courses: French, Spanish, Latin, all 9-12; Math includes Trig & Calculus; Computer Programming, Literacy, Applications. Science: General Science, Biology, Chemistry, Physics, Anatomy & Physiology, Psychology History: U.S. & World. Sociology. Religious Studies req. Remedial Reading & Math. Music: 5 Bands, Composition & Theory. Note: Special Programs-Peer Ministry, Internships, Model U. N.; AP: English, Math, Calculus, History, Chemistry & Physics.

Athletics: Not required. Intramural Basketball. Interscholastic: Football, Basketball, Baseball, Wrestling, Golf, Track, Cross-Country, Tennis, Lacrosse, Soccer, Swimming, and Volleyball.. **Clubs**: Black Student Union, Yearbook, Model U.N., Student Council, Foreign Language. **Publications**: Newspaper, Yearbook, Literary Magazine. **Community Involvement**: 40 hour requirement in junior year as part of religion requirement.

Plant: Library 11,000 vol., Language Lab, 4 Science Labs, Art Studio, Auditorium, Gym, 3 Playing Fields, Weight Room.

Admission: Contact Director of Admissions for information and current procedures. Registration fee $250.

Tuition: (1995-96) $4,350 Books: Rental, $200 **Transportation**: $1,000 both ways
Dress Code: Uniform . **Financial Aid**: Available

Summer Programs: Academic: Remedial English, Science, Math, Religion.
Non-Academic: Football, Basketball Baseball, Soccer Camps.

BLAKE PRE-SCHOOL/ MUNGER ACADEMY............................(703) 430-2781

624 W. Church Road, Sterling, VA 20164
Head : Paula Munger

Grades : N-2 **Enrollment**: 200 Co-ed

Tuition: (1995-96) Call for information

Future Plans: To go up to grade 5

BLESSED SACRAMENT SCHOOL..........(202) 966-6682

5841 Chevy Chase Parkway, N. W., Washington, D. C. 20015
Catholic **Head** Mrs.Frances Scango (Acting)

Grades : K-8   **Enrollment**: 500 Co-ed

Special Programs: **Extended Day** : 7:30 a.m.-6 p.m.

Tuition: (1995-96) K-8, In Parish $2,365;   Non-Parish, $4,260.

BLUE RIDGE SCHOOL..........(804) 985-2811   FAX (804) 985-7215

Dyke, VA. 22935
Episcopal 1909. **Head:** Edward M. McFarlane, Ed. D.

Grades: 9-12. **Enrollment**: 150 Boys, All Boarding. **Faculty**: 32 full-, 3 part-time.
Average Class Size: 9

Special Courses : French I-IV, Spanish I-IV. English electives.   **Math** includes 3 levels of Algebra, Geometry and pre-Calculus. Computer Programming, Introductory thru Advanced, Basic Word Processing. **Science**: Biology, Chemistry, Physics, Earth Science, Anatomy, Physical Science; **History**: World, Modern European, U.S. History & Government, Virginia History; Art.

Athletics: Req.; Interscholastic: Football, Cross Country, Soccer, Wrestling, Basketball, Indoor Soccer, Lacrosse, Tennis, Golf, Baseball, Track & Field. **Clubs**: Choir, Dramatics, Computer, Outdoor Activity (camping, hiking, climbing, caving). **Publications**: Yearbook, Newspaper, Literary Magazine. **Community Involvement**: Recycling, Environmental-Adopt a Highway Program, County Christmas Program.

Plant: 1,000 Acre Campus. Library 11,000 vol., (augmented by easy accessed on-line data-base from U.VA Library) 3 Science Labs, Art Studio, 2 Gyms, Auditorium, 7 Playing Fields, Pool, 12 Tennis Courts (4 Indoor), Computer Lab, Student Center, Chapel, 5 acre lake for fishing, canoeing.

Admission: Rolling Admission; testing may be required. Interview req.; $35 Application fee.

Tuition: (1995-96) $ 18,425   Books: $150. *Dress Code*: Coat and tie. **Financial Aid**: Available

Future Plans: Increasing implementation of Fishburne Learning Center

Summer Program: Academic Enrichment Program offered for students entering grades 7-12 (co-ed). Make up credit or review courses; study skills, reading & writing skills improvement. Afternoon activities both on and off campus.

BOOK OF LIFE ACADEMY..........(410) 263-5377

913 Cedar Park Road, Annapolis, MD. 21401
Annapolis Assembly of God Church. **Head**: April Carpenter, Principal.

Grades: N3-grade 12   **Enrollment**: 210 Co-ed.

Special Courses: Spanish. ABEKA curriculum. **Extended Day**: 7:45 A.M.- 4:30 P.M.

Plant: Library, Gym

Admission: Registration fee $145; Transcript, Interview with parents.

Tuition: (1995-96) Call for information.   **Extended Day**: Extra   *Dress Code*: Uniform req.

BOWIE MONTESSORI LEARNING CENTER..................(301) 464-4506

3501 Moylan Road, Bowie, MD.20715
Head: Suzanne Domadio

Grades: (ungraded) Ages 3 -12

Tuition: (1995-96) Call for information.

BRENTWOOD ACADEMY..........(703) 780-5750

3725 Nalls Road., Alexandria, VA. 22309
Founded 1965. **Head**: Pamela Allen.

Grades: N2-grade 3. **Enrollment**: 90. **Faculty**: 12 full-time. **Average Class Size**: 15
Special Courses: General Science, Computers, Music, Art. **Extended Day**: 6:30 a.m.-6:30 p.m.

Athletics: Swimming, Softball, Ice Skating.

Plant: Library, Playing Fields, 5 wooded acres; use of nearby pool.
Admission: Interview parent and child. Registration fee $50.

Tuition: (1995-96) Half-Day $475/mo.; Full Day $575/mo. Includes Lunch, snacks, &
Extended Day. Books: Extra.

Summer Program: Day Camp. Arts, Computers, Swimming, Field trips, Cookouts, all kinds of
games. 6:30 a.m.- 6:30 p.m. Ages 2-14.

BROADFORDING CHRISTIAN ACADEMY.........(301) 797-8886

13535 Broadfording Church Road, Hagerstown, MD. 21740.
Bible Brethren, 1973. **Head**: Mr. R. William Wyand

Grades: N (2 yrs.) - grade 12. **Enrollment**: 150 Co-ed **Average Class Size**: 15.

Special Courses: French & German, as needed; Spanish, Elem. & 9-12. Math includes Calculus, Computer-Basic Programming, Word Processing, Literacy, Gen'l Business Math. Science: General Science, Biology, Chemistry, Physics. History - World and U.S., American Gov't, World Geography. Religious Studies Req. (Bible class daily). Remedial Reading and Math. Art, Music-Vocal, Instrumental, and Handbell Choir. **Extended Day**: 7:30 a.m.-5 p.m.

Athletics: P.E. req. Intramural: Basketball, Volleyball, Flag Football, etc. Interscholastic: Basketball, Volleyball. Note: Gym class offers Fencing, Orienteering, Football, etc. **Clubs**: Yearbook, Newspaper, Home Economics. **Publications**: Yearbook, Newspaper.

Plant: Library, Science Labs, Gym, Auditorium, Playing Fields.

Admission: Interview, Test; Registration fee $60. Desire to attend the school and to receive a Christian education is important.

Tuition: (1995-96) $1,500, reduction for siblings.. Lunch: Purchase **Transportation**: one way $200 - $500; both ways $400-$850. *Dress Code*: Modest, conservative. **Scholarship Aid**: Some available.

Summer Program: Elementary tutoring in Reading, Math; other courses upon request.
Summer Daycare 7:30 a.m.- 5 p.m.

BROOKSFIELD SCHOOL...................(703) 356-5437

1830 Kirby Road, McLean, VA 22101
Founded 1987 **Head** : Mary Anne Duffus

Ungraded: Ages 2 1/2 to grade 3. **Enrollment**: 70 Co-ed **Faculty**: 7 full-, 8 part-time.
Average Class Size: Pre-school, 20-24; grades 1-3, 10.

Special Courses : Montessori curriculum for pre-school and Kindegarten includes Creative Movement, Art, Music and foreign language; Grades 1 -3: Program includes an integrated reading program, classic and contemporary literature, accelerated Math program, Computer instruction. Science, study of world cultures; Spanish, Art, Music. **Extended Day** : 7:30 a.m.-5:30 p.m.

Athletics : P.E. with special instruction in Horseback Riding and Ice Skating

Admission : For ages 2 1/2-K, Tour, Interview, Informal Evaluation; Grades 1- 3: Tour, Interview, Transcripts, Recommendations.

Tuition: (1995-96) Registration fee $40; Ages 2 1/2-K, $3,990-$7,400 (depends on hours); Grades 1-3, $6, 350-$8,000 (depends on hours); 10% discount for siblings. Note: Tuition may be paid in monthly installments. For occasional **Extended Day Care,** fee is $10/hr., separate charge for an occasional lunch is $8 including 1 hr. of Care.

Future Plans : To build own site to allow for expansion.

Summer Program: Summer camp with swimming instruction daily, nature study, art, music, dance, & crafts.

BROWNE ACADEMY...........(703) 960-3000   FAX (703) 960-7325

5917 Telegraph Road, Alexandria, VA. 22310
Founded 1941. **Head**: Dr. Lois Ferrer.

Grades: Pre-School- grade 8. **Enrollment**: 275 Co-ed. Pupil/Teacher Ratio: 9:1
Faculty: 30 full-, 5 part-time.

Special Courses: Individualized Reading and Math, French, Computer, Art, Music (includes Piano Lessons); Physical Education, Study Skills. Emphasis on dynamic academic program in relaxed, country setting. Special programs for the gifted.
Extended Day: 7 a.m.- 6 p.m.

Athletics: Req. Intramural & Interleague: Soccer, Track & Field, Softball, Basketball, Ballet, Jazz, & Gymnastics. **Clubs**: Arts,Chess, Cooking, Spanish, Scouting, Chorus, Student Government. **Publications:** Newspaper, Yearbook.

Plant: Library 10,000 vol., Math-Science Lab, Computer Lab, Art Lab, Music Building, Swimming Pool, Playing Fields, 11 Acres, Stream, Basketball Court, Outdoor Amphitheater, Par Cours Trail.

Admission: Transcript, Interview, Testing - Seek diversified student body. Application fee $50.

Tuition: (1995-96) Pre-School, $2,885-$7.740; K- 8, $8,745: Lunch for PreK-grade 4 included, 5-8 bring. **Transportation**: $835-$1,465. **Scholarship Aid** : Available

Future Plans: New Library, Multi-purpose Auditorium/Gym. Expansion of student body to 300.

Summer Program: Day Camp - 9 week program ages 2-15. Includes Red Cross swimming instruction, arts & crafts, music, gymnastics, drama, "outdoor education", field sports, pony rides. Summer Studies offering Enrichment and Remedial courses. **Transportation & Extended Day** Available.

BULLIS SCHOOL..........(301) 299-8500   FAX (301) 299-9050

10601 Falls Road, Potomac, MD. 20854.
Founded 1930. **Head**: Dr. Richard K. Jung

Grades: 3-12. **Enrollment**: 513 Co-ed (312 Boys, 201 Girls). **Faculty**: 53 full-, 14 part-time. **Average Class Size**: 14.

Special Courses: Integrated Language Arts Program, 3-6. Math thru AP Calculus. Social Studies: Ancient & Medieval, World Cultures, Modern European, U.S., Economics, Psychology. Science IPS, Earth Science, Biology, Chemistry, Physics. Foreign Language: 7-12: Latin, French, German, and Spanish. Computer Science: req. 3-8; electives 9-12. Fine Arts: daily, 3-8; electives 9-12. Studio Art, Stagecraft, Chorus, Histories. AP: Biology, Chemistry, English, U.S. History, Modern European History, Computer Science, French, Spanish, Latin, Calculus.

Athletics: P.E., 3-5; Interscholastic 6-12. Baseball/Softball, Basketball, Cross Country, Field Hockey, Football, Golf, Lacross, Tennis, Track & Field, Wrestling. **Clubs**: Drama, Honor Society, International, "It's Academic", Key, Multicultural Student Union, Student Council. **Publications**: Newspaper, Yearbook, Literary Magazine. **Community Involvement**: Class and Club sponsored activities support local shelters and causes, and assist area disadvantaged youth.

Plant: Library 15,000 vol., 4 Science Labs, 2 Computer Labs, Playing Fields, Indoor & Outdoor Tennis Courts. Football Stadium, all weather 8 lane track; 3 faculty residences. Athletic Center includes 2 Gyms, Wrestling Center, Physical Fitness Center.

Admission: SSAT or ERB, Interview, Transcript, personal Recommendations. $35 Application fee.

Tuition: (1995-96) Grades 3-5, $9,400; 6-8, $10,975; 9-12, $11,500; includes Lunch. Books: $300. **Transportation** : one way - $825; both ways - $1,400. *Dress Code*: Uniform req. **Financial Aid**: Available

Future Plans: Construction of a Library & Fine Arts Center.

Summer Program: Academic: 6 week program, make-up, enrichment, full credit courses, Grades 7-P.G.; Camps: 1-6 weeks, baseball/softball, basketball, lacrosse, soccer, wrestling, tennis, plus computer/art/writing workshop and drama program. Discovery Day Camp for children.

BURGUNDY FARM COUNTRY DAY SCHOOL..........(703) 960-3431   FAX (703) 960-5056

3700 Burgundy Road, Alexandria, VA. 22303.
Founded 1946. **Head**: Gerald Marchildon
Note: Co-op Parents/Staff Members participate in policy-making & work.

Grades: Pre K-8. **Enrollment**: 280 Co-ed. **Faculty**: 29 full-, 5 part-time. **Average Class Size**: 16-28; PreK-5, 2 teachers full time, per class.

Special Courses: French & Spanish, Transition-8; Computer, Gen'l Science, Biology. Art & Music,Drama Interdisciplinary, hands on approach. Note: Transition class K/1; Grades 1-5, cross-age grouping in two year spans. Middle School grades 6-8. **Extended Day** : until 6 p.m.; Holiday care available.

Athletics: Req.; Intramural Softball, Swimming; Competitive Soccer & Basketball (Middle School) **Publications**: School Magazine, Weekly Newsletter.

Plant: Library 10,000 vol., Middle School Science Lab, Gym/ Auditorium, Art Studios, Heated Pool, Fields. Barnyard farm animals, pond, & woods. 2 new elementary classroom buildings, spring '95. Note: 300 acre campus in West Virginia with three buildings used by grades 2-8 fall & spring.

Admission: Individual Testing with school referred psychologist; References, Student Visit, Parent Interviews and Visits classes; School seeks diverse student body.

Tuition: (1995-96) $8,615-$9,525. **Transportation**: One way $970; rd. trip $1,445 **Extended Day**: Extra. **Financial Aid**: Available.

Future Plans: Continue 10 yr. campus renewal plan

Summer Program: Natural Science Camp at mountain campus in W. Va. (Residential). Day Camp (Alexandria campus)- emphasis on performing and visual arts, natural science, sports - Red Cross swimming, computers. Ages 3-14. **Extended Day**: both a.m. & p.m.

BUTLER SCHOOL...(301) 977-6600

15951 Germantown Road, Darnestown, MD 20874
Founded 1971 **Head**: Rilla Spellman

Grades: N- grade 8   **Enrollment**: 200 Co-ed. **Faculty**: 16 full- 5 part-time.
Average Class Size: 27 primary, 22 elementary.

Special Programs: Spanish K-8, French K-8. Remedial Reading and Math available. Art, Music, Piano lessons. Equestrian program. **Extended Day**: 8 a.m.- 5:15 p.m.

Athletics: All grades, K-8. Intramural. **Publications**: Newspaper

Plant: Library 6,000 vol., Art Studio, Playing Fields, Swimming Pool, Stables, Tennis Courts, 22 acre campus.

Admission: Parent Interview and Classroom Observation.

Tuition: (1995-96) $3,450 Half-day; $5,200 Full-day. **Transportation** : $750 one way, $1,500 both . *Dress Code*: Uniform req. for elementary grades. **Financial Aid**: Available.

Summer Program: Full day camp, 11 weeks- June through August for ages 6-13; Outdoor adventures, equestrian, performing arts, swimming, tennis. Half- day camp, ages 2-4: arts & crafts, swimming, outdoor activities.

CADENCE EPISCOPAL DAY SCHOOL.................(202) 829-5520

7005 Piney Branch Road, N.W., Washington, D. C. 20012
Episcopal   **Head**: Donna Robinson

Grades: N3-grade 2   **Enrollment**: 20 Co-ed

Extended Day: 7:30 - 8:15 a.m. to 5:30 p.m.

Tuition:(1995-96) $4,000 includes Day Care

CALVARY BAPTIST CHURCH ACADEMY.........(410) 768- 5324

407 Marley Station Road, Glen Burnie, MD. 21061.
Independent 1973. **Head**: John Bandy, Principal; Floyd Washburn, Pastor

Grades: K(3)-12. **Enrollment**: 400 Co-ed. **Faculty**: 11 full-, 5 part-time.
Average Class Size: 25

Special Courses: Spanish 9-12. Algebra I & II. General Science, Biology, Chemistry, Physics. History-U.S., U.S. Gov't, World Geography. Religious Studies req. Art, Music, Typing, Computer Science. **Extended Day** : 6 a.m.-6 p.m.

Athletics: req. to grade 10. Soccer, Basketball, Baseball, Softball, Volleyball. **Publications**: Yearbook. **Community Involvement**: Visit the nursing home once a month.

Plant: Library, Science Labs, Auditorium.

Admission: Interview, Individual Testing; $100 Registration fee.

Tuition: (1995-96) N & K Half-day, $1,500; Full-day N & K, $2,250; 1-5 $2,230; 6-8 $2,450; 9-12, $2,760 **Transportation:** $650 round trip. *Dress Code*: Rules stated in student handbook.

Future plans: Build a gym, develop & expand library.

CALVARY LUTHERAN SCHOOL..........(301) 589-4001

9545 Georgia Avenue, Silver Spring, MD. 20910.
Lutheran 1951. **Head**: Melvin P. Schnackenberg.

Grades: K-6. **Enrollment**: 125 Co-ed. **Faculty**: 6 full-, 4 part-time.
Average Class Size: 25 or less.

Special Courses: Remedial Reading & Math, Study Skills, Art, Music. Religious Studies, Group Piano, Science Camp. School subjects taught in Christian environment. Program aimed at developing the natural talents of each child so that he may use these gifts and talents in the services of God and his fellow man. **Extended day**: 7 a.m.-6 p.m.

Athletics: Volleyball, Flag Football, Softball, Track & Field Day. **Community Involvement**: Sing at nursing home. Choir, 10:00 a.m. church service, one Sunday a month.

Plant: Library 3882 vol., Playing Field, Multi-Purpose Room.

Admission: Grades 1-6 - interview with Principal.

Tuition: (1995- 96) K-6 $3,300 (reduced rate for siblings) **Extended Day**: Extra.
Lunch: Extra. *Dress Code*: Neat & clean. **Financial Aid**: Available.

CALVARY ROAD CHRISTIAN SCHOOL...(703) 971-8004

6811 Beulah Street, Alexandria, VA. 22310.
Baptist 1973. **Director**: L. Harold Jones.

Grades: N 2 1/2- 8 **Enrollment**: 200 Co-ed. **Faculty**: 15 full-, 2 part-time.
Average Class Size: 20.

Special Courses: Computer. Religious Studies req. **Extended Day** -6:45 a.m.-6 p.m.

Athletics: Not req. Basketball, Baseball, Soccer, Softball, Volleyball. **Publications**: Yearbook.

Plant: Library, Science Labs, Auditorium.

Admission: I.Q. Test, Grade Placement Test, Interview with Principal. Registration fee $100.

Tuition: (1995-96) PreK, $4,160 includes **Lunch & Extended Day**; Grades K-8, $2,450
Extended Day: Extra. Books: Extra. *Dress Code*: Neatly trimmed hair, girls dress length to top of knee.

Summer Program: Day Camp ages 2 1/2-12.

CALVERTON SCHOOL..........(410) 535-0216 or (301) 855-1922

300 Calverton School Road, Huntingtown, MD. 20639.
Founded 1967 **Head**: Bonnie Miller

Grades: PreK-12. **Enrollment**: 245 Co-ed. **Faculty**: 29 full-, 2 part-time.
Average Class Size: 15.

Special Courses: French PreK-12, Spanish 9-12; Math includes Calculus, Computer. Science:
General Science, Biology, Chemistry, Physics, Biochemistry, Chesapeake Bay Studies. History
European Civilization I & II, American Studies, American Gov't, Economics. Art, Music, Chorus.
Health, Driver's Ed. AP.: English, French, History, Calculus, Computer, Chemistry, Biology.
Extended Day until 6 P.M.

Athletics: Intramural: Tennis, Golf, Volleyball. Interscholastic: Soccer, Lacrosse, Field Hockey,
Basketball, Track & Field, Volleyball. **Clubs**: Photography, Drama, Mock Trial. **Publications**:
Yearbook, Literary Magazine, Newspaper. **Community Involvement**: Community Service,
all levels involved. 30 hrs. of community service graduation requirement.

Plant: 2 Libraries - 15,000 vol.; 2 Science Labs, Gym, Auditorium, Playing Fields, Art Studio.
23 acres with 5 acre marsh on river, 10 miles away.

Admission: Rolling admissions. PreK- grade 2: individual assessment. Grades 3-12, Student
Visits class, Testing. $35 Application fee. Student's academic achievement, character, and
potential taken into consideration.

Tuition: (1995-96) PreK- Full day: $6,635. Grades K-12, $8,350. Bring lunch.
Transportation & Extended Day Extra. *Dress Code*: Uniform req. **Financial Aid:** Some

Future Plans: Outdoor Environmental Camp, Amphitheater, Fine Arts Building.

Summer Program: Day and Specialty camps for ages 5-18.

CANTERBURY SCHOOL..........(301) 292-5535

P.O. Box 509, 600 Farmington Road West, Accokeek, MD. 20607
Episcopal 1961. **Head**: Mrs. Noel Wilson

Grades: 7-12. **Enrollment**: 68 Co-ed. **Faculty**: 4 full-, 5 part-time.
Average Class Size: 10.

Special Courses: French 7-12, Spanish 9-12; Math: Algebra 7-9, Geometry 8-11, Trig 9-12,
Calculus 11-12,, and Computer 9-12. Science: General Science, Biology, Chemistry, Physics.
History: Civics, American, Geography, Anthropology, Western Civilization; Environmental
Studies. Studio Art, Music, Related Arts, Drama. AP.: Biology

Athletics: Not required. Intramural & Interscholastic: Basketball, Soccer, Softball; Volleyball
Intramural only. **Clubs**: Bicycling **Publications**: Yearbook. **Community Involvement**:
River clean-up, Work with the Homeless, Tutoring at local elementary school.

Plant: Library 8,000 vol., Science Labs, Art Studio, Pavilion/Multi-purpose room, 10 acres of
Playing Fields.

Admission: $25 Application Fee; Interview, Class Visitation, Record Review, In-school Testing when indicated.

Tuition: (1995-96) $6,700   Books approx. $250.   **Transportation** : $1,528 yr. *Dress Code*: Must not be offensive. **Financial Aid**: Some available.

CAPITOL CHRISTIAN ACADEMY ....(301) 336-2200 FAX (301) 336-6704

610 Largo Road, Upper Marlboro, MD. 20772
Baptist 1961   **Head**: Wayne P. Baker

Grades: K4-12. **Enrollment**: 480 Co-ed **Faculty**: 22 full-, 9 part-time.
Average Class Size: 22

Special Courses: Spanish K4-12, Remedial Reading and Math. Algebra I & II, Geometry, Computer. Science: General Science, Biology, Chemistry, Physics. Religious studies req. Art, Music, Band, Choir, Typing. Alpha Omega program offers supervised individual progress for accelerated learning, grades 2-8.   Note: Discovery Program for Learning Impaired.
Extended Day: 6:30 a.m.-6 p.m.

Athletics: Req. 7-12. Interscholastic: Volleyball, Soccer, Basketball, Softball, Baseball.
Publications: Newspaper, Yearbook.

Plant: Library 6,000 + vol., Science Lab, Auditorium, Gym, Playing Fields.

Admission: Test, $150 Registration fee, Interview with parents, Transcript.

Tuition: (1995-96) $3,067 (Reduction for siblings). **Transportation**: Available, rate depends on distance.   *Dress Code*: Uniform req. K4-grade 8; grades 9-12, No jeans, Girls must wear dresses; boys traditional haircut. **Financial Aid**: Some available.

Summer Program: Summer school grades 1-12; Math, English, Reading for elem./jr. high. Some academic subjects for high school. "Super Summer" Program for ages 5 through grade 6: swimming, organized games, outdoor recreation, field trips etc.

CAPITOL HILL DAY SCHOOL........... (202) 547-2244

210 South Carolina Avenue, S.E., Washington, D.C. 20003.
Founded 1968. **Head**: Catherine Peterson.

Grades: PreK-8. **Enrollment**: 225 Co-ed.   **Faculty**: 32 full-, 4 part-time.
Average Class Size: 20.

Special Courses: French Pre K-8; Algebra; Computers; General Science; Art. There is a central subject at each grade level around which much of the social studies and science is centered including: Life Cycles, Patterns; Native Americans and Environment; African Cultures and Rain

Forests; Anthropology, Ancient Civilizations; American History. Extensive field trips integrated with curriculum. **Extended Day**: 3-6 p.m.

Athletics: Rigorous physical education program that includes games and creative movement activities for young children. Competitive sports for upper grades including Basketball, Soccer, Softball. **Clubs** : Drama, Chorus. **Publications**: Yearbook. **Community Involvement**: Students work in and provide food for local soup kitchens. parent run community involvement program.

Plant: Library 7,500 vol.; Audio-Visual equipment, Art Studio. Playing fields in 7 acre park across the street.

Admission: Parent Interview, Tour, Application fee $35 (Apply between October and February). Assessment Test, School Recommendation, Transcript, and Class visit.

Tuition: (1995-96) $8,120-$9,070 **Lunch**: Bring **Activitiy/Enrichment Fee** : grades 6-8, $395. Extra School Fee, $150. **Transportation**: $565 one-way, $895 both ways. *Dress Code*: Neat & clean appearance. **Financial Aid**: Available.

Summer Program: Day Camp: 2 week sessions June-July, ages 4-14, Swimming at nearby pools, field trips to historic sites and playgrounds; special programs for older children coordinated with such places as Genesee Valley Outdoor Center/Belle Haven Sailing Marina.

CARDINAL MONTESSORI SCHOOL......................(703) 491-3810

1424 G Street, Woodbridge, VA 22191
Head: Mrs. Leneali Gallegos

Ungraded : Ages 2 1/2-9 (N-4th)

Tuition: Call for information

CHARLES E. SMITH JEWISH DAY SCHOOL..........(301) 881-1400

1901 East Jefferson Street, Rockville, MD. 20852
Founded 1965. **Head**: Dr. Elliot Prager

Grades: K-12. **Enrollment**: 1,057 Co-ed. **Faculty**: 70 Full-, 100 part-time.
Average Class Size: no larger than 23.

Special Courses: French 7-12, Spanish 7-12; Hebrew Language and Literature req. K-12. Math thru Calculus; Computer. Science: General Science, Biology, Chemistry, Physics. History-Geography, U.S., Modern European, Jewish; Senior Seminars: Vietnam and the 60's; Human Growth & Development. Religious Studies req. Remedial Reading & Math. Art & Music, Photography, K-9. Choir 4-6, Drama. Business Management, Computer Keyboarding AP: Biology, Physics, French, Spanish. *Note*: Israel Work/Study Program Senior year.

27

Athletics: Req.; Intramural & Interscholastic. Soccer, Softball, Basketball, Tennis, Baseball, Volleyball, Cross-Country. **Clubs**: Social Action, Student Council, Cooking. **Publications**: Newspaper, Literary Magazine (in Hebrew & English), Yearbook. **Community Involvement**: Service program required in Upper School; intergenerational programs with senior citizens, clothing & food drives for homeless, and other programs.

Plant: 2 Libraries- 27,500 vol., 3 Science Labs, Art Studio, 2 Gyms, Auditorium, Playing Fields, Chapel. Newly equipped playground.

Admission: Interview, Screening Tests, Transcript, Teacher Recommendation. Registration at K, 1, and 7th grade; lateral entry in grades 2-11 if space available.

Tuition: (1995-96) K-6, $7,320; 7-11, $8,690; grade 12, $4,345 1st semester/ $4,700 for 2nd semester work/study program in Poland & Israel. **Books**: extra, grade 7-12 only. **Lunch**: Bring. **Transportation**: one way, $790; round trip $1,130. *Dress Code*: Neat and Clean , no cut-offs, halter tops; no short shorts in grade 7-12. **Financial Aid**: Available.

Summer Program: Sports Camp.

CHATHAM HALL...........(804) 432-2941 FAX (804) 432-2405

Chatham, VA 24531
Episcopal, 1894   **Head**: Mr. Jerry A. Van Voorhis, Rector

Grades: 9-12 **Enrollment**: 125 Girls (113 Boarding) **Faculty**: 25 full-, 5 part-time. **Average Class Size**: 8

Special Courses: Latin, French, Spanish: levels I-AP; **Science**: Introductory Science, Biology, Chemistry, Physics - tri-mester electives: Ethnology, Comparative Anatomy, Genetics. **History**: World Geography and Cultures, U.S. History, Modern European; Psychology; Senior tri-mester electives: Economics, Government, World Affairs. **Math**: Algebra I, intermediate, and II; Geometry, Pre- Calculus, Math V (Statistics, Mathematical Modeling, Intro. to Calculus) AP Calculus, SAT Math Review trimester elective: Math in Nature. Computer 1 (Literacy Basic Programming), Keyboarding and Word Processing. Ethics, 1 tri-mester req.; Religion, 1 tri-mester req. **AP**: English, US History, French, Spanish, Calculus, Biology, Chemistry. Fine or Performing Arts : Note 1 yr. req.-Art, Music (Choir, Voice, Organ, Instrumental), Dance.

Special Opportunities: Sophomore Service Project, Sr. Independent Project, Woodberry Forest in Britain, English Speaking Union, Leadership Seminars.

Athletics: Req. Intramural (all sports) & Interscholastic- Field Hockey, Basketball, Tennis. Also offered-Riding, Swimming, Lacrosse, Softball, Soccer, Volleyball. **Clubs**: French, Spanish, Latin, Ecology, Photography, Riding, Athletic Council, Student Council, Student Senate, Art, Drama, Music, Outdoor. **Publications**: Literary Magazine, Newspaper, Yearbook. **Community Involvement**: Every student is a member of the Service League-either School Life, Church Life, or Community Life.

Plant: Library 16,000 Vol.; 3 Science Labs, Computer Lab, Art Studio, Stables, 3 Playing Fields, 6 Tennis Courts, Greenhouse, 3 Dorms, Community Center, Infirmary, Chapel, New Fine Arts Center, new Gym, new Library with on-line system.

Admission: $35 Application fee; Essay, Questionnaire, Recommendations from English & Math teachers, Transcripts, Campus Visit, Interview, SSAT. First Choice Plan-acceptance date late January, others notified early March.

Tuition: (1995-96) Day $7,000; Boarding $18,000 **Books**: $750 deposit *Dress Code*: Neat appearance req. for classes, Chapel & Dinner. **Financial Aid**: Available.

Future Plans: Note: School's own electron microscope will provide more opportunities for intense research in the sciences; greater focus will be placed on public speaking.

CHELSEA SCHOOL.................(301) 585-1430 FAX (301) 585-9621

711 Pershing Drive, Silver Spring, MD. 20910.
Founded 1976. **Head**: William F. Patterson

Grades: 1-12. **Enrollment**: 126 Co-ed **Faculty**: 54 full-, 1 part-time. **Average Class Size**: 8

Special Courses: All Classes are taught by Special Education teachers. **Math**: Algebra, Geometry, Trig., Computer Programming, Keyboarding. **Science** : Gen'l Science, Biology, Chemistry, Physics, Environmental Science, Nature Skills. **History**: U.S., World, Government, Geography. Psychological and Social Issues. Remedial Reading. Art, includes Independent Seminar, Pottery. Advanced Language Seminar, Journalism, Child Development. College & Careers, Library Skills, Office Practice. Note: Services for LD students including: tutorials, speech & language pathologist, occupational therapist, social skills groups.

Athletics: Not req.; Interscholastic competition; member of Small Schools League - Soccer, Basketball, Softball, Track **Clubs**: Music, Trail, Cinema, Student Government, Pan African Society, Cheerleading. **Publications**: Yearbook, Newspaper. **Community Involvement**: Senior Internship Program, Community Service and Newspaper.

Plant: Library 8,000 vol., Science Lab, Art Studio, Pottery Studio, Darkroom, Gym, Auditorium. 2 buildings- Lower and Upper School

Admission: Tour, Application with Testing. Note: Students must be of average or above average ntelligence with a learning disability.

Tuition: (1995-96) $20,558 **Lunch**: Bag, vending; hot pizza, Tuesdays. *Dress Code*: Clean, neat and presentable clothing. **Financial Aid**: Some available

Summer Program: 5-week s for students with Learning Disabilities. Late June- end of July. .

CHESAPEAKE ABILITY SCHOOL.........(703) 256-1900 FAX (703) 256-1923

5533 Industrial Drive, Springfield, VA 22151
Founded 1979. **Head**: Lois A. Gloor

Grades: K-12; parent/adult education. **Enrollment**: 70 Co-ed. **Faculty**: 12 full-, 2 part-time.
Average Class Size: 15

Special Courses: Individualized instruction, " how to learn", study and communication courses for students at elementary through high school ages. Licensed by Applied Scholastics International to use the study methods developed by L. Ron Hubbard. All basics are learned extreamly well. Emphasis on 100% comprehension and practical application in all subjects. Students move at own rate, and gradiently increase to their full potential as study methods learned and used. Admissions interview required for student and parent; student tested to determine work to be done to repair weak areas in student's earlier education.

Innovative Reading Program raises student literacy level to new heights through individual instruction. Starting with phonics, the program then expands to include dictionary and learning instruction while having the child read great quantity of good literature daily. Emphasis is on having child read lots of good books that gradiently increase in difficulty so child meets many of the important and valuable individuals of his society, culture and heritage through reading.

Job experience considered a priority for high school students. The students are exposed to a moral code, The Way to Happiness, which is based wholly on common sense and is the basis for school counseling services. Graduating student receives diploma certifying competency. College bound program available. **Foreign Languages** : French, Spanish, & German. **Math**: Advanced Geometry, Trig, Calculus. **Science**: Physical Science, Biology, Chemistry, Physics.   Some electives are: Typing, Home Skills, Art, Computer, Word Processing, Basic Programming, Economics, Photography. **Note**: Adult education component includes how to read effectively, study & communication courses, and parent workshops.

Athletics: P.E. daily. **Publications**: Quarterly Newsletter. **Community Involvement**: Participation in environmental clean-ups; Visit senior citizen homes; Volunteer Service at homeless/community centers; other Way to Happiness Projects.

Plant: 4 1/2 acre campus, Soccer Field, Outdoor Basketball Courts (half court),   Library, Film room, Dark Room.

Admission: Interview with student and parents; $50 Application Fee; Student's own interest and goals for education important. Year round enrollment.

Tuition: (1995-96) $5,800. **Materials Fee**: $330/$350. **Lunch**: Bring. *Dress Code*: Casual but neat.

Future Plans: Parent workshops develop into Institute of Parent Education; Teacher/Tutor Training Institute.

Summer Program: 8 weeks (4 week min.); Morning: academics, how to study, communication courses; Afternoon fun : bowling, ice skating, swimming, field trips, arts & crafts, outings

CHESAPEAKE ACADEMY..........(410) 647-9612   FAX (410) 647-6088

1185 Baltimore Annapolis Boulevard., Arnold, MD. 21012
Founded 1980. **Head**: Jane C. Pehlke

Grades: N3-grade 5. **Enrollment**: 240 Co-ed. **Faculty**: 38 full-time, 2 part-time.
Average Class Size: 18

Special Courses: Spanish; Computer; Art; Music; Library, Great Books. Touchpebbles. Individualized enrichment programs. Piano & Strings   **Extended Day**: 7:30 a.m.- 6 p.m.

Athletics: P.E. Req.; Volleyball, Basketball, Soccer, Field Hockey. **Clubs**: Drama, Crafts, Gymnastics; Brownies. **Community Involvement:** Children perform community service.

Plant: Library 8,000 vol.; Science Room, Auditorium, Playing Fields, Computer Lab.

Admission: Application fee $55; Tour, Interview, Testing: Preschool-Early Learning Screening and Diagnostic test; Elementary Grades, 2 day visit includes Otis Lennon and Brigance testing.

Tuition: (1995-96) $1,785-$6,950   **Extended Day** : Extra.   *Dress Code*: Uniform req.
Financial Aid: Available

Summer Camp: "Super Summer" 9 a.m.-3 p.m., Care provided 7:30 a.m.-6 p.m.. Arts and crafts, sports, swimming, nature study, games, drama, music, cooking, field trips, overnights.

CHESAPEAKE MONTESSORI SCHOOL..........(410) 757-4740

30 Old Mill Bottom Road North, Annapolis, MD. 21401
Founded 1977. **Head**: Anne Locke.

Ungraded: Ages 2-1/2 through 11. **Enrollment**: 110 Co-ed. **Faculty**: 4 full-, 3 part-time.
4 class-room assistants. **Average Class Size**: 25

Special Courses: French - all ages, Art, Music, Athletics K-5, Montessori Method;
Extended Day Care: 7 a.m.-6 p.m.

Publications: Yearbook   **Community Involvement**: Jump Rope for Heart; Holiday sharing program

Plant: Central Library & Libraries in classrooms, Playing Fields, Swimming Pool, Multi-purpose Room.

Admission: Interview with parents and child; Observation; Test age 6 and over; $25 Application fee, $250 Registration fee. <u>Note</u>: Child must be at least 2-1/2 and toilet trained to be admitted.

Tuition: (1995-96) Half- day N, $3,680; full day K $5,175; Elementary $5,485. **Extended Day**: additional charge. **Financial Aid**: Available

Summer Program: Three 2-week sessions late-June through July for ages 3-8; includes swimming, singing, nature walks, field trips, arts & crafts. Morning or full day programs.

CHILDREN'S LEARNING CENTER............(301) 871-6600   FAX (301) 871-6015

4511 Bestor Drive, Rockville, MD 20853
Jewish 1978   **Head**: Ms. Rena Popkin

Grades: N- 5   **Enrollment**: Co-ed: N, 260; K-5, 57. **Average Class Size**: 12-20 depending on age. **Faculty** Use of Resource teachers in K-5.

Special Programs: Judaic/Hebrew Curriculum inclusion. <u>Extra-curricular</u>:: Computer tots, Group Piano Lessons, Dance Lessons, Gym on Wheels.. **Extended Day**: 7 a.m. - 6 p.m.

Plant: Use of former public elementary school building

Admission: Registration fee, $75-$100. Interview with parents.

Tuition: (1995-96) N: depends on number of days and hours; Half-day K, $335/mo.; Full-day K grade 5, $640/mo. Registration fee $100-$125. <u>Lunch, Activity Fees, and</u> **Extended Day** Extra. **Transportation**: $75/mo, **Financial Aid**: Available.

Summer Program: Camp for ages 2-6.

CHRISTCHURCH SCHOOL...........(804) 758-2306   FAX (804) 758-0721

Rt. 33 Christchurch School , Christchurch, VA 23031
Episcopal 1921   **Head**: C. Jackson Blair

Grades: 9-PG   **Enrollment**: 200 Co-ed (170 Boys, 30 Girls) 140 Boarding (Boys only 9-12, PG) 60 Day (Co-ed 9-12). **Faculty**: 30 full-, 5 part-time. **Average Class Size**: 12.

Special Courses: Latin, French, Spanish: 9-12. <u>Math</u> includes Trig, Calculus, Basic & Advanced Computer. <u>Science:</u> Introduction to Physical Science, Biology, Chemistry, Physics, Marine Sciences;   <u>History</u>: World, U.S., U.S. Gov't, 20th Century World, World Geography, Comparative Idealogies, Future Studies. Economics. Religious Studies, req.; Art, Music, Drama. Remedial Reading and Math . Learning Skills Program for students diagnosed as having a learning skills disability <u>Note</u>: Complete program for Learning Disabled. <u>AP</u>:: Chemistry; Honors English.

Athletics: Req.; Intramural: Softball, Volleyball. Interscholastic: Soccer, Football, Wrestling, Basketball, Cross Country, Track, Baseball, Lacrosse, Tennis, Golf, Indoor Soccer, Weight Lifting, Indoor Track, Sailing, Crew **Clubs**: Syudent Gov't; Social Activities, Sailing, Scuba, Marine Science. **Publications**: Newsletter, Yearbook, Literary Magazine. **Community Involvement**: Work with Local civic club & organizations, nursing homes; Participate in Adopt a Highway Program.

Plant: Library, 7,000 vol.; 2 Science Labs, 2 Gyms, Art Studio, 4 Playing Fields, 2 Swimming Pools, 6 new Tennis Courts with lighting;. Waterfront location used for Marine Science projects and Sailing.

Admission: Interviews are conducted all year. Recommendations: teachers, counselor and family friend. Note: Candidates for the Learning Skills Program may use outside tests administered within the last two years.

Tuition : (1995-96) Boarding $18,500; Day, $9,5000, Includes Lunch Books: $300-$400. *Dress Code:* Boys: Shirts with collars, trousers with belt, shoes & socks (No jeans, running shoes, etc. for classroom dress). **Financial Aid:** Available

Future Plans: Refurbishment of Dormitory, Construction on waterfront of new field house and Marine Science classroom with lab facility.

Summer Program: Academic classes in Math, History, Languages, etc.
Summer Camp: Junior Marine Science Institute which studies Chesapeake Bay Ecology. Also an all sports Camp which includes sailing, scuba, soccer, & tennis.

CHRIST CHURCH DAY SCHOOL...........(301) 934-1477

East Charles Street, (P.O. Box 1467) La Plata, MD 20646
Head: Barbara Merrick

Grades: N- grade 5 **Enrollment**: 100 Co-ed **Average Class Size**: 15

Special Programs: French; Science Fair, Odssey of the Mind. **Extended Day**: 7:30 a.m.-6 p.m.

Tuition: (1995-96) N 1/2 day, 2 days a wk: $610; PreK, 1/2 day, 3 days a wk. $830; K $1,700; Grades 1-5, $2,400. **Financial Aid**: Limited

CHRIST EPISCOPAL SCHOOL..........(301) 424-6550 FAX (301) 424-0494

109 S. Washington Street, Rockville, MD. 20850
Episcopal 1966. **Head**: Dana F. Beane

Grades: PreK-8. **Enrollment**: 196 Co-ed. **Faculty**: 12 full-, 7 part-time.
Average Class Size: 18.

Special Courses: Spanish K-8; Algebra, Computer K-8. General Science. Social Studies 5-8 Great Books K-6; Shakespeare. Library Skills K-8. (Learning Resource teacher on staff). Art, Music (Recorders, Chimes), Chapel req. (daily), Drama. Builders Club.
Extended Day: 7-8:30 a.m. and 3-6 p.m..

Athletics: Required and includes Soccer. **Publications**: Yearbook, Monthly Newsletter.
Community Involvement: Outreach programs

Plant: Library, Science Lab, Art Studio, Playing Fields, Chapel (located in church).

Admission: Interview, Transcripts, Testing, Class Visit. Fee for Screening. Recommendations from previous schools.

Tuition: (1995-96) Pre K- 2 days $1,260; 3 days, $1,890; 5 days, $3,150; K-8 $5,900.
Dress Code: Uniform req. **Financial Aid**: Some Available.

Summer Program: Summer Camp, Pre K-and K

CHRISTIAN ASSEMBLY ACADEMY.....(703) 698-7458   FAX (703) 698-9860

8200 Bell Lane, Vienna, VA 22182-5299
Founded 1984. **Head**: Richard T. Chrisinger, Principal; Martin R. Reeve,Administrator

Grades: K-8 **Enrollment**: 92 Co-ed **Faculty**: 7 full-, 8 part-time.
Average Class Size: 10-11

Special Courses: Algebra, Earth Science, Music, Art, Health

Athletics: P.E.; Basketball, Soccer, Softball (5-8)

Plant: 7 Classrooms, Art/Health room, Cafeteria, Library, Soccer Field, Blacktop Basketball Court.

Admission: Application and Interview

Tuition: (1995-96) Call for information in summer.

CHRISTIAN CENTER SCHOOL..........(703) 971-0558/0559

5411 Franconia Road, Alexandria, VA. 22310
Interdenominational 1976. **Head**: Mercedes S. Morrison, Principal

Grades: K4-grade 6. **Enrollment**: 157 Co-ed. **Faculty**: 27 full-, 1 part-time.
Average Class Size: 20.

Special Courses: Art, Bible, Computer, Co-Curricula Studies, Health Safety and Manners; History and Geography, Language Arts, Math, Music, Science, Science Lab, Spanish; Morning & Afternoon Extended Learning Center, Speech Therapy. **Extended Day** : 7 a.m.-6 p.m.

Athletics: P.E. req. all grades: Intramural: Basketball, Baseball, Volleyball, Softball, Soccer, Dance (Tap, Jazz, Ballet), Gymnastics. **Clubs**: Art **Publications**: Yearbook.

Plant: Gym, Playground, Classrooms

Admission: Parent/child Interview with Principal, Test, Transcript.

Tuition: (1995-96) Call for information. **Transportation**: depends on distance *Dress Code*: Uniform req.

CHRISTIAN FAMILY MONTESSORI...........(301) 927-7122

3628 Rhode Island Avenue, Mt. Rainier, MD. 20712
Christian, 1982. **Head**: Heinz Bondy, Director

Ungraded: Ages 2 1/2-9. **Enrollment**: 75 Co-ed. **Faculty**: 3 full-, 4 part-time. **Average Class Size**: 25.

Special Courses: Montessori method. Elementary Math and Science studies. History and Social Science included in cultural areas. Religious Studies req.; Art and Music. Note: Catechesis of the Good Shepherd, a religious education program based on Montessori, developed by Sophia Cavaletti, that stresses the spiritual life and child's relationship with God, offered after school, one day a week.

Athletics: P.E. for elementary grades only.

Plant: Library 2,400 Vol.; 4 classrooms, playground

Admission: Contact Director; Interview; Transcript

Tuition: (1995-96) N & K, Half-day, $1,650, 1-2, $2,500 **Financial Aid**: Some available.

Future Plans: Add 3rd primary and upper elementary program

CLINTON CHRISTIAN SCHOOL..........(301) 599-9600

6707 Woodyard Road., Upper Marlboro, MD. 20772 (K3-grade 12)
also: Bannister Circle, Waldorf, MD 20601 (K4-grade 6)
Baptist 1966. **Head**: William G. Spence, Administrator; Larry Spencer, Pastor.

Grades: N-12. **Enrollment**: 600 Co-ed. **Faculty**: 33 full-, 6 part-time.
Average Class Size: 20.

Special Courses: French 1-6. Computer Instruction 1-12. Religious studies req. Bible;
Piano, Chorus, Drama. **Extended Day**: 7 a.m.-6 p.m.

Athletics: Req. 1-12. Interscholastic. Flag Football, Volleyball, Basketball, Softball,
Cheerleading. **Clubs**: Journalism, Yearbook. **Publications**: Yearbook. **Community
Involvement**: MS Read-a-Thon, Thanksgiving Basket project.

Plant: Auditorium, Playing Fields, Gym.

Admission: Registration (conference before child is registered). Testing. Registration fee $100.

Tuition: (1995-96) Half- day, $1,800-$2,000; Full Day, $3,000-$3,400 includes hardback
Books. **Extended Day & Lunch**: Extra. **Transportation**: $940 plus zone charges.
Dress Code: Specific regulations.

Summer Program: Summer school - Elementary level work in Phonics, Reading & Math.
Summer Camp - Day program offering Swimming, Riding, Fishing, Field trips, Organized games,
Bible stories.

CLOVERLAWN ACADEMY..........(703) 538-4022

3455 North Glebe Rd. (at Ditmar Rd.), Arlington, VA 22207
Founded 1953. **Head**: Mary Harper Clark.

Grades: N-7. **Enrollment**: 65 Co-ed. **Faculty**: 6 full-, 3 part-time.
Average Class Size: 11.

Special Courses: French, Holt Unlimited Math; Computer; Enrichment Reading, Creative &
Expository writing; Accelerated Science Program; Social Science & Geography; History. Art,
Music. Humanities. **Extended Day**: 7 a.m.-5:30 p.m.

Athletics: P.E. req. **Clubs**: Newspaper & Science. **Publications**: Newspaper.
Community Involvement: Services to the community   including sandwich making for the
homeless. Environment.

Plant: Science Lab, Computers, Playing Fields, & Auditorium.

Admission: Interviews; Referrals; some Testing; Transcript. Classroom visits.

Tuition: (1995-96) $2,750-$4,500 *Dress Code:* Uniform req. in grades.
Scholarship Aid: 2 full, 2 partial.

Summer Program: Combined recreational and academic program .

COLUMBIA ACADEMY...................(410) 312-7413

10350 Old Columbia Road, Columbia, MD 21046
Head : Tracy Underwood

Grades: K-4

Tuition: (1995-96) Call for information

Future Plans: to go to grade 6.

CONCORD HILL SCHOOL.........(301) 654-2626   FAX (301) 654-1374

6050 Wisconsin Avenue, Chevy Chase, MD. 20815.
Founded 1965. **Head**: Mrs. French McConnaughey

Grades: N-3. **Enrollment**: 90 Co-ed. **Faculty**: 11 full, 3 part-time.
Average Class Size: 18 with 2 teachers

Special Courses: Art, Music, Computer (all levels); General Science, Social Studies, Field Trips.
Note: Small classes allow much individual attention: a ratio of 1:9 teacher/ pupil maintained
throughout the program. Optional After School enrichment classes.

Athletics: PE **Clubs**: Cub Scouts and Brownies.

Plant: Library 3,500 vol.; Computers at all levels, Science Lab. Playground. Spacious
classrooms with indoor play/assembly facilities.

Admission: $55 Application fee; Transcripts and Teacher Recommendations; Parent Interview,
then child visits . Interviews begin in Oct. 1. for following year, notification mid-March..

Tuition: (1995-96) N $5,600; K $7,425; Grades 1-3 $7,920 includes all fees & Books.
Lunch: Brown bag, milk provided. *Dress Code*: Comfortable, appropriate school clothes.
Financial Aid: Limited, partial scholarships.

Summer Program: Day Camp for 3-5 yr. olds, 3 two-week sessions. Arts Camp, K-grade 5.

CONCORDIA LUTHERAN SCHOOL.........(301) 927-0266

3799 East-West Highway, Hyattsville, MD. 20782.
Lutheran 1944. **Head**: Mrs. Nancy Ann Grandel, Principal.

Grades: PreK-grade 8. **Enrollment**: 275 Co-ed. **Faculty**: 16 full-time.
Average Class Size: 28.

Special Courses: Algebra, Computer. Gen'l Science. World & U.S. History;   World & U.S. Geography. Religious studies. Note: Language Arts & Math, grouped according to performance. Music, Chorus, Band. **Extended Day** : 7 a.m. - 6 p.m.

Athletics: P.E. Req. grades 1-8. Interscholastic Basketball. **Publications**: Yearbook. **Community Involvement**: Students participate in various charity drives, Hyattsville Clean-up, Canned goods for "Help by Phone", "Jump for Heart", and annual mission projects.

Plant: Three facilities- Library 12,000 vol.; Science Labs, Computer Lab, Gym, Playing Fields..

Admission: Open application policy. Interview, Transcript, Teacher & Principal Recommendations.

Tuition: (1995-96) Half-Day N & K available; Full-day K, $3,335. grades 1-8, $3,100 **Transportation**: Available. *Dress Code*: Neat and in good taste. **Financial Aid**: Limited..

Summer Program: Summer program for age 3 to grade 6, daily.

CONGRESSIONAL SCHOOLS OF VIRGINIA...........(703) 533-9711

3229 Sleepy Hollow Rd., Falls Church, VA 22042
Founded 1939. **Head**: Shirley K. Fegan

Grades: N (infant)-grade 8. **Enrollment**: 427 Co-ed. **Faculty**: 38 full-time. **Average Class Size**: Pre -school (Age 2-5), Teacher/pupil ratio 1:7, 1:9; grades 1-8, 15-22.

Special Courses: French l-8, Spanish 6-8. Computer Pre-K- grade 8, Algebra 8. General Science 6, Life Science 7, Physical Science 8; Art, Music. **Extended Day**: available 7 a.m. -6 p.m., for Pre-school-grade 8.

Athletics: P.E. Program. Note: after-school program for grades 5-8. Soccer, Basketball, Softball, Track and Field, Swimming. **Clubs**: Service, Student Gov't, Drama, Art, Chess. **Publications**: Yearbook, Literary Magazine. **Community Involvement**: Through Service Club: Recycling project, Volunteer at W.S.P.C.A. (Humane Society), Nursing Homes, and Ronald McDonald House; Collect canned goods for local shelters.

Plant: 2 Libraries, 2 Science Labs, Computer Lab, Art Studio, Assembly Room, 3 Playing Fields, 2 Swimming Pools.

Admission: Interview, Transcript & Recommendation from previous school. Testing. Application fee $50.

Tuition: (1995-96) $6,300-$8,262. **Extended Day** : Extra. Lunch: $436-$548. **Transportation**: $1,761-$2,483. *Dress Code*: Uniform req. grades 1-8.

Summer Program: Recreation for ages 2 1/2-14 ; Swimming, riding, archery, art, music, outdoor sports.

CONNELLY SCHOOL OF THE HOLY CHILD.........(301) 365-0955   FAX (301) 365-0981

9029 Bradley Boulevard., Potomac, MD. 20854.
Catholic 1961. **Head**: Maureen K. Appel, Headmistress

Grades: 6-12. **Enrollment**: 310 Girls. **Faculty**: 29 full-, 10 part-time.
Average Class Size: 15   Note: 20% of students, non Catholic.

Special Courses: French & Spanish- 7-12.   Math includes Calculus BC; Computer Science;
Science: Gen'l Science, Biology, Chemistry, Physics. History: Western Civilization, World
Cultures. Multidisciplinary Humanities; Religious Studies. 4 yr. Studio Art Program, Music,
Consortium Courses. AP : Biology, Chemistry, U.S. History, European History.

Athletics: Intramural & Interscholastic: Basketball, Tennis, Cross-Country, Swimming,
Volleyball, Soccer, Lacrosse, Hockey, Softball. **Clubs**: Art, Debate, GAA, Pep, Library, Nat'l
Honor Society, Black Awareness, Environmental, SADD, Service, Drama, Model OAS.
Publications: Newspaper, Yearbook. **Community Involvement**: Service Program; Annual
Musical Production.

Plant: Library 10,000 vol., 4 Science Labs, 2 Art Studios, Gym, 2 Playing Fields, 2 Tennis
Courts. Campus is in a pastoral setting.

Admission: Archdiocese Entrance Test or SSAT; School Visit, Interview. Recommendations;
$35 Application Fee.

Tuition: (1995-96) 6-8, $7,950; 9-12, $8,950   Books: Extra. *Dress Code*: Uniform req.
Transportation: reached by #36 Ride on and T-2 Metro bus. **Financial Aid**: Available.

Summer Program: "Express Yourself": a Day Camp for girls entering grades 8 & 9.

CORNERSTONE CHRISTIAN ACADEMY.........(301) 262-7683

16010 Annapolis Road, Bowie, MD 20715
Head Mrs. Dee Lehmann

Grades : PreK3 - grade 8 **Enrollment**: 40 Co-ed **Faculty**: 5 full-time
Average Class Size: 8

Special Programs: ABEKA, Bob Jones 7 & 8; small classes, individual attention
Extended Day : 2:30 - 6 p.m.

Tuition: (1995-96) $2,600

The COUNTRY DAY SCHOOL OF JEFFERSON COUNTY.........(304) 725-1438
FAX (304) 725-1439
P.O. Box 659, Charles Town, West VA 25414

Founded 1982   **Head** : Thomas H. Gast

Grades: K-9 **Enrollment**: 91 Co-ed **Faculty**; 17 full-, 8 part-time
Average Class Size : 18

Special Courses : Academic oriented: French K-9; Latin 6-9; Computer K-9; Art, Music, Math through Geometry; Science through Biology. Current Events. Drama. Field trips: one per grade, per month and grade 3 visits Williamsburg, Jamestown, Yorktown. Latin Certamen 6-9; National Mythology Exam and National Geography Bee.

Athletics : P.E. K-9; Intra-mural programs for girls & boys in soccer and basketball. Skiing, Swimming, Horseback Riding, and Roller Skating.

Plant : Library, Language Lab, Computer Lab, Art/Music Facility, Playing Fields, Basketball Court

Admission : Interview parent & child; Placement Testing; Transcript. Application fee $25.

Tuition : (1995-96) $3,200-$4,330   Books: extra **Financial Aid** : Some available

Future Plans: Addition of a sports/auditorium

Summer Program : Tutoring

DeMATHA CATHOLIC HIGH SCHOOL..........(301) 864-3666   FAX (301) 864-0248

4313 Madison Street, Hyattsville, MD. 20781
Catholic 1946. **Head**: Mr. John L. Moylan.

Grades: 9-12. **Enrollment**: 880 Boys. **Faculty**: 54 full-, 6 part-time.
Average Class Size: 25.

Special Courses: Latin I-II, French I-IV, Spanish I-IV, Math through Calculus BC, Basic I-II, Pascal, Computer Survey, Computer Graphics "C" & Design. Science: Biology, Chemistry, Physics, Human Anatomy & Physiology, Environmental Science. Business Law, Accounting Journalism, Mech. Drawing, Art History. Religious Studies req. Extensive Music program: Music Theory, 7 performing bands; Concert Band I-II, Wind Ensemble, Percussion Ensemble. Fundamental Art & Color Ceramics, Advanced Drawing, Architectural Drawing. AP.: English, French, Government, History, Biology, Chemistry, Physics, Calculus: Regular and Honors courses also offered in these areas. Students are ability grouped and performance determines mobility. Strong counseling program to help students evaluate own potential both educationally and vocationally. Levels of Courses: Some students attend University classes; some take courses at DeMatha to earn college credits by examination; can participate in specialized study.

Athletics: (Not req.) Intramural & Interscholastic. Football, Basketball, Baseball, Cross-Country, Track, Ice Hockey, Softball, Soccer, Swimming, Wrestling, Lacrosse, Tennis, Golf.

Clubs: Nat'l Honor Society, Science, Black Student Union, etc. **Publications**: Yearbook, Newspaper, Literary Magazine. **Community Involvement**: Social Action Groups and campus ministry program.

Plant: Library 14,000 vol., 5 Science Labs, Art Studio, Gym. Use of public parks for playing fields. Large new addition to academic building.

Admission: For grades 9 & 10 - Students in Catholic Elementary schools apply through Elementary schools; those in public school take High School Entrance Exam. School Records, standard Test scores, and character References. Grades 11 & 12 - Students must submit Transcript, References, High School Entrance Exam. Upon acceptance, $125 Registration fee.

Tuition: (1995-96) $4,320 plus fees. *Dress Code*: Uniform Blazer and Gray Dress or Khaki Trousers. **Books**: $200. **Lunch**: Cafeteria. **Financial Aid**: Available.

Future Plans: Addition of student activities building.

Summer Program: 5-week program for high school level repeat and preparatory courses.

DIFFERENT DRUM, INC..........(703) 971-0778

7150 Telegraph Road, Alexandria, VA. 223410
Founded 1973. **Director**: Mrs. Robin Harviel

Ungraded: Ages 14-18. **Enrollment**: 25 Co-ed. **Faculty**: 7 full-, 5 part-time.
Average Class Size: 8.

Special Courses: LD & ED Program. Remedial Reading & Math Program is individualized -student is taught at his level. Computer, General Science, Biology. All required Va. Social Studies, History, Math, English courses on secondary level. Elective courses include Typing, Vocational Class, Photography. Individualized curriculum for students who have been unsuccessful in public schools. Note: additional services include individual, group, and parent counseling.

Athletics: Informal sports program - all grades. **Publications**: monthly newsletter.

Plant: Basic Science Lab, Volleyball Court.

Admission: Social history, previous Testing (psychological & academic). Transcript req. prior to Interview with parents and students.

Tuition: State & County contract fees. **Transportation**: Available

DIVINE PEACE LUTHERAN SCHOOL..........(301) 350-4522

1500 Brown Station Road, Largo, MD 20772

Lutheran, 1983   **Head**: John Mittelstaedt

Grades: 1-8   **Enrollment**: 25 Co-ed   **Faculty** : 2 full, 1 part-time   **Average Class Size**: 4
Extended Day: Available

Tuition: (1995-96) $2,100   **Financial Aid**: Some available

DuPONT PARK SCHOOL..........(202) 583-8500

3942 Alabama Avenue, S.E., Washington, D.C. 20020
Seventh Day Adventist, 1914. **Head**: Mrs. Lafese Quinones

Grades: Pre K-10. **Enrollment**: 215 Co-ed. **Faculty**: 15 full-, 3 part-time.
Average Class Size: 20.

Special Courses: Biology, Gen'l Science; America: Its People and Values, History. Bible
K-10 (req.); Classroom worship service. Choir, Band, Typing, Home Ec. **Extended Day** :
7 a.m - 6 p.m.

Athletics: Req. Clubs: Many older students participate in Pathfinders (church-sponsored -
like Scouts). **Publications**: Weekly newsletter.

Admission: Transcript, Interview, Test. Healthy children with no disciplinary problems.

Tuition: (1995-96) $150-$260/mo. (3 or more, reduced rate) **Extended Day**: Extra. *Dress
Code*: Uniform req. Books: Included in Registration Fee.

EARLY YEARS ACADEMY.......(703) 590-3659   FAX (703) 590-3755

13817 Spriggs Road, Manassas, VA 22111
Founded 1987   **Head**: Samia Harris

Grades: Infant (3 wks) - grade 6 **Enrollment**: 140 Co-ed **Faculty**; 15 full-, 5 part-time
Average Class Size: Maximum, 15.

Special Courses: Bi-lingual, individualized curriculum. Spanish; Music: piano lessons
available; Algebra, grade 5; Phonics based curriculum. Hands on work shop in all areas.
Computer network in all areas; Internet. **Extended Day**: 5:30 a.m.-6:30 p.m.

Athletics: Sports program.

Plant: 5.5 acre campus: includes 3 buildings, sports field, Basketball court, 2 large playgrounds

Admission: Interview; Evaluation

Tuition: (1995-1996) $2,772 for grades 1-6; call for information on pre-school tuition.

Transportation: $60 mo. **Financial Aid**: Very Limited

Future Plans: To expand to 8th grade

Summer Program: Summer school and active summer camp

EARLY YEARS MONTESSORI..........(703) 237-0264

3241 Brush Drive, Falls Church, VA 22042
Founded 1990 **Head**: Mrs. Ahmad

Ungraded: Age 2-8 (grade 3) **Enrollment**: 40 Co-ed

Special Programs: **Extended Day**: 7 a.m.-6 p.m.

Tuition: (1995-96) $440/mo.

Summer Camp: Ages 2-8; Call for information

EDLIN SCHOOL...........(703) 758-1855

10922 Vale Road, Oakton, VA 22124
Founded 1989   **Head**: Elaine Mellman & Linda Schriebstein

Grades: K-8 **Enrollment**: 75 Co-ed **Average Class Size**: 12

Special Courses: Latin & French K-8. Extensive Math program with many computer courses. Science. History. English Language Arts program with emphasis on Shakespeare. Art, Music, Drama.. Note: An alternative school for gifted students.

Athletics: P.E. req. all grades.

Admission: IQ. & Achievement Tests, Testing fall and spring. Child spends 3 days visiting in class.

Tuition: (1995-96) $7,000 **Transportation** : $2,500 yr.

Future Plans: A summer program.

EDMUND BURKE SCHOOL..........(202) 362-8882   FAX (202) 362-1914

2955 Upton St., N.W., Washington, D.C. 20008
Founded 1968. **Head**: (Mr.) Jean Mooskin and Richard Roth.

Grades: 6-12. **Enrollment**: 245 Co-ed. **Faculty**: 30 full-, 8 part-time.
Average Class Size: 14

Special Courses: Rigorous college preparatory studies with full attention to basic skills, innovative course offerings, and intellectual challenge. Writing Center & Math Center for students of all grades; Math program integrates Algebra, Geometry, and Higher Mathematics; 7th Grade Linguistics Course; large array of Upper School electives, ranging from Peace Studies to Japanese History to Pascal Programming; AP courses in all disciplines; extensive use of city and the surrounding outdoor area.

Athletics: Intramural & Interscholastic. 20 Varsity, Jr. Varsity, and Middle School Teams for males and females in 8 sports (Potomac Valley Athletic Conference winner in Girls Soccer, '94) PE and Health req. to 11th grade; Outdoor program. Full range of extra-curricular activities including a thriving Theater program. **Clubs:** Debate Team, Model U.N. **Publications** : Yearbook, Literary Magazine, Newspaper. **Community Involvement**: Community Service Program for all grades.

Plant: Library 10,000 vol.; 4 Science Labs, Computer Lab, Art and Pottery Rooms, Gym, Playing Fields, Dark Room. School's center is an architecturally attractive atrium that is used for assemblies, meetings, recitals, etc.

Admission: SSAT or equivalent, plus Essay; Interview with parents; Student visits for a day. Application fee $40. Transcript and Teacher Recommendations.

Tuition: (1995-96) $11,200. *Dress Code*: Neatness & cleanliness. **Financial Aid**: Available.

Summer Program: Academic: Developmental and College Preparatory Math; Science, Languages, Verbal Skills, Study Skills. SAT Review, Computer courses among others. Camp: Basketball Camp in late June; Musical Theatre Workshop.

ELFLAND SCHOOL..........(703) 971-4337

4511 Glenwood Drive, Alexandria, VA. 22310
Head: Elizabeth Hathorn

Grades: N2- grade 1. **Enrollment**: 75 Co-ed. **Faculty**: 9 full-time, 5 part-time.
Average Class Size: 9.

Special Courses: Phonics, Whole Language, Spanish. **Extended Day** : 7 a.m.-6 p.m.

Plant: 2-1/2 acres of playing area.

Admission: Tour of school; Complete Registration Form.

Tuition: (1995-96) $435/mo. includes Lunch & **Extended Day**. Discount for 2nd child.

Summer Program: Reading, Arts & Crafts, Field Trips, Sports, Picnics, Cook-outs. 7 a.m.-6 p.m., June-Sept..

ELIZABETH SETON HIGH SCHOOL.......... (301) 864-4532

5715 Emerson Street, Bladensburg, MD. 20710
Catholic 1959. **Head**: Mrs. Geraldene Buckley

Grades: 9-12. **Enrollment**: 500 Girls. **Faculty**: 66 full-time. **Average Class Size**: 20-23

Special Courses: Besides the general college prep offerings: Careers in Art, Ceramics, Sculpture, Drawing and Painting; Business Education Word processing and Basic programming; Honors Program Latin, French and Spanish; Chorus, Concert Band, Symphonic Band; Nutrition, Clothing-Interior Design, Consumer Survival, The Family and the Child. Religious Studies. Honors Psychology, Introduction to Philosophy/ Theology, Sociology. **AP**: Biology, U.S.History, English, Government, Spanish, French, Calculus.

Athletics: Interscholastic. Basketball, Softball, Soccer, Volleyball, Track, Swimming, Cheerleading. **Clubs**: French, Spanish, Latin, Ecology, Mock Trial, Drama, Art, National Honor Society, SADD, Photography, Dance, Lacrosse. **Publications**: Newspaper, Yearbook. **Community Involvement**: Tutor in public schools, visit aged and help in Day Care centers; charity drives and involvement with S.O.M.E. and organizations helping the homeless in D.C..

Plant: Library 17,000 vol., Computer Center, Language Lab, Science Labs, Art Studio, Gym-Auditorium, Playing Fields, Tennis Courts, Home Economics Labs.

Admission: Arch-Diocese Entrance exam (call 202-853-4597 for dates) Transcript. Registration fee $100.

Tuition: (1995-96) $4,100. **Books**: $150 *Dress Code:* Uniform: Req. **Scholarship Aid**: Available through Archdiocese and work/study.

EMERSON PREPARATORY SCHOOL..........(202) 785-2877:

1324 18th Street, N.W., Washington, D.C. 20036
Founded 1852. **Head**: Dr. John J. Humphrey; Margot Ann Walsh, Administrator

Grades: 9-12 & PG. **Enrollment**: 150 Co-ed (over 12 months) **Faculty**: 2 full-, 12 part-time. **Average Class Size**: 12; Students are assigned to classes on basis of preparation and ability.

Special Academic Program : Note Intensive and accelerated program, ages 13-20 which allow students to complete high school in fewer than 4 years because of concentrated program (90 minute classes   per day per class) French, Spanish, German, Japanese & Russian: all 9-12. Math includes Calculus, Computer Programming. Science: General Science, Ecology, Biology Chemistry, Physics. History: U.S., World Geography,   American Government; Law, Economics. The Individual & Society. Remedial Reading & Math. Typing, AP.: Math & Foreign

Languages. There are two terms each year. (There are no extra-curricular activities). Small classes . **Community Involvement** : Some involvement in community service.

Plant: Library 5,000 vol., Science Lab, 11 classrooms, Bookstore, Recreation Area.

Admission: Personal Interview, Placement Exams- ETS, Math & English, Formal Application ($35 fee), Transcripts, Recommendations req..

Tuition: (1995-96) $4,000 per term. Books: Extra. *Dress Code*: Good taste. **Financial Aid**: Limited.

Summer Program: Intensive 6 week academic program.

ENGELSIDE CHRISTIAN SCHOOL..........(703) 780-4332

8428 Highland Lane, Alexandria, VA. 22309
Baptist 1972. **Head**: Pastor, Robert Purdue

Grades: K4-12. **Enrollment**: 150 Co-ed. **Faculty**: 15 full-, 3 part-time. **Average Class Size**: 13.

Special Courses: Spanish, 9-12. Math includes Calculus, Computer. Gen'l Science, Biology, Chemistry, Physics. History-Geography, World, Government, U.S., World Studies, New Republic. Religious Studies, req.; Speech, Music, Choir & Ensemble. **Extended Day**: 7 a.m.- 5:30 p.m.

Athletics: P.E. Req. to Grade 10. Boys: Soccer, Basketball, Baseball; Girls: Volleyball, Basketball, Softball, Cheerleading. **Publications**: Yearbook.

Plant: Library 5,000 vol., Science Lab, Auditorium, Playing Fields.

Admission: Application, Interview, Testing. Registration fee.

Tuition: (1995-96) Call for informattion *Dress Code*: Conservative.

EPISCOPAL HIGH SCHOOL..........(703) 379-6530 FAX (703) 931-8546

1200 N. Quaker Lane, Alexandria, VA. 22302
Episcopal 1839. **Head**: Lee S. Ainslie, Jr.

Grades: 9-12. **Enrollment**: 400 Co-ed: 260 Boys, 140 Girls   (All Boarding). **Faculty**: 54 full-,5 part-time. **Average Class Size**: 12, Student/teacher 7:1.

Special Courses: Episcopal is committed to the spiritual, intellectual, moral and physical development of its students and offers a comprehensive, college-preparatory curriculum with 22 AP courses as well as Honors Courses in most subjects. Many courses draw on learning resources in Washington, D.C. such as a Washington Quarter-students go regularly into the nation's capital; Senior Seminar: a month-long, off-campus internship. There are Language and Cultural Exchange programs in France, Austria, Russia, and Japan and summer language immersion programs in France, Spain, and Austria; a classics program in Italy.

Ecology, Astronomy, History and Science of Flight, Ethics, Comparative Religion, East Asian Studies, International Relations, Developing Nations, Journalism, Creative Writing, Shakespeare, Russian, German, Latin, Computer Science, AB and BC Calculus, and History of Art.

Athletics: Req. Interscholastic -3 seasons for boys' and girls' Varsity, JV, and Jr. Team Play for fielding 39 teams in 14 sports: Baseball, Basketball, Cross Country, Field Hockey, Football, Golf, Lacrosse, Soccer, Squash, Tennis, Indoor & Outdoor Track, Volleyball, Wrestling. Participate in Independent School League and Interstate Athletic Conference.
Clubs and Activities: Student Monitors, Honor Committee, Activities Program, Model U.N., Model Judiciary, International Relations, Pep, Student Vestry, Science, Chess; Choir, Performing Arts Group, Orchestra, Rock Band. **Publications**: Yearbook, Newspaper, Literary Magazine.
Community Service: Youth in Philanthropy, Peer Counseling, Student Health Awareness Committee, Stop AIDS for Everyone Chapter, Envionmental Club.

Plant: Automated Library Media Center with more than 28,000 books, videos and CDs, 12 Newspapers, 150 periodicals, microforms and CD-Roms. 2 Computer Labs, 4 Science Labs, Art Studio, Dance Studio, Auditorium and Performing Arts Center; Chapel, 7 Dorms, 3 Student Lounges, Book Store, Infirmary; Stadium, Field House with 3 Indoor Tennis Courts, 3 Basketball Courts, 220 yd. Track, and Batting Cage. Gym with Basketball Court and Free-Weight room, 7 Playing Fields, 6 Squash Courts, Swimming Pool, 6 lane-400 meter Outdoor Track, 12 all-weather Tennis Courts. Baseball Diamond, Wrestling Cage. Faculty Housing, etc.

Admission: SSAT, Campus Visit and Interview; additional Tests if needed.

Tuition: (1995-96)) $19,850 Comprehensive Fee. **Books**: $250-$300. *Dress Code*: Boys: Shirt & tie to classes, Coat & tie for meals and chapel; Girls: Dresses, Skirts amd pants to classes, Blazers for chapel and meals. **Financial Aid**: More than $1,000,000 available for full and partial tuition scholarships

Summer Program: Academic-three week program includes ESL and SAT preparation.
Sports Camp: Ages 7-12; Tennis Academy: Players, ages 10-18; Computer Camp: ages 7-15; Johns Hopkins University Center for Talented Youth,: ages 8-11; Women's Lacrosse Camp, girls ages 12-18. Georgetown Lacrosse Camp boys, ages 10-16; National Championship Lacrosse Camp, boys, ages 8-15; Field Hockey Camp: girls, ages 12-18.

ETS CHAIYIM SCHOOL..........(301) 424-0721

215 W. Montgomery Avenue, Rockville, MD 20850
Head: Lee Cooperman

Grades: K4-8   **Enrollment**: Co-ed

Special Programs: ABEKA; small classes, individual attention, students advance at own speed.

Admission: Registration, $75

Tuition: (1995-96) Call for information.

EVANGEL CHRISTIAN SCHOOL..........(703) 670-7127

14836 Ashdale Avenue, Dale City, VA 22193
Head: Mr. Weinberg

Grades: K-12   **Enrollment**: 234 Co-ed   **Faculty** 12 full-, 6 part-time
Average Class Size : 15

Special Programs: Traditional College Preparatory Program in High School.
Extended Day: 6 a.m.-6 p.m.

Athletics: Interscholastic. Soccer, Volleyball, Baseball, Basketball, Softball, Track & Field.

Tuition: (1995-96) Call for information.

EVERGREEN MONTESSORI SCHOOL..........(301) 942-5979   FAX (301) 946-0311

10101 Connecticut Avenue, Kensington, MD. 20895
Founded 1964. **Head**: Lynn Pellaton.

Ungraded: Ages 2-1/2 to 12 (N-grade 6). **Enrollment**: 110 Co-ed. **Faculty**: 11 full-, 1 part-time
Average Class Size: primary 22, elementary, 20.

Special Courses: Integrated curriculum taught using the Montessori method, including (on elementary level): Language Arts, Spanish, Geography, Computer, History, Science, Music, Art, Math. **Extended Day**: 7:30- 8:30 a.m.; 3-6 p.m. Note: Holiday Care, Winter & Spring Breaks.

Athletics: P.E. req. for all levels--Includes: Motor development, Soccer, Gymnastics.
Community Involvement: Older children spend time with younger children as part of the Student Service Corps. Community Outreach Program

Plant: Library; 7 classrooms Playground: adjacent to public park with fields, basketball court, and play equipment for ages 6-12.

Admission: $75 Application fee. Interview; preference given to siblings and children with Montessori experience.

Tuition: (1995-96) N-K, $5,250-$7.200 depending on number of days, hours, etc.; Grades 1-6, $7,500. Lunch: Bring. **Transportation**: $1,200. **Financial Aid**: Available.

Future Plans: Long range plan to purchase school building.

Summer Program: 10 week summer component: 2 1/4- 12 years: field trips, swimming, fishing, sports and fun.

FAIRFAX BAPTIST TEMPLE ACADEMY.........(703) 323-8100

9524 Braddock Road, Fairfax, VA. 22032
Baptist 1976. **Head**: Gil Hansen, Administrator.

Grades: K - Grade 12. **Enrollment**: 260 Co-ed. **Faculty**: 5 full-, 10 part-time.

Special Courses: Strong Phonics Program: Grades K-1, based on Pensacola Curriculum; Grades 2-12, Accelerated Christian Education, ABEKA and Bob Jones curriculum. Higher Math & Science, Piano & instrumental instruction available.   Note: Emphasis on individual learning based on diagnostic testing. Child's ability determines level. Purpose of the Academy is to give academic training throughout with a solid Bible foundation. **Extended Day**: to 5:30 p.m.

Athletics: P.E. req. in Jr. & Sr. High. Intramural: Softball, Volleyball, Basketball, Soccer. **Clubs**: Choir K-12. **Publications**: Yearbook. **Community Involvement**: All through association with the Fairfax Baptist Temple and ODACS.

Plant: Use church facilities which include 4 acres, Auditorium, Resource Center.

Admission: Interview, parent & child. Transcript & Recommendations. Registration fee, $75.

Tuition: (1995-96) K, $190/mo.; 1-12, $250-$260/mo.: Discount for Siblings. **Books**: Extra. *Dress Code*: Uniform req.

FAIRFAX-BREWSTER SCHOOL.........(703) 820-2680 FAX (703) 820-6940

5860 Glen Forest Drive, Baileys Crossroads, VA. 22041
Director: Mr. & Mrs. William J. Brill, Jr.

Note: Fairfax Academy of Early Learning......(703) -671-5555
        820 S. Carlin Springs Road, Arlington , VA 22204
        Ages 2 yrs-K   Call for information

Grades: Jr. K-grade 6. **Enrollment**: 215 Co-ed. **Faculty**: 35 full-, 4 part-time; **Class Size**: 20 Maximum.

Special Features: Spanish, Music, Computer for all grades.
Extended Day: 6:30 a.m.-6 p.m.

Athletics: P.E., Basketball, Soccer, Cheerleading, **Clubs**: Spanish, Daisey's, Brownies, Girl Scouts, Tiger Cubs, Cub Scouts, Jr. and Sr. Chorus, Dance.

Plant: Pre-primary building and elementary school building; separated Playgrounds; Computers, Lab; Cafeteria.

Admission: Interview, parent & child; Transcript; Evaluation Testing.

Tuition: (1995-96) $400/mo(base fee) **Transportation:** $75 mo,/one way, $140 mo./both ways. *Dress Code:* Uniform grades 1-6. **Extended Day:** Extra.

Financial Aid: 10% reduction for siblings.

Summer Camp: ages 4-12. June-August:. Swimming, field trips, sports, arts & crafts, ceramics, bowling, roller skating, etc.

FAIRFAX CHRISTIAN SCHOOL...(703) 759-5100   FAX (703) 759-2143

1624 Hunter Mill Road, Vienna, VA. 22182
Founded 1961. **Head:** Robert L. Thoburn II

Grades: K4-12. **Enrollment:** 300 Co-ed. **Faculty:** 15 full-, 5 part-time.

Special Courses: French 1-12,   Math includes Calculus, Computer (6-12).   General Science, Biology, Chemistry, Physics, Economics, History - U.S., World. Religious Studies req. Note: Advanced curriculum offered.   **Extended Day:** to 5.30 p.m.

Athletics Req., Intramural. Baseball, Basketball, Soccer.
Plant: 28 acre campus off Dulles Toll Rd.; Playing Fields, Basketball Courts.

Admission: $150 Registration fee; Interview req.; Possible Testing; Transcript.

Tuition: (1995-96) K-7,$3,800; 8-12, $5,500; (can be paid in 10 installments)
Books and Milk: Included   **Transportation:** $1,500 first child, $750 each additional child
Extended Day: Extra

Future Plans: Additional Buildings, Expand Student Body.

Summer Program: English for Foreign Students

FAIRFAX COLLEGIATE SCHOOL.......(703) 538-6928

301 North Washington Street. Falls Church, VA 22046
Founded 1993   **Head:** Laura A. Snyder

Grades: 5-8   **Enrollment:** 35 Co-ed   **Faculty:** 4 full-, 1 part-time **Average Class Size:** 12
Extended Day: 7:30 -8 a.m.; 4:15 -6 p.m.

Special Courses: Academic challenging liberal arts curriculum emphasizing writing, analytical reasoning, discussion, creative activities, and independent thinking. Spanish, Art, Computers, Accelerated Math. Music.

Athletics: Req. P.E. Daily; Soccer, Football, Basketball, Cross-country **Clubs**: Current Events Drama. **Publications**: Newspaper

Admission: Parent Interview; Child Visit. Transcript, Recommendations, Testing.

Tuition: (1995-96) $6,250 includes Books.(may be paid in monthly installments) **Financial Aid**: Limited

Future Plans: Add high-school grades: grade 9 by September 1996.

Summer Program: Four two-week activity programs and two one-week, end of summer academic refresher programs.

FAITH CHRISTIAN SCHOOL..........(703) 430-0499   FAX (703) 430-6402

21393 Potomac View Road, Sterling, VA. 20164-3559
Independent Bible. Founded 1980. **Head**: David K. Duffy.

Grades: PreK- grade 8. **Enrollment**: 380 Co-ed. **Faculty**: 29 full-, 3 part-time.
Average Class Size: 22

Special Courses: Religious studies req. Traditional academic program; Spanish;
LD (Learning Differences) Program.   Band;   **Extended Day**: 7 a.m.-5:30 p.m.

Athletics: P.E. req.; Basketball, Volleyball & Soccer. **Clubs** Band, Jr. High Student Council. **Publications**: Yearbook, Student Newspaper.

Plant: Library, 16 Classrooms, Gym, Auditorium, LD Centers, Playing Fields.

Admission: Interview

Tuition: (1995-96) PreK, $900-$3,400 (depending on hrs.);   grades 1-5, $2,500;   6-8 $2,600;
discount for siblings.   Books Extra   **Financial Aid** : Available

Future Plans: Additional classrooms.

Summer Program: Pre-school, 4-6 yrs.

FALLS CHURCH CHILDREN'S HOUSE OF MONTESSORI..........(703) 573-7599

3335 Annandale Road, Falls Church, VA. 22042
Founded 1971. **Head**: Carol Bowers.

Ungraded: Ages 2-1/2 - 7. **Enrollment**: 92 Co-ed. **Faculty**: 6 full-, 13 part-time. **Average Class Size**: 23.

Special Features: Montessori method, ungraded classes. French, Enrichment program one day a week. Children learn about nutrition, travel, science, etc. - special snack and art project always related. **Extended Day** : 7:30 a.m.-5:30 p.m.

Admission: $100 Registration fee. Not accepted after age 4 unless previously enrolled in Montessori school.

Tuition: (1995-96) Half-day, $340/mo.; Full day only - $600/mo. (includes hot Lunch and two snacks).

Summer Program: Program with special crafts, gardening and "splash pools".

FIELD SCHOOL ....(202) 232-0733

2126 Wyoming Avenue, N.W., Washington, D.C. 20008
Founded 1972. **Director**: Mrs. Elizabeth C. Ely

Grades: 7-12. **Enrollment**: 180 Co-ed. **Faculty**: 19 full-, 9 part-time. **Average Class Size**: 10.

Special Courses: Latin, French, Spanish - all 7-12. Art, Music, Drama, Photography, Pottery. Science: General Science, Biology, Chemistry, Physics. History: Modern European, American, Chinese History & its impact on Western Civilization in 20th Century. Note: Curriculum is integrated (Literature/ History/ History of Art/ Music History) by historical period for each grade. Language & Math are ability grouped. Composition taught as separate class for each grade. Study skills incorporated into humanities curriculum. Foreign language exchange programs to France & Spain. Theater presentations, Chorus. Typing. AP.: Physics American History, Calculus, Computer Science, American Literature, Advanced Writing. *Peer tutoring is available in writing.

Athletics: Req.; Intramural & Interscholastic. Member PVAC. Soccer, Tennis, Baseball, Volleyball, Basketball, Aerobics, Track & Field, X-Country. **Publications**: Yearbook, Newspaper, Literary Magazine. **Community Involvement**: 2 week intern program for students in community service. Youth in Philanthropy program.

Plant: Library 2,500 vol., Science Labs, Art Studio, Photo Studio & Darkroom, Ceramics Studio, Small Theater. Gym, Volleyball Court; Access to playing fields. Friends Meeting House is used for all school assemblies. Adjunct campus, Leesburg, VA., 93 acres.

Admission: $50 Application fee; Student spends day at school followed by Interview with Director which includes parents. SSAT strongly recommended; Essays req.

Tuition: (1995-96) $11,500 includes Books. Lunch: Bring. *Dress Code*: decent attire. **Financial Aid**: Some available.

Summer Program: Academic- Math Summer School and Typing Class. Recreational- one week sports camp in August.

FIRST BAPTIST SCHOOL OF LAUREL..........(301) 490-1076

811 Fifth Street, Laurel, MD 20707
Head: Brenda Schilling

Grades: N-6 **Enrollment**: Pre-school, 170; K-6, 135 Co-ed. **Average Class Size**: 16

Special Courses: P.E., Music, Day Care for ages 2-4; **Extended Day**: 7 a.m.-6 p.m.

Tuition: (1995-96) Half-day N, $85-$105/mo; K $2,200; 1-6, $2,400-$2,600
Extended Day : Extra   **Lunch**: Bring.

Summer Program: only for children enrolled yr. round.

FLINT HILL SCHOOL..........(703) 242-0705   FAX (703) 242 0718

10409 Academic Drive, Oakton, VA. 22124
Founded 1956. **Head**: Thomas C. Whitworth.

Grades: JK-12. **Enrollment**: 560 Co-ed **Faculty**: 60 full-, 7 part-time.
Average Class Size: 16.

Special Courses: Latin 7-12, French & Spanish 8-12, German 10-12. Math includes AP Calculus. Computer-Graduation requirement. Biology, Chemistry, Physics, Field Ecology. Outdoor Field Studies. History: U.S., Modern European, Comparative World Cultures, Soviet Studies, War & Peace in the 20th Century, Ancient Civilization. Music- Choral, Guitar; Drama. Note: Learning Center available for mild learning style differences. AP.: English, Calculus, Biology, Chemistry, Physics, U.S. History, Latin, Spanish, French. **Extended Day**: 3:30-6 p.m.

Athletics: Req. grades 6-8; Six seasons req. grades 9-12. Golf, Basketball, Baseball, Swimming, Softball, Soccer, Tennis, Track, Lacrosse, Cross-Country. Clubs: Latin, Spanish, French, Model U.N., Outing, Bird Banding, Recycling, Friends of Diversity, Chess, Non-traditional Sports, Service. **Publications**: Yearbook, Newspaper, Literary Magazine.
Community Involvement: 60 hours of community service req. for graduation in upper school; 8 service trips per year req. in Middle School (6-8)

Plant: 2 Libraries, 30,000 vol.;   Science Labs, Art Studios, Activity Center with Gym, Playing Fields.

Admission: K-5: Entrance Test, Teacher Recommendations, Visit, Transcript; Grades 6-12: SSAT, Interview, Teacher Recommendations, Transcript. Application by February.

Tuition: (1995-96) JK, $7,285; K-3, $10,010; Gr. 4-12, $11,500. **Transportation**: $1,100-$1,580. Books: Extra. *Dress Code*: Uniform req. **Financial Aid**: Available.

Summer Program: Enrichment & Summer Studies for all grades, end of June-1st week of Aug, Overseas & U.S. Travel Opportunities. Day Camp: ages 4-11, 9 a.m.- 3 p.m. **Extended Day Care**: 7:30 a.m.-6 p.m.; Summer Sports Academy: Baseball, Softball, Soccer, Lacrosse, Golf, Tennis, Basketball.

FLOWER HILL COUNTRY DAY SCHOOL.................(301) 840-8448 FAX (301) 948-3731

8507 Emory Grove Road, Gaithersburg, MD 20877
Founded 1987 **Head**: Donna Allen

Grades: N-2 **Enrollment**: 120 Co-ed **Faculty**: 3 full-, 2 part-time **Average Class Size**: 20-25

Special Courses: Montessori Pre-school; Elementary: Spanish, Music, Art

Plant: 3 acre wooded site in quiet, residential community

Admission: Rolling admission

Tuition (1995-96) Half-day, $390/mo; Full-day, $505/mo.

Summer Program: Registration on weekly basis. Summer 1995 "Capture the Medieval Magic of Renaissance Days" (Castles, Knights, Dragons, Food & Feasting, Art, Inventions) Each week is centered around a different theme.

FORCEY CHRISTIAN SCHOOL...(301) 622-2281

2130 E. Randolph Road, Silver Spring, MD. 20904
Founded 1977 **Head**: Mr. T. Kenneth Roussey, Jr.

Grades: N3-grade 6 **Enrollment**: 450 Co-ed. **Faculty**: 22 full-, 8 part-time. **Average Class Size**: 18

Special Courses: Religious Studies req.; Language Arts, Math, Social Studies, Science, Bible, Art, Music. After School Programs in Piano, Band.

Athletics: P.E. required in all grades. Publications: Yearbook.

Plant: Library, 8,000 vol.; Gym.

Admission: Registration fee, K $160; grades 1-6, $200. Achievement Tests. Open enrollment, March 6 until classes fill.

Tuition: (1995-96) Call for information Note:discount for siblings.

Summer Program: Day camp for grades 1-6. Call 301-622-3498

FORK UNION MILITARY ACADEMY............(804) 842-3212 or 800-462-3862
FAX (804) 842-5035

P.O. Box 278, Fork Union, VA 23055
Baptist 1898 **Head**: Lt. General John J. Jackson, Jr.

Grades: 6-12, PG **Enrollment**: 655 Boys; 30 Day, 625 Boarding (all grades).
Faculty: 45 full-time **Average Class Size**: 15

Special Courses: Spanish, French, German, all 9-PG; Science:Gen'l Science, Biology, Chemistry, Physics, Astronomy; History: World, U.S.; Economics, World Geography, Asian Studies, U.S. Gov't, Sociology. Religious Studies req. of all 11th graders or new 12th graders. Band, Chorale, Computer Science, Health & P.E.; Driver's Ed. **AP**: U.S.History, Calculus, English, Biology.

Athletics req. Intramural, Interscholastic. Football, Basketball, Baseball, Lacrosse, Wrestling, Track, Cross-Country, Swimming and Diving, Tennis, Golf, Soccer, Riflery. **Clubs**: (According to student interest) Boy Scouts, Explorers, Bicycling, Canoeing, Computer, Civil Air Patrol, Flight Training, Art, Bayonet, Military History, Debate, Fishing, Weight Lifting, Model Building, Fellowship of Christian Athletes,National Rifle Assoc., Jr. Rifle, Chess, Science, Quadrille (arranges school dances). **Publications**: Newspaper, Yearbook. **Community Involvement**: Cadets participate in Community activities for various churches & charities.

Plant: Library, 19,000 vols.; 5 Science Labs, 3 Gyms, Auditorium, 6 Playing Fields, 2 Swimming Pools, 4 Tennis Courts.

Admission: Interview recommended; $50 Application fee; Two letters of Recommendation req.; Quotas established for each grade level. Applicants accepted on basis of character and ability.

Tuition: (1995-96) Day $5,500 includes Lunch; Boarding $11,900 Books and fees: $200. *Dress Code*: Uniform req.(approx. $1,700) **Financial Aid**.: Available

Summer Programs: Summer School, non-military; grades 7-12 for enrichment, remediation, and review. Summer Camp: One week Basketball Camp for Boys.

FOUNDATION SCHOOL...................................(301) 468-9700

6000 Executive Boulevard, Suite 605, Rockville, MD 20852
Developmental School Foundation 1981 **Head** : Dr. Sheila Kaler
    (Formerly the Broschard School)

Grades: K-12 **Enrollment**; 150 **Faculty**: 25 full **Average Class Size**: 8-10

Special Courses: Foreign Language tutoring available; Biology, Chemistry, Gen'l Science, Earth Science. History: U.S., World, Contemporary Issues; Psychology, Sociology, Street Law, Government, Art, Drama, Computer, Typing. Career Education. AP Math, English, Social Studies, Science. *Note*: Also LD/ED

Athletics: PE; Individual & Dual Sports: Volleyball, Basketball, Weight Training, Softball. **Publications** School Newsletter & Magazine.

Plant: Library, Science Lab, Art Studio, Gym, Auditorium, Playing Fields.

Admission: All adolescents admitted to the Psychiatric Institute of Montgomery County are enrolled in this school; Day Student-any student who does not require hospitalization but needs a more restrictive enviornment than offered by public schools. Students enrolled in the residential treatment program at the Psychiatric Institute of Montgomery County (Fairbridge). Tests: Education evaluation; Transcripts, Interview with parents & student.

Tuition: (1995-96) $100 per day **Transportation**: Day Students- no charge, provided by county school bus. *Dress Code* Appropriate school attire, may include jeans. **Financial Aid**: Available

Summer Program: Full academic/enrichment; outings related to course of study.

FOXCROFT SCHOOL..........(703) 687-5555   or (800) 858-2364   FAX (703) 687-3675

P.O. Box 5555
Middleburg, VA. 22117
Episcopal 1914. **Head**: Mary Louise Leipheimer.

Grades: 9-PG. **Enrollment**: 161 Girls (126 Boarding, 35 Day). **Faculty**: 27 full-time. **Average Class Size**: 10-12

Special Courses: French, Spanish: 9-P.G. Math includes advanced Algebra & Trig, Calculus, Computer;   Science: General Science-Biology, Chemistry, Physics, Anatomy, and Physiology, Ecology; Introduction to Psychology. History- U.S., World Civilizations, European, Africa, World Cultures, Nazi Germany. Art includes Drawing, Painting, Art History, Printmaking; Music includes History, Theory, Chorus, Ballet, Dance, Drama. Independent Study in grades 11-12. E.S.L. Program, Interim term with Senior Projects. AP.: in all disciplines.

Athletics: Req. to grade 12.; Intramural & Interscholastic: P.E.; Hockey, Soccer, Basketball, Tennis, Lacrosse, Softball, Riding, Volleyball. Dance Technique **Clubs**: Art, Drama, Outing, Athletic, Activities, Riding, Camera, Vaulting, Social Service, Octet, Blue Planet Society, Afternoon Delights. **Publications**: Yearbook, Literary Magazine, Newspaper. **Community Service**: Students must complete a certain amount of community service each year.

Plant: Library 50,000 vol.; Science Labs, Math Lab, Computer Lab, 4 Playing Fields, 5 Dormitories, Dance Studio, Pool, Art Studio, Gym, Stables (Trails & Rings), 8 Tennis Courts, Indoor Riding Ring, Fields, Observatory, 500 Acres, Auditorium.

Admission: SSAT req., Transcript & personal information req. Applications due mid-Feb.-early March but Rolling Admission. Fee $35, $45(foreign). Interview at school req. of U. S. students, recommended for overseas students. (Parent asking financial aid must complete SSS form).

Tuition: (1995-96) $15,735 Day; $20,980 Boarding. Books: $300-$350 **Transportation**: Available, Cost varies. *Dress Code*: Neat and orderly appearance, no jeans, no printed T-shirts. **Financial Aid**: Available.

Summer Program: Co-ed, 5 Day Residential Camp for ages 9-13; Adventure Program, for ages 11-13; Day Camp for ages 5-13: Riding, swimming, canoeing, arts & crafts, sports, music, hiking, & camping.

FREDERICK ACADEMY OF THE VISITATION..........(301) 662-2814 FAX (301) 695-8549

200 East Second Street, Frederick, MD. 21701
Catholic 1846. **Head**: Kenneth P. Moore (Headmaster), Bernadette Emerson (Principal)

Grades: PreK4-grade 8. **Enrollment**: 160 Girls - Boarding 18; (grades 5-8)
Faculty: 12 full-, 6 part-time. **Average Class Size**: 15

Special Courses: French, Spanish, Computer, Music. P.E. after school for borders.
Extended Day: 7 -8:15 a.m. & 3-6 p.m.

Tuition: (1995-96) Day $2,350; Boarding $11,000.

Summer Program: Summer Camp

FREDERICK CHRISTIAN ACADEMY..........(301) 473-8990

6642 Carpenter Road, Frederick, MD. 21702
Founded 1974. **Head**: Rev. Roger Salomon.

Grades: K3-12. **Enrollment**: 315 Co-ed. **Faculty**: 20 full-, 3 part-time.
Average Class Size: 15-22

Special Courses: Foreign Languages; English; History, Government, Geography; Science, Math, Computer; Accounting, Business Law, Business Procedures; Drama ,Speech, Drafting, Photography; Fine Arts. **Extended Day**: 6:45 a.m.-6 p.m.

Athletics: Req.; Intramural sports. Soccer, Basketball, Volleyball, Cheerleading. **Clubs**: Yearbook, Photography. **Publications**: Yearbook.

Plant: Library, Science Lab, Gym, Auditorium, Playing Fields.

Admission: Entrance Test ; $75 Registration fee

Tuition: (1995-96) $2,640 (reduction for siblings) **Transportation by zone**: $600-$795. Lunch: Available. *Dress Code*: Uniform req. **Financial Aid** : Available

Summer Program: For pre-school, age 3-4yrs ; Super Summer camp for K5-grade 6.

FREDERICK SEVENTH DAY ADVENTIST SCHOOL.........(301) 663-0363

80-A Adventist Drive, Frederick, MD. 21701
Adventist, 1951.   **Head**: Dan Goddard, Pastor; Lois Folkenberg, Principal

Grades: K-8. **Enrollment**: 60 Co-ed. **Faculty**: 4 full-6 part-time.
Average Class Size: 18-22

Special Courses: Remedial Reading & Math. Economics. Religious Studies, req. Art, Music, Bell Choir; Computer. **Extended Day**: 8 a.m.-5:30 p.m.

Athletics: P.E. req. **Clubs**: Yearbook staff.   **Publications**: Yearbook   **Community Involvement**: Students visit Nursing Home

Plant: Library 3,500 Vol., Science Lab, Gym, Auditorium, Playing Fields.

Admission: Iowa Test of Basic Skills, grades 3-8. $125 Registration fee.

Tuition: (1995-96) Call for information.   *Dress Code*: No tank tops; No tight jeans, No shorts in grades 4-8. **Financial Aid**: Some .

FREEDOM CHRISTIAN ACADEMY..........(301) 736-2500

2916 East Avenue, Forestville, MD 20747
Head: Willetta Langon

Grades: PreK-12 **Enrollment**: Co-ed

Special Courses: **Extended Day** to 6 p.m.

Tuition: Call for information

FRENCH INTERNATIONAL SCHOOL..........(301) 530-8260

9600 Forest Road, Bethesda, MD. 20814
Founded 1967. **Head**: Pierre Hudelot

Grades: N-13. **Enrollment:** 980 Co-ed. **Faculty**: 70 full-time. **Average Class Size**: 20-25.

Special Courses: Latin 8-12, French K-13, Spanish 9-13, German 9-13, Remedial Reading, Art, Music, Biology, Chemistry, Physics, General Science, Economics. American History, French History & Geography. Computer Learning; Video Tape. Note: All classes are taught in French. The academic program follows the French School system except for additional English.

Athletics: Req. Intramural: Soccer. Interscholastic: Volleyball, Basketball.
Publications: Yearbook.

Plant: Library 10,000 vol., Language Lab, Art Studio, Gym, Playing Fields, Media Center.

Admission: Interview, Tests. Registration fee $110. Note: Students must be fluent in French except in N. Student body represents 52 nationalities.

Tuition: (1995-96) Call for information. **Transportation**: Available

Summer Program: Two Sessions- Ages 4-14;

FRIENDS COMMUNITY SCHOOL..........(301) 699-6086

4601 Calvert Road, College Park, MD. 20740
Quaker 1986 **Head**: Jane Manring

Grades: K-6 **Enrollment**: 137 Co-ed **Faculty**: 9 full-, 5 part-time.
Average Class Size: 16

Special Courses: Multi-age classes; conflict resolution program. Whole Language Approach; Spanish; Science units;. Social Science is integrated with field trips. Great Books, Writer's Workshop; Art, Music; Note: Diversity Committee; Cultural Arts Committee; Computer Committee.. **Extended Day** : 8 -9 a.m.; 3-6 p.m.

Athletics: Gymnastics, Basketball, Swimming, Co-operative Games, Skills. **Publications**: Weekly Newsletter **Community Involvement**: visit to Nursing Home; donations to soup kitchens; Ecology projects.

Plant: Library, Playground and Playing Fields, Art Room, Music Room...

Admission: Application Fee $40; Interview, Tour; open house in early December..

Tuition: (1995-96) $5,400 includes Books. Lunch: Bring **Financial Aid**: Some Available.

Summer Camp: 2 week sessions, mid June-July. Soccer, arts & crafts, Spanish.

FROST SCHOOL AND COUNSELING CENTER..........(301) 933-3451 FAX (301) 933-3330

4915 Aspen Hill Road, Rockville, MD. 20853
Founded 1975. **Head**: Brother Sean McLaughlin, S.D.S.

Ungraded: Ages 11-19 **Enrollment**: 35 Co-ed. **Faculty**: 15 full-time. **Average Class Size**: 5-6. Note: Related Services offered by psychologists, psychiatric nurse, social worker, consulting psychiatrist, and speech pathologist.

Special Courses: Program is for emotionally troubled adolescents and their families and is designed to give academic instruction and counselling in a supportive and stuctured enviornment. Adolescents are referred to this program for the treatment of a variety of emotional and adjustment problems such as difficulty with school, peers, parents, and self. The General Education program may serve as a transitional placement from residential treatment or as alternative to it.

The program provides schooling on a year 'round basis, 5 days a week , 8:30 a.m.- 3 p.m., and, one evening counselling session per week with parent or guardian. The Frost School also offers a component which integrates vocational assessment, work placement, independent living skills, special education classes, and group and family therapy. This is designed for adolescents ages 15-19 experiencing emotional problems who need help in pursuing a work career as an important part of their adjustment process.

Plant: Library 4000 vol., Science Lab, Art Studio, Playing Fields, Gym.

Admission: Interview-exchange information, 2 evaluation sessions . Students may be referred by physician, social service agency or school system.

Tuition: May be paid in part or in full by local school system. Counseling fee may be covered by family's health insurance.

Future Plans: To have Extended Day Program

Summer Program: Call for information

GAITHERSBURG INTERNATIONAL SCHOOL ....(301) 840-9335

429 West Diamond Avenue. Gaithersburg, MD. 20877
Founded 1977. **Head**: Mrs. Barbara Herold

Ungraded: Ages 2-1/2 -6. **Enrollment**: 52 Co-ed.(Capacity 75) **Faculty**: 4 full-time, 7 assistants. **Average Class Size**: 22.

Special Courses: Montessori method. French, Computer, Creative Movement, Music.
Extended Day: 7 a.m.-6 p.m.

Plant: Library in each room, Playing Field.

Admission: Interview parent & child; Application & Registration $50

Tuition: (1995-96) Half-day, $142/mo.-$355/mo.; Full, $210/mo.- $525/mo.; depends on number of days (2 up to 5). Bring Lunch. **Extended Day**: included

60

Summer Program: Camp - ages 2-1/2 -8. Swimming, arts & crafts, nature study, music, drama. Hours: 7 a.m.-6 p.m.

GARRISON FOREST SCHOOL.........(410) 363-1500   FAX (410) 363-8441

300 Garrison Forest Road, Owings Mills, MD 21117
Founded 1910. **Head**: G. Peter O'Neill, Jr.

Grades: Pre K-12. **Enrollment**: Note: N & K is Co-ed. Grades 1-12, Girls only. Total Enrollment, 500; Day-415, Boarding 85 (Boarding begins grade 8) **Faculty**: 65 full-, 15 part-time. **Average Class Size**: 12.

Special Courses: Latin 7-12, French & Spanish, 1-12. Math: Algebra -Calculus; Computer-practical, programming; Finite Math. Science: Biology, Chemistry, Physics, Physical Science, Field studies in Ecology, Current Issues in Science, Animal Behavior, Geology. History- World, U.S., Contemporary World Issues, Ethnicity in 20th Century America, Major Religions, Modern China, Russian/Soviet History; America since 1945. Economics; Child Development. Art, Music, Theater Arts, Dance. AP. English, French, Spanish, Latin, U.S. History, Calculus, Biology, Studio Art, Art History. **Extended Day** : 3:30 - 6 p.m.

Athletics: Req.; Interscholastic. Riding, Polo, Field Hockey, Basketball, Lacrosse, Tennis, Cross Country, Badminton, Soccer, Softball. **Clubs**: Activities, Athletics, Black Student Union, Cultural Awareness Explorations, Singing Groups, Foreign Language Clubs, Drama, Outing, Riding, Tour Guides, Model U.N., Community Service. **Publications** : Yearbook, Newspaper, Literary Magazine. **Community Involvement**: Comprehensive Community Service Program run by students with a faculty advisor.

Plant: Library 16,000 vol., 3 Science Labs, Art Studio, Auditorium, 2 Gyms, Weight Training Center, Music Practice Room, Dance Studio, 3 Dorms, Tennis Courts, Chapel, Stables, Outdoor Riding Rings and Indoor Arena, Playing Fields.

Admission: Apply by Jan 31; Testing-SSAT, Upper School; ERB, Otis Lennon Middle School; Stanford Achievements Lower School. Interview on campus, req., Transcript, Teacher Recommendations. Application fee: Upper & Middle School, $35.

Tuition: (1995-96) Day: $1,400- $10,980; Boarding: $20,860   Lunch: $2.50/day-Lower; $3.00/day, Middle & Upper. Books $200 **Transportation**: $400-$600 for day students. *Dress Code*: Uniform req. **Financial Aid**: Some Available

Future Plans: Fine Arts Center, Student Center. Master plan to improve all sections of the campus.

Summer Program: Camp for Pre and Lower School Children; Pony Club.

GEORGE SCHOOL..........(215) 579-6547   Fax (215) 579-6604

Admissions Office, Box 4000, Newtown, PA 18940
Quaker, 1893   **Head**: David L. Bourns

Grades: 9-12   **Enrollment**: 532 Co-ed (295 Boarding)   **Faculty**: 70 full-, 8 part-time.
Average Class Size: 15

Special Courses: College Preparatory, AP & International Baccalaureate Programs; ESL,
IB, Fine Arts, Performing Arts Courses; Outdoor Adventures.

Athletics: 101 Team Sports for Boys and Girls, including: Basketball, Football, Baseball,
Softball, Lacrosse, Field Hockey, Soccer, Swimming, Diving, Riding, Tennis, Track & Field,
Cross-Country, Cheerleading, Dance, Wrestling; **Clubs** : 40 Clubs and **Community Service**
Workcamps.

Plant: 265 Acre Campus: Library, 25,000 vol.; 5 Classroom Buildings, Meeting House;
2 Girls Dorms, 4 Boys Dorms; Word Processing Center; 9 Playing Fields, 14 Outdoor Tennis
Courts, Indoor Tennis Courts, 2 Gyms, Cross-Country Course, Cinder Track, Swimming Pool,
Stables, Barn; Alternate Energy Center houses Solar Greenhouse & Dance Studio.

Admission: SSAT, Application, Essay, 3 School Recommendations, Interview, Transcript

Tuition: (1995-96) Day $13,200; Boarding $20,150. **Fiinancial Aid**: Available

GEORGETOWN DAY SCHOOL..........(202) 333-7727,   H.S. (202) 966-2666
                                                                                FAX (202)338-0480

4530 MacArthur Blvd., N.W., Washington, D.C. 20007 (Lower, Middle School)
4200 Davenport Street, N.W., Washington, D.C. 20016 (H.S.)
Founded 1945 (parent owned). **Head**: Gladys M. Stern.

Grades: Pre K-12. **Enrollment**: `1000 Co-ed. **Faculty**: 114 full-, 16 part-time.
Average Class Size: Lower/Middle - 20; High School - 15.

Special Courses: French & Spanish 4-12; Latin 6-7, 9-12. Math includes Calculus. Computer
Programming. Science: Gen'l Science, Biology, Chemistry, Physics, Human Behavior. History-
U.S.Gov't & Politics, Western Civilization to Middle Ages, Global History, U.S., European,
Anthropology, Cultural Anthropology. Art, Music Drama, Band, Photography. AP.: Art,
Computer Science, French Literature, Spanish Literature, Calculus, Biology, Chemistry, Physics,
U.S. History. **Extended Day** : 3 p.m.-6 p.m.

Athletics: Req. through 4 semesters of H.S.; Intramural & Interscholastic. Soccer, Basketball,
Track & Field, Volleyball, Lacrosse, Cross Country, Softball, Tennis. **Clubs**: Debate,
Newspaper, Literary Magazine, Chess, Math, Model U.N, Model Congress, " It's Academic",
SADD, Amnesty International, Women's Issues, Black Issues, Yearbook. **Publications**: Yearbook
Newspaper, Literary Magazine. **Community Involvement**: Each High School student is Req. to

complete 60 hrs. of community service.

Plant: 2 Libraries - Lower/Middle; 12,000 vol., H.S. 12,500 vol. Science Labs, Art Studio, Gym, Auditorium, Theater, Playing Field. Photography Lab, Computer Labs.

Admission: Parents Interview and Tour; Student Visit. $50 Application fee. SSAT req. grades 7-12. Committee begins meeting March 1.

Tuition: (1995-96) $10,800-$12,925; Extra fees $400 for first 3 yrs. Bring Lunch. **Financial Aid**: 144 partial.

Summer Program: "Hop into Summer", all day program for grades PreK-5; Explore and Discover for grades 5-8; Counselor apprentice program; **Extended Day** and early morning programs.

GEORGETOWN PREPARATORY SCHOOL..........(301) 493-5000 FAX (301)493-5905

10900 Rockville Pike, North Bethesda, MD. 20852
Catholic 1789. **Head**: Dr. James Patrick Power SJ

Grades: 9-12. **Enrollment**: 400 Boys, 100 Boarding. **Faculty**: 50 full-time. **Average Class Size**: 17.

Special Courses: Latin, French, Spanish, German: all 9-12; Greek. Math through Calculus Computer. Science: Biology, Chemistry, Physics. History-American, Western Civilization. Economics. Religious Studies req.; Art, Music. ESL program. AP: English, Calculus, Biology, Physics, Computer Science, Chemistry, Modern European History, Art History, Studio Art, Music, Economics.

Athletics : Not req. Intramural & Interscholastic: Football, Track, Basketball, Cross Country, Swimming, Tennis, Golf, Lacrosse, Soccer, Wrestling, Baseball. **Clubs**: Forensics, German, French, Russian, International Relations, Math Team, Chess Team, Drama, Fencing, Computer, Photography, Student Council. **Publications**: Yearbook, Newspaper. **Community Involvement**: Required Service Projects for all students.

Plant: Library 15,000 vol., Language Lab, 3 Science Labs, 3 Computer Science Labs, Theater, Art Studio, Gym, Playing Fields, Swimming Pool, Indoor Tennis Courts, Chapel, Golf Course, Synthetic Track.

Admission: Application Deadline Feb. 1.; SSAT, Interview, Transcripts, Recommendations from 2 teachers, auto-biographical essay. Reply date March 1.

Tuition: (1995-96) Day, $11,650, includes Lunch.   Boarding, $21,400 Books: $350. *Dress Code* : Jacket and tie req. **Financial Aid**: Available..

Summer Program: Summer Day Camp - co-ed, ages 6 to 13.
Summer School: For foreign students, co-ed, ages 14-18, Day & Boarding; intense English

language and academic enrichment program.

GEORGETOWN VISITATION PREPARATORY SCHOOL.........(202) 337-3350
FAX (202) 342-5733

1524 35th Street, N.W., Washington, D.C. 20007
Catholic 1799. **Head**: Daniel M. Kerns, Jr.

Grades: 9-12. **Enrollment**: 403 Girls. **Faculty**: 32 full-, 19 part-time.
Average Class Size: 20.

Special Courses: AP courses in the following subjects: English, Modern European History, U.S. History, Comparative Politics, Calculus, Biology, Chemistry. Electives in Creative Writing, Anthropology, Law, Psychology, among others. Bridge Program with Georgetown University enables selected students to take courses for college credit. Language Consortium with area high schools in Chinese, Japanese, and Russian.

Athletics: P.E. Req.; Interscholastic athletic teams: Volleyball, Basketball, Soccer, Field Hockey, Cross Country, Track, Swimming, Diving, Softball, Lacrosse, Tennis. **Clubs**: Co-curricular activities include over 35 Clubs: Model U.N., Prism Multicultural, Photography, Forensics Team, Madrigal Choir, Environmental Awareness, Chorus, Drama, Dance, Great Books, Service, Black Women's Society, Language; Speakers Forum.. **Publications**: Yearbook, Newspaper, Art & Literary Magazine.

Plant: 24 acre campus includes four-story main academic building; Library 10,000 vol., 4 Science Labs, Art Studio, Auditorium, Gym, 4 Tennis Courts, 3 Playing Fields; Lodge & cabin.

Admission: Applications should be filed by Dec.15; Process includes a personal statement, student Interview, Recommendations from Math & English teachers; Transcript; Archdiocesan Entrance Exam..

Tuition: (1995-96) $8,400. **Lunch**: Catered, may be purchased. **Books**: $300 approx. *Dress Code*: Uniform req. **Financial Aid**: Available.

Summer Program: Courses offered in pre-Algebra, English, and Word-processing, U.S. History, SAT Prep Course, First Aid and CPR. **Note**: Week prior to Labor Day: Camps in Field Hockey, Soccer, Tennis, and Volleyball.

GERMAN SCHOOL..........(301) 365-4400

8617 Chateau Drive, Potomac, MD 20854-4599
Founded 1961. **Head**: Peter Kasper

Grades: K-13. **Enrollment**: 560 Co-ed. **Faculty**: 41 full-, 8 part-time.
Average Class Size: Lower School, 20; Upper School, 20-24.

Special Courses: Art 5-13, Music 5-13, Latin 9-11, French 7-13, German 1-13, English 1-13. General Science 5 & 6, Biology, Chemistry, Physics. History-World, American History, Social Science. AP.: 11-13 English, French, German, Math, Biology, Chemistry. Computer Science. Religious studies. Typing, Drama, Choir, Orchestra. Note: Grades 5-13 are University preparatory; curriculum taught in German similar to that of a University preparatory school within Germany.

Athletics: Req. Swimming, Basketball, Soccer, Volleyball. **Publications**: Yearbook.

Plant: Library 25,000 vol., Science Lab, Art Studio, Auditorium, 2 Gyms, Playing Fields, Swimming Pool, Photography Lab, Music Lab.

Admission: Test, Interview, Transcript. Must be German speaking.

Tuition: (1995-96) K, $2,500; 1-13, $3,700-$4,200 **Transportation**: Call for information on rates. Books: Extra.

GESHER JEWISH DAY SCHOOL..........(703) 978-9789

8900 Little River Turnpike, Fairfax, VA 22031
Jewish, 1982   **Head**: Rabbi Reuven Taff

Grades: K-6. **Enrollment**: 140 Co-ed **Faculty**: 23 **Average Class Size**: 15.

Special Courses: General Studies & Judaic program, Hebrew Language, Resource Program. Religious Studies req.; Art, Music, hands- on Science, Computer. **Extended Day**: Monday through Thursday, until 6 p.m.

Athletics: P.E.req. Intramural. **Publications**: Weekly Community Newsletter. **Community Involvement**: Choir performs at secular and religious celebrations.

Plant: 15,000 sq. feet in Jewish Community Center of Northern Virginia building.

Admission: K: current teacher Recommendation; Observation. Grades 1-6: current teacher Recommendation, Transcripts, Interview with parents and child.

Tuition: (1995-96) $6,300 **Transportation**: Available at neighborhood sites. **Financial Aid**: Available.

Future Plans: Relocation to permanent site; expansion to grades 7 & 8

GIBSON ISLAND COUNTRY SCHOOL..........(410) 255-5370

5191 Mountain Road, Pasadena, MD 21122
Founded 1947. **Head**: Carol Keenan

Grades: Pre K-5. **Enrollment**: 105 Co-ed. **Faculty**: 12 full-, 4 part-time. **Average Class Size**: 15.

Special Courses: French, Pre K-5. Art, Music, Environmental   Studies, 4-5. **Extended Day** : to 6 p.m.

Athletics: Req. Intramural   **Clubs**: Science, French, Student Gov't. **Publications**: Weekly Newspaper, Literary Magazine.

Plant: Library 6,000 vol.; Computer Lab, Science Lab, Gym, Art Studio, Playing Fields.

Admission: Parent Visit; Testing; Interviews.

Tuition: (1995-96) Half-day Pre K, $3,800; Half-day K, $4,950; K-5, $6,280 includes **Books**. *Dress Code*: Uniform req. **Transportation** : $750 both ways **Financial Aid**: Some .

Summer Program: Summer camp, Half-day, for ages 4-12.

GLENELG COUNTRY SCHOOL..........(410) 531-2229   FAX (410)-531-5142

12793 Folly Quarter Road, (P.O. Box 190) Glenelg, MD 21737
Founded 1954   **Head** Ryland O. Chapman, III

Grades: PreK-12 **Enrollment**: 430 Co-ed **Faculty**: 50 full-, 15 part-time **Average Class Size** :16

Special Courses : French, Latin, Spanish; Computer Science, Art, Music, Chorus, Drama; Remedial Reading; Integrative Seminar, Active Citizenship Training Program. **Extended Day** : PreK-6, 7:30-8 a.m.; 1-6 p.m., PreK; 3:20-6 p.m., K-6.

Athletics: Req.; Intramural & Interscholastic; Soccer, Field Hockey, Cross- country, Basketball, Lacrosse, Tennis. **Publications**: Yearbook, Newspaper, Literary Magazine.

Plant: 2 Libraries, 3 Science Labs, Gym, 3 Art Studios, Fields, Pool, Performing Arts Room, 2 Computer Rooms.

Admission: Interview, Class Visit, Tests req.

Tuition: (1995-96) PreK, $4,150; K $7,600; grades 1-4, $8,150; 5-8, $8,580; grade.9-$9,100; grades 10-12 $9,680 **Books**: Extra. **Transportation**: $950 round trip.. *Dress Code*: Good taste.   **Financial Aid**: Available

Future Plans: New Middle School Building by 1997

Summer Program: Summer School - Grades 1-9, Remedial or Enrichment. Summer Day Camp - Ages 6-13. Pre-K Camp, ages 4-5.

GONZAGA COLLEGE HIGH SCHOOL..........(202) 336-7100   FAX (202) 336-7164

19 Eye Street, N.W., Washington, D.C. 20001
Roman Catholic/ Jesuit 1821. **Head**: Dr. Joseph Ciancaglini/ Rev. Allan Novotny (President)

Grades: 9-12. **Enrollment**: 750 Boys. **Faculty**: 54 full-, 8 part-time.
Average Class Size: 25.

Special Courses: Latin, French, Spanish, German - all 9-12; Greek 3 yrs. Math thru Calculus, Computer Science, Math Analysis and Statistics. Science: Biology, Chemistry, Physics, Psychology, Marine Biology, Anatomy, Earh Systems Science.   History- World Cultures, European and American. Politics, Economics, and Social Justice. Religious Studies req.; Art, Music, Choral Arts Program, Band. *Learning Development; Driver's Ed., Drama, TV. Communications. Extensive Retreat Program. AP.*: Languages, Science, Math, History, English, Computer Science.

Athletics: Not Req. Intramural & Interscholastic. Football, Soccer, Rugby, Ice   Hockey, Basketball, Baseball, Softball, Cross-Country, Track & Field, Tennis, Golf, Swimming, Diving, Crew.   **Clubs**: Languages, Forensics, Drama, TV Communications, Booster, Chess, Bridge, Math, Science. etc.   **Publications**: Newspaper, Yearbook, Literary Magazine.
Community Involvement: Mandatory Social Justice Program for all Seniors. Enrichment program for neighborhood children. Appalachian project. Work Project in inner city of Philadelphia;   Summer Project: working in orphanage in Puerto Rico.

Plant: Library 15,000 vol., Language Lab, Science Lab, Art Studio, Gym, Auditorium, Playing Fields, Tennis Courts, Track.

Admission: Grade 9: Application, Achievement Test, Transcript, Recommendations of teacher. Apply by Dec. 15. For other grades, contact Director of Admissions.

Tuition: (1995-96) $7,350. Lunch: & Books: Extra. *Dress Code*: Dress pants, shirts, shoes. **Financial Aid**: Available

Summer Program: Academic but remedial for those who may need to review or complete a course; Academic enrichment program. Also Purple Eagle Basketball Camp, Football Camp.

GOOD COUNSEL HIGH SCHOOL..........(301) 942-1155 FAX (301) 942-3656

11601 Georgia Avenue, Wheaton, MD. 20902
Catholic 1958. **Head**: Mr. Michael E. Murphy

Grades: 9-12. **Enrollment**: 980 Co-ed **Faculty**: 78 full-time. **Average Class Size**: 26

Special Courses: Latin, French, Spanish; Art, Instrumental Music, Math; Religion Req.
Typing, Driver's Ed., Mechanical Drawing. Honors level available, AP.: English Literature, French, Spanish, Calculus Biology, Physics, U.S., European History, Politics.

Athletics: P.E. req. through Grade 10. Intramural & Interscholastic. Football, Basketball, Soccer, Cross Country, Track & Field, Indoor Track, Swimming, Wrestling, Tennis, Baseball, Softball, Golf, Lacrosse. **Clubs**: Booster, Drama,Chess, Spanish, French, Math, Political Science, Volunteers, Speech & Debate, Sportsmen, National Honor Society, Student Council. **Publications**: Yearbook, Newspaper, Literary Magazine. **Community Service**: Project req. for Seniors; underclasses encouraged to volunteer in day camp or recreation programs for the underprivileged.

Plant: Library, Language Lab, 3 Science Labs, 2 Art Studios, Music Center, College Resource Room, Computer Center, Cafeteria, Gym, Auditorium, Playing Fields, Weight Room, Lighted Field, Chapel.

Admission: Contact Director of Admissions.

Tuition: (1995-96) $6,150 **Lunch**: Cafeteria. **Books**: Extra. **Financial Aid**: Available

Summer Program: Full academic credit and extra credit courses. **Camp**: Boys and Girls Basketball camps. Day Camp for underprivileged children; Driver's Ed.

GRACE ACADEMY..........(301) 733-2033

530 N. Locust Street, Hagerstown, MD. 21740
Founded 1976. **Head**: George F. Michael

Grades: K-12. **Enrollment**: 310 Co-ed. **Faculty**: 13 full-, 1 part-time.
Average Class Size: 22

Special Courses: Gen'l Science, Biology, Chemistry, Physics. History: U.S. & World. Gov't, Economics; Religious Studies, req.-Study of the Bible in grades 9-12. Remedial Reading & Math-limited. Computer Science, Accounting, Typing Emphasis on Grammar, Language, Literature. **Extended Day Care**: 8 a.m.-5:30 p.m.

Athletics: Not Req. Soccer (Jr. High), Softball (Girls), Volleyball (limited basis). **Clubs**: Christian Service Club (student leadership) **Publications**: Yearbook **Community Involvement**: Christian Service Club projects.

Plant: Library 10,550 Vol.;   Science Labs, Gym/Auditorium

Admission: Interview, Achievement Test for placement, Recommendations; Note: emphasis is on Christian character development and on developing a Christian world-view for students.

Tuition: (1995-96)) $1,900; reduced rate for siblings. Bring **Lunch**. *Dress Code*: Modest & clean.

GRACE BRETHREN CHRISTIAN SCHOOL...(301) 868-1600;   FAX (301) 868-9475

6501 Surrets Road, Clinton, MD. 20735 (N-12)
Grace Brethren Church 1965. <u>Head</u>: Pastor Howard Mays.

<u>Grades</u>: N-12. <u>Enrollment</u>: 850 Co-ed. <u>Average Class Size</u>: 25

<u>Special Courses</u>: Spanish 6-12, French 8-12; General Science, Biology, Chemistry, Physics; Computer Literacy and Math. Art, Music, Religion req., Bible; Chapel once a week. Drama, Band, Typing, Yearbook <u>Note</u>: L.D. Therapy Program; College Classes-11 and 12; Dinner Theater. <u>Structured Educational Supervision</u> 3 -6 p.m.

<u>Athletics</u>: Req. to grade 9. Soccer, Basketball, Baseball, Softball Volleyball.

<u>Plant</u>: Library, Playing Fields, Chapel, Gym, Science Labs.

<u>Admission</u>: Parent/child interview. Registration fee $60. Required   Testing.

<u>Tuition</u>: (1995-96) Half- day $211/mo.;   K-8, $342/mo.;   9-12, $374/mo. <u>Lunch</u>: Bring. <u>Books</u>: $50-$110. *Dress Code*: Neat.

GRACE CHRISTIAN SCHOOL..........(301) 262-0158   FAX (301) 262-4516

7210 Race Track Road, Bowie, MD 20715
Baptist 1975. <u>Head</u>: Mrs. Kathy Brown

<u>Grades</u>: K 5 - grade 8. <u>Enrollment</u>: 312 Co-ed. <u>Faculty</u>: 19 full- time. <u>Average Class Size</u>: 25

<u>Special Courses:</u> Algebra, 8. Computer Science & Lab all grades. Art, Music-Vocal & Instrumental. Religious Studies req.; P.E.

<u>Athletics</u>: Not req. Interscholastic: Boys Soccer (grades 6-8) in fall; Girls Volleyball in fall; Boys/Girls Basketball (grades 6-8) in winter; Softball, Baseball, Track.. <u>Publications</u>: Yearbook. <u>Community Involvement</u>: MS. Readathon competition, Jump Rope for Heart, Math-a-thon Community Service Programs.

<u>Plant</u>: Library 9,000 vol., Computer Lab, Auditorium, Playground, Large Indoor Multi-purpose Room.

<u>Admission</u>: Screening Tests all students. Application & Testing Fee $50. Enrollment Conference.

<u>Tuition</u>: (1995-96) K half-day $2,110; K(all day)- grade 8, $2,780 (Discount for siblings) <u>Lunch</u>: Bring . <u>Transportation</u>: Privately contracted.   *Dress Code*: Uniform req. <u>Financial Aid</u>: Limited; after 1 year enrollment.

GRACE EPISCOPAL SCHOOL..........(703) 549-5067   FAX (703) 549-2832

3601 Russell Road., Alexandria, VA. 22305
Episcopalian 1959. **Head**: Mrs. Shirley N. Tyler, Director

Grades: N-5. **Enrollment**: 90 Co-ed. **Faculty**: 13 full-, 3 part-time.
Average Class Size: 15

Special Courses: Grades-Strong individualized academic program. French, grades. 4-5; Art,
Music. Religion.; Computer literacy. **Note**: Small instructional groups, low pupil/staff ratio, and
Developmental Pre-school Program; **Extended Day**: 7:30 a.m.- 5:30 p.m.

Athletics: P.E/ Creative Movement req. **Publications**: Newsletter
Community Involvement: Outreach Projects

Plant: Library 2,500 vol. Auditorium/Gym (shared); Multi-purpose rooms. Playgrounds, including
semi-wooded area for nature study.

Admission: Application fee $50; Parent/Child Interview; Transcript, Testing as necessary.

Tuition: (1995-96) $1,550-$5,800. **Supplies/Activities fee**: $125-$160; Grades Bring Lunch,
Milk Fee. **Extended Day**: Extra   *Dress Code*: Comfortable, washable clothing; no sandals.
Financial Aid: Available.

Future Plans: Summer Camp, 1996

GRACE EPISCOPAL DAY SCHOOL..........(301) 949-5860   FAX (301) 949-8398

9411 Connecticut Avenue, Kensington, MD. 20895 (1-6)
9115 Georgia Avenue, Silver Spring, MD. 20910 (N- K)
Episcopalian 1960. **Head**: Mrs. Carol Hjortsberg.

Grades: N-6. **Enrollment**: 275 Co-ed. **Faculty**: 16 full, 15 part-time.
Average Class Size: 14-18.

Special Courses: Spanish K-6, Latin 5 & 6, Gen'l Science, Computer, Math Enrichment class
grade 4-6. Geography. Religious Studies req., one semester in grades 5 & 6. Library, Music, Art,
Group Piano. **Extended Day** : 7:45 a.m.- 6 p.m.

Athletics: P.E. req. **Publications**: Yearbook, Literary Magazine of Children's Work.
Community Involvement: Community out-reach programs.

Plant: 11 Acre Campus with Playing Fields and woodlands; All-purpose room, Library, Science
room, Art room, Computer Lab.

Admission: Parents Interview and Tour School; Testing K-6 and child visits class for a day.
Teacher Recommendations and Transcripts. Earliest admissions decisions made by March 1.

Tuition: (1995-96) $6,600 **Lunch**: Bring Books and milk included. *Dress Code* : Uniform req.
Financial Aid: Available, awarded on need basis.

Summer Program: Day camp for age 3 -5, (in Silver Spring) two three-week sessions each
with thematic program. For ages 6 -10, (in Kensington)program includes environmental and
natural sciences, arts & crafts, rehearsal & performance of a play; Soccer skills, Computer.

GRACE LUTHERAN SCHOOL..........(703) 534-5517

3233 Annendale Road, Falls Church, VA. 22042
Head: Steve Balza

Grades: K-8. **Enrollment**: 30 Co-ed.

Tuition: (1995-96) K, $1,000; 1-8, $2,350; Reduction for siblings **Transportation**: Some
available-van route from the south.

GRANITE BAPTIST CHURCH SCHOOL..........(410) 761-1118

7823 Oakwood Road, Glen Burnie, MD. 21061
Head: Rick Scarfi

Grades: K4-12 **Enrollment**: 250 Co-ed

Special Programs: Bob Jones curriculum, Saxon Math Program. Sign language choir, Band.
P.E. grades 4-12. **Extended Day**: 7 a.m. to 5:30 p.m.

Tuition: (1995-96) K, Half-day, $1,460; full day, $2,195; 1-6, $2,150; 7-12, $2.300
Reduction for siblings

GREEN ACRES SCHOOL..........(301) 881-4100   FAX (301) 881-3319

11701 Danville Drive, Rockville, MD. 20852
Founded 1934. **Head**: Dr. Arnold S. Cohen

Grades: PreK-8. **Enrollment**: 300 Co-ed. **Faculty**: 35 full-, 5 part-time. **Cooperative**:
Parent/teacher owned, team teaching, small instructional groups. **Average Class Size**:
16 in the grades.

Special Courses: Spanish. Algebra, Computers; General Science, Biology; Contemporary &
American History, Global Issues; Art, Music, Drama, Family Life Education, Library,
Outdoor Education, Physical Education, Research & Study Skills. Note: Older students
work with younger students.

Athletics: Req.; Soccer, Basketball, Softball, Volleyball, Gymnastics, Track & Field, Creative Movement, Outdoor Education. **Clubs** : After school enrichment classes. **Publications:** Yearbook. **Community Involvement:** 20 hours of community service for grades 7 & 8 other grades participate in community drives for food & clothing, etc.

Plant: Library 11,000 vol., Science Lab, Art Studio, Swimming Pool (for camp only) , Playing Fields, Wooded area, Basketball Courts, Gym/Theater Building.

Admission: Parent Interview/Tour; Child Interview. Child must be age 4 by June 1 for PreK Applications due by Feb. 1st.

Tuition: (1995-96)Full Day PreK-8, $9,085; **Lunch**: Bring. **Books**: grades 5-8, Extra. **Transportation**: $1,385 Round Trip, $855 one way; reduced rate for siblings. **Financial Aid**: Some Available.

Summer Program: Summer Day Camp ages 4-12. One 6 week session.

GREEN HEDGES SCHOOL..........(703) 938-8323   FAX (703) 938-1485

415 Windover Avenue, Vienna, VA. 22180
Founded 1942. **Head**: George Schumacher

Grades: N3 -grade 8. **Enrollment**: 181 Co-ed **Faculty**: 28 full-, 2 part-time. **Average Class Size**: 20, grades 1-8

Special Courses: Latin, French K-8, Spanish 5-8. Computer 1-8. Individualized Reading, Drama, Art, Music.   Note: School offers accelerated Math, Science and English courses at least one year ahead of grade level. Pre-school Montessori Program; Enriched Elementary 1-5, Innovative Middle School. Leadership opportunities and off campus experiences. **Extended Day**: until 6 p.m.

Athletics: Req.; Daily P.E., after school sports club available. **Publications**: Yearbook, Monthly Newsletter.

Plant: Library 6,000+ vol.; Auditorium, Playing Fields, Science Lab, Computer Lab.

Admission: Children must be able students who would benefit from enriched curriculum. Admission based on Transcripts, Recommendations, Testing, and Interview. Contact Marian T. White, Director of Admissions

Tuition: (1995-96) $6,300-$9,700   *Dress Code*: Uniform req. for special occasions. **Financial Aid**: Available.

Summer Program: Enrichment program, ages 3-10. **Extended Day**: Available.

THE GRIER SCHOOL..........(814) 684-3000   FAX (814) 684-2177

Tyrone, PA. 16686 (165 miles from Washington, D.C.)
Chartered 1853. **Head**: Angelica Wutz

Grades: 7-PG. **Enrollment**: 136 Girls Boarding **Faculty**: 21 full-, 4 part-time.
Average Class Size: 8

GUNSTON SCHOOL............(410) 758-0620 or 1-800 758-0620

P.O. Box 200 Centreville, MD. 21617
Founded 1911. **Head**: Peter A. Sturtevant, Jr.

Grades: 9-12. **Enrollment**: 70 Girls (60 Boarding, 10 day). **Faculty**: 14 full-, 6 part-time.
Average Class Size: 9.

Special Courses: Note: College Preparatory & Chesapeake Bay Studies. Spanish I-IV,
French I-V; Math includes Calculus Computer. Science: Adv. Biochemistry, Natural History,
Biology, Chemistry, Physics. History: American, Modern European, Eurasian Studies,
Women's History through Literature, Social Issues of the 90's, Political Science, World
Geography. World Religions. Photography, Ecology, Advanced Composition, Creative Writing,
Shakespeare, Studies in Poetry, Drama, Piano, Guitar, Art, Music History, Typing, Music
Appreciation; AP courses offered. Independent study week, Individualized instruction, Private
tutoring. Full range of English and Mathematics courses.

Athletics: Req.; Intramural & Interscholastic. Field Hockey, Biking, Lacrosse, Volleyball,
Sailing, Canoeing, Swimming, Ice Skating, Aerobics, Basketball, Riding, Dance, Tennis, Softball.
Clubs: Drama, French, Chorus, Candy Stripers, Amnesty International, Photography, Pep Club,
Literary. **Publications**: Literary Magazine, Yearbook. **Community Involvement**: 45 hrs. of
Community Service req.; Candy Stripe program, Church & civic aides.

Plant: Library 5000 vol., Science Labs, Language Lab, Auditorium, Art Studio, Stables, Playing
Fields, Tennis Courts, Field House. Note: Located on the Corsica River for swimming, canoeing
and sailing.

Admission: Interview, (fall or winter) $50 fee with application .

Tuition: (1995-96) Day Students: $8,850; 5 Day Boarding $17,200, 7 day Boarding $19,900.
Lunch & Books Included. *Dress Code*: Uniform req. **Financial Aid**: Available.

HADLEY ACRES SCHOOL..........(301) 926-0337   FAX (301) 926-8905

20101 Woodfield Road, Gaithersburg, MD. 20882
Seventh Day Adventist 1957. **Head**: Robert Dornburg

Grades: K-8. **Enrollment**: 75 Co-ed. **Faculty**: 5 full-, 1 part-time. **Average Class Size**: 15.

Special Courses: Spanish K-8. Religious studies req.; Art, Music. **Extended Day**: 7 a.m. -6:15 p.m., Mon.-Thurs; 7 a.m.- 4 :30 p.m. Friday.

Athletics: P.E. Req.; Gymnastics **Publications**: Yearbook Newsletter.
Community Involvement: Participate in food drive for the homeless, Nursing Home visitation, and individual needs.

Admission: Registration fee before June 8, $62.50; after June 8, $125. All new students are accepted on a 30 day probationary period. For entrance to K, must be 5 by Sept. 15; for grade 1, 6 by Sept. 15. Reading readiness testing.

Tuition: (1995-96) Church member, $1,800; Adventist, non-constituent, $2,495; Non-Adventist, $2,960; Books: $85. *Dress Code*: Neat & modest.

HARBOR SCHOOL.........(301) 365-1100   FAX (301) 365-7491

7701 Bradley Boulevard, Bethesda, MD. 20817
Founded 1972. **Head**: Nancy Harmon

Grades: Pre school, Jr. K, K-grade 2. **Enrollment**: 143 Co-ed. **Faculty**: 11 full-, 11 part-time. **Average Class Size**: 15. .

Special Courses: Computer; Art, Music, Movement, Science, P.E.. Optional full day Pre-school (9:15 a.m.-3:30 p.m.) **Extended Day** : 8:15 a.m. - 3:30 p.m.; 5 yrs. and up may stay until 6 p.m.

Plant: Library, Gym, Playground

Admission: Application fee, $40 Pre school; $50, Jr. K-2nd grade. Parent visits and observes.

Tuition : (1995-96) Half Day N, $4,200; Jr. K, $7,750; K, $8,200; Grades 1-2. $8,600 **Extended Day**: Extra. **Financial Aid** : Available

HARBOUR SCHOOL.........(410) 974-4248

1277 Green Holly Drive, Annapolis, MD 21401
Founded 1982   **Head**: Dr. Linda Jacobs

Grades: N-12 **Enrollment**: 75(49 Boys, 26 Girls) **Faculty**: 39 full-, 4 part-time **Average Class Size**: 4

Special Courses: Algebra, Computer. General Science, Biology, Chemistry, Physics. American History (2 yrs.), Government, World History, Economics. Remedial Reading and Math. Art, Drama Note: School is ungraded N-8 and is designed for Learning Disabled; program is completely individualized to meet each student's needs.

Athletics: Not required. **Clubs**: Drama, Computer, Crafts, Student Council. **Publications**: Yearbook, Newspaper. **Community Involvement**: Seniors are required to complete a Senior Community Service project.

Plant: Library, 5,000 vol.

Admission: Application Fee, Submit all previous Test Records; Interview and School Visit for half-day. Note: Student should have some type of learning problem.

Tuition: (1995-96) Lower, $18,800; Middle & High School, $19,500.   **Books & Lunch**: included.   *Dress Code:* No holes, No Sex, Drugs, Alcohol on T-shirts or other apparel. **Scholarship Aid**: 8 partial.

Future Plans: Expansion into large new building

Summer Program: Tutoring & Recreation.

HARGRAVE MILITARY ACADEMY...,......(800) 432-2480 FAX (804) 432-3129

Military Drive, Chatham, VA 24531
Southern Baptist 1909   **Head**: Colonel Thomas Cunningham

Grades: 7-12, PG **Enrollment** : 410 (Girls, 22 Day only); Boys, 388 (328 Boarding)
Faculty: 40 full-, 3 part-time, **Average Class Size**: 12

Special Courses: Spanish, French, & Latin; Math thru Calculus; Science: Physical Earth ,Enviornmental, Biology, Chemistry, Physics; Computer I & II, Pascal; American & World History, Government;   Mechanical Drawing, Art; Bible, Health, Public Speaking, Business Law, Journalism; English as a Second Language; How to Study, SAT Prep.; Band, Horsemanship.

Athletics: P.E.; Football, Soccer, Cross-Country, Riflery, Basketball, Wrestling, Baseball, Track, Golf, Tennis, Lacrosse, Swimming

Plant: 240 Acre Campus;Library, Computer Lab, 2 Science Labs, Chapel, Auditorium, 2 Gyms, Olympic Size Indoor Pool, Outdoor Pool, 4 Athletic Fields, Weight & Nautilus Room, Rifle Range, Skeet Range, Stables, Outdoor Track, 5 Dormitories.

Admission : $50 Application fee, Transcripts, Campus visit or interview

Tuition: (1995-96) $13,450 includes Books, Laundry, Uniforms, Haircuts, Lab pass, Accident insurance. **Financial Aid**: Available

Future Plans: To build a Science Building

Summer Program: 5 week, non-military summer school

HEBREW ACADEMY OF GREATER WASHINGTON.........(301) 587-4100
FAX (301) 587-4341

2010 Linden Lane, Silver Spring, MD. 20910
Orthodox Jewish 1943. **Head**: Principal, Pinchos Hecht

Grades: N3-12. **Enrollment**: 623 Co-ed. **Faculty**: 25 full-, 50 part-time.
Average Class Size: 20.

Special Courses: Remedial Reading, Remedial Math, Art, Music, Religious studies req.,
Hebrew N-12, Half- day; Academic studies, Half- day. **Extended Day**: until 5:30 p.m.

Athletics: Req.; Intramural & Interscholastic: Tennis, Touch Football, Basketball, Volleyball,
Softball.
Plant: Library 12,000 vol., Science Lab, Auditorium, Gym, Playing Fields, Tennis Courts.

Admission: Interview, req.; Transfer student-require knowledge of Hebrew.

Tuition: (1995-96) N $1,995-$4,130 (depends on number of days & hours) K-12, $4,755 -
$7,880 **Lunch**: Extra. **Transportation**: Availble free for N. *Dress Code*: No extreme styles.

HEBREW DAY INSTITUTE...........(301) 984-2111

11710 Hunters Lane, Rockville, MD 20852
Jewish, 1973 **Head**: Moshe Schreiber

Grades: N2- 4, K-grade 6 **Enrollment**: 200 Co-ed **Faculty**: 9 full, 35 part-time.
Average Class Size: N, 13; Grades K-6, 18

Special Courses: Hebrew K-6; Enrichment programs in Science and Math; Computer K-6.
Religious Studies req. Remedial Reading & Math. Art, Music, Library Science. Note: Skills
Augmentation Program for gifted & talented. **Extended Day** : 7:30 a.m.-6 p.m. except Friday in
winter, then day ends earlier.

Athletics: P.E. req. **Clubs**: Chorus, Chess, Science. **Community Involvement**: Chorus
performs regularly throughout the community at nursing homes, etc. Students participate in
special projects related to Jewish & Israeli causes.

Plant: Library, 6,000 vol. Gym, Auditorium, Playing Fields. Recent renovation to Nursery
School.

Admission: Application fee $55 for N, $85 for K-6; Interview req. for placement in K-6.
(Registration fee applied to tuition).

Tuition: (1995-96) K-6, $6,095 **Lunch**: Bring **Books**: $115 **Transportation**: Limited, from
the Jewish Day School. Mornings only. *Dress Code:* Modest attire. **Financial Aid**: Need based

HEBREW DAY SCHOOL OF MONTGOMERY COUNTY.........(301) 649-5400

1401 Arcola Avenue, Silver Spring, MD 20902
Jewish **Head**: Peretz Hochbaum

Grades: K-6. **Enrollment**: 100 Co-ed. **Faculty**: 9 full-, 11 part-time. **Average Class Size**: 15.

Special Courses: Hebrew. Religious Studies req. -full curriculum of Judaic Studies. Remedial Math & Reading. Art, Music, Choir, Drama. Individualized instruction in all areas-child progresses at own rate. **Extended Day**: to 6 p.m.

Athletics: P.E. req. all grades. Soccer. **Publications**: Weekly and quarterly Newsletter.

Plant: Library 3,000 vol., All-purpose room, Playing Fields, Auditorium.

Admission: Interview with parents & student; Testing where indicated.

Tuition: (1995-96) K - $4,975; Grades 1-6, $5,560. Note: Registration Fee for K-6, $150.
Financial Aid: Available.

THE HEIGHTS SCHOOL..........(301) 365-4300   FAX (301) 365-4303

10400 Seven Locks Road, Potomac, MD. 20854
Catholic, 1969 **Head**: Joseph W. McPherson, J.D.

Grades: 3-12. **Enrollment**: 365 Boys **Faculty**: 18 full, 2 part-time. **Average Class Size**: 20.

Special Courses: Latin 9-12, Spanish 6-10, Greek 11 & 12. Science Biology, Chemistry, Physics, Nature Study. History U.S. & European History.   Physiology, Art History, Economics, Logic, Shakespeare Seminar. Religious studies for Catholic students. Band 3-8. Entire program has traditional liberal arts orientation - program pace requires academically-motivated students - all courses at secondary level are accelerated. AP Spanish, Latin, Economics, Calculus, History.

Athletics: Req.; Intramural & Interscholastic: Tennis, Soccer, Basketball, Baseball,
Clubs: Drama, Computer, Chess **Publications**: School Yearbook, Newspaper.

Plant: 3 Classroom Buildings, Playing field, 3 Tennis courts, Gym.

Admission: Application, Transcript, Recommendations, Interview. $25 fee.

Tuition: (1995-96) grades: 3-5 $5,900; 6-8, $6,800; 9-12 $7,400. Books, $100
Dress Code: Jacket & Tie. **Financial Aid**: Available.

Summer Program: Natural History Camp, boys, grades 3-5; Sports Camp/ Exploration Camp, boys, grades 6-8.

HELLENIC AMERICAN ACADEMY........(301) 299-1556   (301) 299-0187

10701 South Glen Road, Potomac, MD 20854
Greek Orthodox   **Head**: Mrs. Marianne Monek

Grades: PreK2-grade 5   **Enrollment**: 90 Co-ed **Faculty**: 8 full-, 4 part-time.
Average Class Size: 10

Special Features: Enriched Math and Reading Courses; Art, Music all classes. Greek taught
as a second language. Computer, General Science.   **Extended Day**: 7 :30 a.m.- 6 p.m.
Note: Piano instruction available; also Dance and Karate.

Athletics: P.E. all grades. **Publications**: Newsletter. **Community Involvement**: Visit &
sing in Nursing Homes.

Plant: 25 acre woodland property with pool and stables; playground

Admission: Interview parent/child; Child Visits classroom for a day if applying for elementary
grades.   Testing for elementary grades.

Tuition: (1995-96) $1,900-$6,000 includes Books   *Dress Code*: Uniform req. K-5.
Financial Aid: Some Available.

Summer Program: Camp Potomac Woods

HENSON VALLEY MONTESSORI SCHOOL..........(301) 449-4442

7007 Allentown Road, Temple Hills, MD. 20748
Founded 1965. **Head**: Mr. Gordon Maas

Ungraded: Ages 2-1/2 -12. **Enrollment**: 210 Co-ed. **Faculty**: 11 full-2 part-time, 5 aides.
Average Class Size: 25.

Special Features: Montessori primary and elementary ungraded programs. Computers in
Elementary classes. Spanish all ages. Art, Music, P.E.   Comprehensive integrated program in
Math, Science. Note: LD Specialist on staff. **Extended Day**: 7:30 a.m.-6 p.m.

Plant: 4 acres of land for play and study. Library. Building especially designed to accommodate
Montessori Classes.

Admission: Interview, $25 Application fee. Not accepted after age 4-1/2 unless previously
enrolled in Montessori school.

Tuition: (1995-96) Half-day, $3,320; Full day N & K, $4,200; grades 1-6, $4,450. Equipment
fee, Books: $125. Bring Lunch. *Dress Code*: Clean & Neat.   **Financial Aid**: Available after
one year.

HERITAGE ACADEMY CHRISTIAN SCHOOL..........(301) 582-2600

12215 Walnut Point West, Hagerstown, MD 21740
Founded 1969. **Head:** Kathleen Mallory.

Grades: K4-12. **Enrollment**: 240 Co-ed. **Faculty**: 17 full-, 4 part-time.
Average Class Size: 24; Resource Room in elem., 20.

Special Courses: Spanish 9-10, Science through Physics, Computer science, Math includes Advanced Math & Business Math. Typing, Music, Art, Journalism. Note: Resource room for Talent Development

Athletics: P.E. req.; Intramural & Interscholastic. Boys - Soccer, Basketball, Girls - Volleyball, Softball, Basketball, Cheerleading.

Plant: Library, Science Lab, Gym - All purpose room, Playing Fields, Auditorium.

Admission: Interview & Testing ($60 fee); Registration fee $45.

Tuition: (1995-96) Age 4-Grade 6, $l,963; Grades 7-12, $2,119; Reduction for siblings **Books & Activities**: Extra. Note: For grades 1-6, if student enrolled in Talent Development, (LD/ED) 2 subjects, $259 but cost is included in tuition for 3 or more subjects (tuition is then $2,588) **Transportation**: Depends on distance & number of students in family. **Lunch**: Cafeteria. *Dress Code*: Uniform req. **Financial Aid**: Details on Request.

HERITAGE ACADEMY & CHILD CARE CENTERS, INC..........(703) 922-6600

6318 May Boulevard, Alexandria, VA. 22310 (K-6)
7136 Telegraph Road, Alexandria, VA. 22310 (N only)
Founded 1948 **Head**: Judy Miller

Grades: Age 4-Grade 6. **Enrollment**: 140 Co-ed. **Faculty**: 15 full-time.
Average Class Size: 12

Special Courses: French, Spanish, Music, Computer Studies. Remedial Reading (Phonovisual method used for reading) Individual Learning Program for special needs.
Extended Day : 6:30 a.m.- 6:30 p.m.

Plant: Library 1,300 vol., Playing Fields, Swimming Pool, Tennis Courts, Computer Lab, Gym.

Tuition: (1995-96) K-6, $145/wk; includes Books, Lunch. **Extended Day Transportation** : Available.

HIGHLAND SCHOOL..........(703) 347-1221 FAX (703) 347-5860

597 Broadview Avenue, Warrenton, VA 22186
Founded 1928. **Head**: David P. Plank

Grades: PreK-8. Enrollment: 230 Co-ed. Faculty: 30 full-, 4 part-time.
Average Class Size: 15.

Special Courses: Latin , French, Spanish;. Algebra, Geometry, Computer; Grammar, Science,
Social Studies. Extended Day: 2:15 -5:30 p.m..

Athletics: Req. daily; Intramural & Interscholastic: Skiing, Riding, Softball, Tennis, Soccer,
Field Hockey, Lacrosse, Basketball, Track and Field. Clubs: Yearbook Publications: Yearbook
Literary Magazine. Community Involvement: Community Service Programs.

Plant: Library , C.D. Rom/ 9,000 vol.; 14 acre campus: Science Lab, Art Studio, Gym, Playing
Fields, 3 Academic Buildings..

Admission: Interview, Placement Test. $50 Application fee. Transcript,

Tuition: (1995-96) K-2 $6,170; grades 3-8, $6,730 includes Books. Transportation:
Available. Financial Aid: Available.

Future Plans: Addition of grades 9-10, Sept. '96; expansion for secondary school campus

Summer Program: Art; Day camps, soccer & lacrosse.

HIGHLAND VIEW ACADEMY..........(301) 739-8480

10100 Academy Drive, Hagerstown, MD 21740
Seventh Day Adventist 1949. Head: Mogan Hellgren

Grades: 9-12. Enrollment: 160 Co-ed, (70 Boarding). Faculty: 12 full-time.
Average Class Size: 20.

Special Courses: Physical Science, Chemistry, Biology, Human Physiology, Physics; Math,
Mini-Business Courses. History: U.S., World, Civil War, Government. Computers. Religious
Studies req. Typing, Mechanical Drawing, Shop, Home Economics, Architectural Drafting,
Photography, Woodworking, Band, Automechanics, Small engines. Note: Grades 9 & 11 have
classes from 1 p.m.-5:30 p.m. -work in the morning either in school maintenance jobs, in the
school office, or assisting the teachers. Grades 10 & 12 have classes 7 a.m.-11:30 a.m., and work
in the cafeteria or other jobs. Opportunities available to work in Pretzel Factory or Bakery.
Complete combination of work experience with educational experience
Extended Day: 6:45 a.m.-7:30 p.m.

Athletics: Boys: Varsity & Jr. Varsity Basketball, Varsity Soccer; Girls Varsity Volleyball
and Basketball. Clubs: Boys & Girls Club, Student Association. Publications Newspaper,
Yearbook.

Plant: Gym, Computer Lab, Dormitories, Cafeteria, Music Building, Playing Fields.

Admission: Application, Interview, Transcript.

Tuition: (1995-96) Day, $4,782; Boarding $8,162 **Lunch**: Extra for day students. **Books**: Extra. *Dress Code*: Girls, Dresses; Boys - No jeans; sports shirts slacks.

HILL SCHOOL..........(703) 687-5897   FAX (703) 687-3132
130 South Madison Street,
P.O. Box 65, Middleburg, VA 22117.
Founded 1926. **Head:** Thomas Northrup.

Grades: K-8. **Enrollment**: 195 Co-ed. **Faculty**: 24 full- time. **Average Class Size**: 12.

Special Courses: Spanish 8, Latin 7-8. Algebra 8, Computer 1-8. General Science 1-8.
Art & Music, K-8.

Athletics: Req.; Intramural, K-8; Interscholastic 4-8. Soccer, Field Hockey (Girls), Basketball, Gymnastics, Lacrosse, Track & Field. **Clubs**: Outing, Hiking/Camping, Skiing.
Publications: Yearbook, Literary Magazine.

Plant: Library 12,000 vol.; Science Lab, Art Studio, Gym, Playing Fields, Auditorium, 30 Computers, Outdoor Science Center..

Admission: Interview, Achievement Testing, $20 fee.

Tuition: (1995-96) K $5,000; Grades 1-8, $8,500-$8,900 *Dress Code*: No blue jeans, T shirts, sweatshirts. **Financial Aid**: Available.

The HILL SCHOOL ....(610) 326-1000   FAX (610) 326-7471 (Admissions)

717 East High Street, Pottstown, PA 19464
Founded 1851 **Head**: Mr. David R. Dougherty

Grades: 8-12, PG **Enrollment**: 450 Boys (Boarding 385) **Faculty**: 71 full-, 4 part-time
Average Class Size: 11

Special Courses: Latin, Greek , French, Spanish, German, Russian; Math, Computer, Pascal
History: European, U. S. (req); Economics; _Science_: Biology, Chemistry, Physics;
Theology/Philosophy (one yr, req.), Judeo-Christian roots; Discussion of Dimensions,
Encounters Beyond and Within, Religion through Literature, The Nature of Religious Experience,
Philosophy Seminar, Psychology; Transitional English, Study Skills. Theatre I, II; Music Theory,
Photography, Studio Art, Wood shop, _AP_: English, Humanities, Math, Pascal, French, Spanish,
History: European and U.S., Economics, Biology, Chemistry, Physics. Note The Hill School is an
an associate member of The School Year Abroad Program: Open to Juniors who have
completed two years of French (program in Rennes, France) or Spanish (Barcelona, Spain).

Athletics: Req.; Interscholastic and Intramural; Soccer, Football, Cross Country, Water Polo, Basketball, Ice Hockey, Wrestling, Swimming, Squash, Ski-racing; Winter Track, Lacrosse, Baseball, Golf, Tennis, Track.

Clubs: Model U.N., Spanish, Glee, Chamber Orchestra, Jazz,Ensemble, Hilltones, String Quartet, Drama, Radio Station. **Publications** : Newspaper, Yearbook **Community Service** : Students participate in various ways.

Plant Library, Extensive Athletic Facilities, Large Physical Plant

Admission : Apply by Feb. 15; Transcript, Recommendations from English & Math teachers, SSAT. and Interview on campus.

Tuition: (1995-96) $21,000 **Financial Aid**: Available

Future Plans : 150th Anniversary Celebration and Capital Campaign

Summer Program: Academic Enrichment, Sports

HOLTON ARMS SCHOOL..........(301) 365-5300

FAX (301) 365-6071 (Admissions office)

7303 River Road, Bethesda, MD 20817
Founded 1901. **Head**: Diana Coulton Beebe

Grades: 3-12. **Enrollment**: 650 Girls, expands at Grades 7 & 9. **Faculty**: 69 full-, 10 part-time. **Average Class Size**: 15.

Special Courses: Latin, French & Spanish, all 7-12. Math through Calculus & Computer, Statistics; Discrete Math. General Science, Biology, Chemistry, Physics, Botany, Environmental, Earth Science. History & Social Science- Western Civilization, History of U. S. and Europe, Asian History, Anthropology, Western Philosophy, Contemporary History, Geography, Government & Economics. Art, Art History, Art & Music. AP.: English, U.S. History, Biology, Calculus, Computer Science, French Literature, Spanish, Latin. **Extended Day**: 3:30 - 6 p.m.

Athletics: Req.; Intramural & Interscholastic. Field Hockey, Soccer, Tennis, Softball, Track, Volleyball, Cross Country, Basketball, Swimming, Lacrosse. **Clubs**: Amnesty International, Boosters, Community Service, Cultural Awareness, Debate, Environmental Awareness, Model U.N., Peer Counseling, It's Academic, Drama, Chorus, Swing Choir, Orchestra. **Publications**: Literary, Newspaper, Yearbook. **Community Involvement**: Long tradition of service by graduation requirement requiring 30 hours of voluntary service during one 12 month period of four years of high school.

Plant: Library: Upper School 22,000 vol., Lower School, 6,000 vol.; Language Lab, 2 Computer Centers, Science Labs, 2 Art Studios, 2 Gyms, Playing Fields, Tennis Courts, Dance Studio, Swimming Pool, Theater, Amphi-Theater.

Admission: SSAT Req. 7-12. Individual aptitude and achievement testing 3-6; Tour and Interview. Application fee $50; Feb. 1 deadline.

Tuition: (1995-96) Gr.3-6, $12,300; Gr. 7-12, $12,995 includes Lunch; Books: $300.
Dress Code: Uniform req.   **Transportation**: one way $425, both ways $750.
Financial Aid: Available.

Summer Program: Creative Summer - Programs for boys and girls ages 7-14; Art, Music, Dance, Drama, Tennis, Swimming, Computer, Science. Creative Sixes: day program for age 6. Creative Morning: half-day program for ages 4-6.

HOLY COMFORTER SCHOOL- ST. CYPRIAN..........(202) 547-7556 FAX (202) 547-5686

1503 East Capitol Street, S. E., Washington, D. C. 20003
Catholic   **Head**: Sister Mary Charlotte Marshall, OSP

Grades: PreK- grade 8   **Enrollment**: 204 Co-ed **Average Class Size**: 20

Special Courses : IBM Computer Lab   **Extended Day** : 2:35-5:55 p.m.
Athletics: CYO Basketball   **Clubs**: Glee

Tuition: (1995-96) $2,000

Summer Program: Camp Harambe.

HOLY CROSS ELEMENTARY SCHOOL..........(301) 949-1699

4900 Strathmore Avenue, Garrett Park, MD 20896
Catholic   **Head**: Sister Miriam R. Brosnan CSC

Grades: K-8 **Enrollment**: 240 Co-ed

Special Programs: Emphasis on Reading, Writing, Math, Science & Social Studies; Enrichment courses in Art, French, Drama, Music, Spanish, Computer Science, Library Skills. Religion req.
Extended Day: 7:15 a.m.- 6 p.m.

Athletics: P.E. req.

Plant: Library, 10 acre park-like campus

Admission: Interview, child Visits school for day, Transcript.

Tuition: (1995-96) In parish, $2,600; Out of parish, $3,200

HOLY FAMILY SCHOOL..........(301) 894-2323

2200 Callaway Street, Hillcrest Heights, MD 20748
Catholic   **Head** : Sister Jude Boyce

Grades: PreK- grade 8   **Enrollment**: 200 Co-ed

Special Courses: **Extended Day** : 7 a.m.-6 p.m.

Tuition: (1995-96) Catholic, $2,020; Non-Catholic, $2,820; Reduction for siblings.
Extended Day: Extra, $10/wk before school care; $35/wk after school care

HOLY NAME SCHOOL..........(202) 397-1614

1217 West Virginia Avenue, N. E., Washington, D. C. 20002
Catholic   **Head** : Sister Owen Patricia Bonner, SSJ

Grades: PreK-8   **Enrollment**: 225 Co-ed

Special Courses: Choral and Instrumental Music, P.E., Track & Basketball
Extended Day : 7 a.m. until 6 p.m.

Tuition: (1995-96) K4, $2,030; K-8, $1,825; Reduction for siblings.

HOLY REDEEMER SCHOOL...........(301) 942-3701

9715 Summit Avenue, Kensington, MD 20895
Catholic 1951   **Head** : Mrs. Rosemarie Garten

Grades: K-8 **Enrollment**: 400 Co-ed   **Faculty** : 19 full-, 6 part-time.
Average Class Size: 22

Special Courses : French, Spanish,.Math, Social Studies, Science, English. Religion req.:
Art, Music, Learning Center (Enrichment & Remedial). **Extended Day**: 7:15-8:15 a.m.; 3-6 p.m

Athletics: P. E.; Soccer, Basketball, Football, Baseball, Softball, T-Ball. **Clubs** : Drama,
Chorus, Hands on Science Program

Admission : Interview, Testing

Tuition: (1995-96) Parishioner, $1,900;   Non-Catholic, $3,100. *Dress Code*: Uniform req.
Financial Aid: Available

HOLY REDEEMER SCHOOL..........(202) 638-5789

1135 New Jersey Avenue, N. W., Washington, D. C. 20001
Catholic, 1954   **Head**: Angela Kittrell

Grades: Pre K-8   **Enrollment**: 258 Co-ed   **Faculty**: 13 full-, 2 part-time
Average Class Size: 26

Special Courses Reading, Math, Language Arts, Science, Social Studies, Computer. Religion req: Conformity of Christian Doctrine. **Extended Day**: 7-8 a.m., 3-6 p.m.

Athletics: P.E.; Basketball, Double Dutch, Track and Soccer.

Admission: Birth Certificate. Testing, Health Records.

Plant: Computer Lab, Use of nearby Gym for athletic program.

Tuition: (1995-96) $!,980. Family rates available.

HOLY SPIRIT LUTHERAN SCHOOL......... (410) 255-1852

109 Burns-Crossing Road
P.O. Box 937, Severn, MD 21144
Plan to open Fall of 1996   **Head**: Teresa Steger ,President

Grades: 6-8

HOLY TRINITY EPISCOPAL DAY SCHOOL..........(301) 262-5355 FAX (301) 262-9609

13106 Annapolis Road, Bowie, MD. 20720
Episcopal 1963. **Head**: Margaret C. Reiber

Grades: K-8. **Enrollment**: 320 Co-ed. **Faculty**: 20 full-, 9 part-time.
Average Class Size: 16-20

Special Courses: French (K-5), Spanish (6-8), Latin,(8); Art, Music. Computer, Gen'l Science, Religious studies; Outdoor Ed.; Chorus, Band. **Extended Day**: 7 a.m.-6 p.m.

Athletics: P.E. Req.; Intramurals; Interscholastic Sports, 6-8.

Plant: Library 5,000 + vol.; Two campuses: K-5(Lower) and 6-8 (Middle); All Purpose Room, Playing fields. Two fully-equipped Computer Labs.

Admission: Free application. As openings occur applicants are called in order and Tested;$50 fee; Interview. Preference given to siblings & parish children.

Tuition: (1995-96) K-5, $4,375; gr. 6-$4,850; gr. 7 & 8- $5,725; **Extended Day**: Extra. Lunch: Purchased daily, Beverage provided.   **Transportation**: Limited; Queen Ann School bus service, car pools. *Dress Code*: Suitable.   **Financial Aid**: Available.

Future Plans: Continued growth & development

Summer Program: Six week : For children entering grades 1-8; Variety of offerings with weekly themes, on and off campus: academics, sports, crafts, music, etc.

HOLY TRINITY SCHOOL..........(202) 337-2339

1325 36th Street, N.W., Washington, D.C. 20007
Catholic 1860's   **Head**: Ms. Ann Marie Santora

Grades: N-8   **Enrollment**: 330 Co-ed **Faculty**: 23 full, 6 part-time.
Average Class Size: 15-30

Special Features: French 2-8. Algebra, Geometry, Computer. General Science, Biology.
Religious Studies req; Remedial Reading & Math   Note : LD tutoring/ Speech & Language
Therapy/ Developmentally appropriate ED program. Art, Music. **Extended Day**: 7:30 a.m.
-6 p.m.

Athletics: P.E. req. 1-8 **Clubs**: Student Council, Environmental Club. **Publications**: Yearbook,
Newspaper. **Community Involvement**: Food collections for hungry; Special events for
seniors; Recycling.

Tuition: (1995-96) N-K $4,850; 1-8, $3,740; Reduction for parish member and siblings. .
Fees, 1-8, $325. *Dress Code*: Uniform req. **Financial Aid**: Some Available.

HOPE CHRISTIAN ACADEMY..........(301) 982-6405, 982-6400 FAX (301) 982-9280

5301 Edgewood Road, College Park, MD 20740
Head: Leslie D. Bennett

Grades: Pre-School -grade 6   **Enrollment**: 110 Co-ed **Average Class Size**: 16

Special Programs: Spanish, Computer Applications; Character education; Critical Thinking
component.   Note: Pre-school is a yr. round day care alternative for 3 & 4 yr.olds.
Extended Day: 6:30 a.m.- 6:30 p.m.

Clubs: After school clubs, interactive satellite network.

Admission: Family Interview; Student Visits school for day; Academic Screening.

Tuition: (1995-96) $2,300

Summer Program : 8 week camp; character development, computers, academic enrichment and
remediation.

IDEAL SCHOOL OF WASHINGTON..........(202) 726-0313

1501 Gallatin Street N. W., Washington, D. C. 20011
Head: Mr. Taiwo Inman

Grades: N 2 1/2- Grade 6   **Enrollment**: Co-ed

Special Programs: LD/ED program, **Extended Day**: 7:30 a.m.-6 p.m.

Tuition: Call for information

IMMACULATE CONCEPTION SCHOOL..........(202) 234-1093

711 N Street, N. W., Washington, D. C. 20001
Catholic   **Head**: Sister Carolann Knight

Grades: K4- grade 6   **Enrollment**: Co-ed

Special Courses: **Extended Day**: 2:45-6 p.m.

Tuition: (1995-96) $1,500

IMMANUEL CHRISTIAN SCHOOL..........(703) 941-1220

6915 Braddock Road, Springfield, VA. 22151
Founded 1976 **Head**: Stephen Danish

Grades: Pre K-8 **Enrollment**: 290 Co-ed

Special Programs: Well-rounded academic program. Daily Bible. Computer Science program. High parent involvement.   Strong music program.   Sports and other activities in the upper grades.

Tuition: (1995-96) N $725-$1,325; K $1,600; 1-5 $3,200; 6-8, $3,350.

IMMANUEL LUTHERAN SCHOOL.......... (703) 549-7323

109 Belleaire Road, Alexandria, VA. 22301
Missouri Synod, Lutheran 1945. **Head**: Celinda Claxton

Grades: K-6. **Enrollment**: 100 Co-ed. **Faculty**: 5 full-, 1 part-time.
Average Class Size: 15-20

Special Courses: Spanish; General Science. Music Program. Religious studies req. Strong academic & religious programs. **Extended Day**: 3- 6 p.m.

Athletics: Req., all grades. Softball, Volleyball.

Plant: Library 5000 vol., Playing Fields.

Admission: Interview, Application fee $50 , Registration fee $175; Entrance Exam and Placement test in Math & Reading.

Tuition: (1995-96) $2,750, Reduction for siblings and church members.   **Extended Day**: Extr up to $170/mo. *Dress Code*: Uniform req. **Fnancial Aid**: Some available.

INDEPENDENT BAPTIST ACADEMY..........(301) 856-1616 FAX (301) 856-8234

9255 Piscataway Road, P.O. Box 206, Clinton, MD. 20735
Independent Baptist 1972. **Head**: Mr. Frank Burton

Grades: K4-12. **Enrollment**: 139 Co-ed. **Faculty**: 9 full-, 6 part-time.
Average Class Size: 20.

Special Courses: Spanish; <u>Math</u> thru Algebra. Physical Science; World Geography; Literature; Typing. Religious studies **Extended Day**: 7 a.m.-6 p.m.

Athletics: Flag Football, Basketball, Softball, Volleyball.

Plant: Gym; use of nearby Library & Playing Fields.

Tuition: (1995-96) $2,540; Reduction for Siblings. <u>Books</u>: $120. <u>Registration Fee</u>: $125

INDIAN CREEK SCHOOL..........(410) 987-0342   FAX (410) 923-2159

Evergreen Road, Crownsville, MD. 21032
Founded 1973. **Head**: Anne Chambers.

Grades: PreK-8. **Enrollment**: 425 Co-ed. **Faculty**: 47 full-, 1 part-time.
Average Class Size: PreK & K, 1:10; grades 1-5, 1:20; grades 6-8, 1:15.

Special Courses: Spanish N-8th. Algebra, Computer. General Science, Biology. <u>History</u> includes Maryland, American, European. Civics, World Geography. Remedial Reading and Math(within classroom). Art, Music, Library. note: Learning Specialist on staff, parallel program for grade 6-8; Enrichment Program. **Extended Day**: 7:30 a.m.- 6 p.m.

Athletics: Required all grades. Intramural: Soccer, Field Hockey, Lacrosse, Basketball, Wrestling, Rugby **Clubs**: Grades 1-5 meets Friday afternoon; Swimming, Mind Olympics, Drama, Cooking, Crafts, Computer. **Publications**: Yearbook, Newspaper. **Community Involvement**:   Extensive holiday sharing program.

Plant: Library, Science Lab, Gym, Art Studio, Auditorium, Playing Field, Computer Lab.

Admission: Application fee $35; In-House Testing(fee $30): Brigance Metropolitan Readiness, Iowa Achievements; Transcript, Teacher Recommendations.

Tuition: (1995-96) $4,280, half-day PreK; $5,620 full day PreK; K, $5,890;   Pre 1st-grade 8, $6,690- $7,525. Lunch: $1.50 day. *Dress Code*: Uniform req. **Transportation**: $465, one way, $925 both-ways; Reduction for siblings. **Extended Day** Extra, several plans offered. **Financial Aid**: Available.

Summer Program: Computer Camp, Art Camp, Play Care

ISLAMIC SAUDI ACADEMY...........(703) 780-0606

8333 Richmond Highway, Alexandria, VA 22309
11121 Popes Head Road, Fairfax, VA 22309
Muslim   **Head**: Dr. Saad H. Al Adwani

Grades: K-12   **Enrollment**: 1,150

Special Courses: Advanced academic program all grades for Muslim students. Arabic Language, Islamic Studies Program.

Tuition: (1995-96) $1,000

JEWELS OF ANN SCHOOL..........(202) 529-5446

2011 Bunker Hill Road, N.E., Washington, D.C. 20018
Founded 1970. **Head**: Dr. Ruth H. Baxter.

Grades: N-6. **Enrollment:** 70 Co-ed. **Faculty**: 10 full-, 2 part-time.
Average Class Size: 10.

Special Courses: Foreign Language K-6, Remedial Reading & Math as needed; Art, Music; British method - reading readiness program at 4 yrs. - open education, ability grouping. **Extended Day Care**. 7 a.m.-6 p.m. and in and out of the country trips.

Admission: Registration fee $60. K Interview, 1-6 Interview & Aptitude Test. Fee $75.

Tuition: (1995-96) N- grade 3, $350/mo.; 4-6, $ 450/ mo.; Tuition includes **Extended Day**. Books: (rental fee) K-3 ,$50; 4-6,$70. *Dress Code* Uniform req. Pre-K-6.

Summer Program: Day Camp ages 3-12; (End of June - end of August). Arts & crafts, swimming, physical education; week-ends away from home, field trips.

JEWISH PRIMARY DAY SCHOOL of ADAS ISRAEL..........(202) 362-4446
FAX (202) 362-4961 att: JPDS
2850 Quebec Street, N. W., Washington, D. C. 20008
Head: Susan Koss, Director

Grades: K-5   **Enrollment**: 104 Co-ed   **Faculty**: 14 full-, 9 part-time.   **Average Class Size**: Maximum, 16

Special Courses: Integrated curriculum combining General and Judaic studies along with Hebrew as a modern spoken language. Developmental orientation and Hands-on Learning. at all grade levels. Writer's Workshop, Journals, Math, Science, Music, Art, Drama; Computers introduced in K and used throughout the school day in all grade levels. Frequent Field Trips integrated into the curriculum. Focus on development of a postitive self image, social awareness, and cultural identity. Strong emphasis on ethical values and actions.
Extended Day Care: Provided on site by the DCJCC; Monday-Thursday, 3-6:30 p.m.; Friday , until 6 p.m.; Also available for special programs, school holidays and vacations.

Athletics: P.E. twice wkly.   **Clubs**: Student Council in upper grades   **Publications**: Newsletter for Parents. **Community Service** : Activities within both metropolitan D. C.and Jewish Communities.

Plant: Two or more computers in each classroom Use of synagogue Library, auditorium, multipurpose rooms. Two outdoor play areas.

Admission: Applications accepted Sept.-Jan., (later if space permits); Parents visit at Open Houses Nov.-Jan.; Application fee $50; K- Child visits for a play session and a Kindergarten Readiness Screening (fee). Teacher recommendations. For grades 1-5, call for application requirements.

Tuition: (1995-96) $6,300; Activities fee: $150 Voluntary Building Fund Contribution $150.
Financial Aid: Some Available

Future Plans: To add Grade 6, 1996-97.

JOHN NEVINS ANDREWS SCHOOL..........(301) 270-1400   FAX (301) 270-1403

117 Elm Avenue, Takoma Park, MD. 20912
Seventh Day Adventist 1907. **Head**: Dr. Leroy Kuhn, Principal

Grades: Pre-school - grade 8. **Enrollment**: 286 Co-ed. **Faculty**: 20 full-time.
Average Class Size: 23.

Special Courses: Computer. Gen'l Science; Remedial Reading & Math. Religion req. - General Bible for all classes. Steel Band.   **Extended Day**: until 6 P.M.

Athletics: Req.; Intramural Basketball, Full P.E. Program. **Clubs**: Student Council.
Publications: Yearbook, Newspaper. **Community Involvement**: Musical programs, Nursing Home visits.

Plant: Library 10,000 vol., Gym, Playing Fields.

Admission: Interview, Transcript, Achievement/readiness tests req. of all new students. Gesell testing for admission to K.; Metropolitan testing for grade 1; WRAT testing for all new students. Additional testing may be given to identify children with learning disabilities.

Tuition: (1995-96) $1,700-$3,500. Registration $125-$140. <u>Books</u>: $85-$100. <u>Lunch</u>: $2.50 / day. **Transportation**: $375-$700 one way; $560-$1,000 both ways. *Dress Code*: Must be neat & clean; No jewelry or heavy make-up. **Financial Aid**: Some available

Future Plans: Junior High Computerized Curriculum

JULIA BROWN MONTESSORI SCHOOLS...........(301) 498-0604 FAX (301) 622-5045

9450 Madison Avenue, Laurel, MD 20723
1300 Milestone Drive, Silver Spring, MD 20904
Head: Julia Brown, Director

Grades: Pre-school- grade 3 **Enrollment**: 185 Co-ed **Average Class Size**: 24

Special Programs: Montessori method; Language & Movement **Extended Day**: 7 a.m.-6 p.m.; Extra.

Tuition: (1995-96) Pre-school, half-day: $268-$275/mo.; all day, $545-$570; grades 1-3, $450-$480

Summer Program: call for information

JUNIPER LANE SCHOOL.............(703) 533-8890

3106 Juniper Lane, Falls Church, VA. 22044-1814
Head: Robert J. Bishton (Administration) Christine H. Bishton (Academic Programs)

Grades: N-3 **Enrollment**: 50 Co-ed **Average Class Size**: 7-10

Special Courses: Spanish (optional; extra fee) for children age 3 and older; Gymnastics (extra fee)

Plant: "Home-like" Building in residential neighborhood. Large 1/2 acre Playground

Admission: Interview (Sept.-March); Admission decision made in April.

Tuition: (1995-96) $2,550-$6,300 depending on age (Note: half-day for Nursery 3 or 5 days,etc) Registration -Supplemental Fees $155-$375. **Transportation**: $400-$1,250

Summer Program: Camp-Limited to new and returning students only: 12 sessions, 3 days a week, 9 a.m.-noon, for one month beginning the end of June.

KENWOOD/GRASSHOPPER GREEN SCHOOLS.........(703) 256-4711

4955 Sunset Lane, Annandale, VA. 22003
Founded 1957/1939. **Head**: Nancy Griffin.

Grades: N-6. **Enrollment**: 200 Co-ed. **Faculty**: 20 full-, 5 part-time.
Average Class Size: 16.

Special Courses: Computer, Spanish, P.E., Music; High priority placed on mastery of Reading skills and Math concepts as basis for ongoing educational development. Small classes and groups with individual attention. Before & after school supervision & activities available. **Extended Day** 7 a.m.-6 p.m.

Plant: 3 Classroom Buildings, Library, Gym, Playing Fields.

Admission: Interview, $30 Registration fee; Testing for placement.

Tuition: (1995-96) Half- Day $280/mo.; All Day $535-$540/mo. **Lunch**: Provided for Pre-School; Kenwood-Bring. **Books**: Extra. *Dress Code*: Neat, no jeans or tee shirts.

Summer Program: Year round program for pre-school. School age, Day Camp 12 weeks, ages 5 1/2-12. Swimming instruction, field trips, ice & roller skating, soccer, picnics, camp-out & overnights, arts & crafts. **Extended Hours** 7 a.m.-6 p.m.

KEY SCHOOL..........(410) 263-9231

534 Hillsmere Drive, Annapolis, MD. 21403
Founded 1958. **Head**: Ronald S. Goldblatt

Grades: Pre-K - grade 12. **Enrollment**: 565 Co-ed. **Faculty**: 48 full-, 19 part-time.
Average Class Size: 15.

Special Courses: Latin 8 & 9, French 1-12; Greek & Spanish 9-12. Math includes Calculus, Computer, Analytical Geometry, Logic, Economics. Biology, Chemistry, Physics, Earth Science, Estuarine Biology, Physiology. History- Ancient, European, American, American Civilization. Education/ Psychology, Introd. to Philosophy. Russian Studies. Remedial Reading & Math. Art, Music. **AP**.: French, Calculus, Biology, Physics, Art History. **Extended Day** : to 5:30 p.m.

Athletics: Req. thru grade 11. Intramural & Interscholastic: Soccer, Lacrosse, Field Hockey, Basketball, Softball. **Clubs**: Chess, Journalism, Drama, Chorus, Ensemble, Dance, Typing. **Publications**: Yearbook, Newspaper, Literary Magazine.

Plant: 2 Libraries, 2 Language Labs, 3 Science Labs, 2 Art Studios, 4 Playing Fields, Gym, Auditorium, Amphitheater, 2 Computer Labs.

Admission: Rolling (yr. round); $35 Application fee; Testing (ERB)

<u>Tuition</u>: (1995-96) PreK & K, $4,815; 1-4, $8,190; 5-8, $8,550; 9-12. $9,390.
<u>Lunch</u>: Bring or buy **Transportation:** Available. **Financial Aid**: Available

<u>Summer Program</u>: Pre K-grade 5, Day Camp; Ages 10-15, Outings and Overnight trips.
Tutoring.

THE KINGSBURY DAY SCHOOL...........(202) 232-1702   FAX (202) 667-2290

2138 Bancroft Place N.W., Washington, D.C. 20008
Founded 1984 <u>Note</u>: 1938, founded as Kingsbury Center **Head**: Marlene S. Gustafson

<u>Grades</u>: K-5 **Enrollment**: 58 Co-ed **Faculty**: 7 full-time, 10 part-time.
Average Class Size: 6-8

<u>Special Courses</u>: "Hands on Science", Art, Music. Remedial Reading & Math. School offers
intensive intervention for students with learning disabilities. Occupational therapy and
language therapy are available on site and integrated with classroom learning. <u>Note</u>: The
Kingsbury Center offers assessment and tutoring for all ages. **Extended Day**: 3- 6 p.m.

<u>Athletics</u>: P.E., non-competitive games.

<u>Plant</u>: Library 5,000 Vol.; New Arts Studio; Computers in classrooms.

<u>Admission</u>: Rolling admissions: applicants should apply as early as possible; $50 fee. Submit any
previous tests or arrange for Testing to be done at parent expense. Child must Visit school for
minimum of two days. The school seeks students who have diagnosed learning disabilities and
who would benefit from early intervention. Students accepted as old as 9 in September of school
year.

<u>Tuition</u>: (1995-96) $13,600 $150 Activities fee. <u>Lunch</u>: Bring. **Financial Aid**:
Limited.

<u>Summer Program</u>: For students ages 5-11.

LAB SCHOOL OF WASHINGTON..........(202) 965-6600

4759 Reservoir Road, N.W., Washington, D.C. 20007
Incorporated, Non-profit 1967. **Head**: Mrs. Sally L. Smith.

<u>Grades</u>: Ages 5-18, ungraded in elementary. **Enrollment**: 250 Co-ed. **Faculty**: 85
Average Class Size: Individualized tutortials and small groups (3-11).

<u>Special Features</u>: Program designed for primary, elementary, junior and senior high school
students of average or better intelligence with learning disabilities. Primary and elementary
students spend half-day in classrooms with highly individualized prescriptive programs taught
by master teachers; half-day learning academic skills through art forms (Graphics, Woodwork,

Ceramics, Photography, Music, Dance, Drama, and Film making) with outstanding artists trained in learning disabilities. History, Geography, Civics, and academic readiness skills are taught through a unique method called Academic Clubs in the elementary school. The junior - senior high school programs emphasize college preparatory courses, arts, electives, and sports. Spanish offered in High School. Math includes Calculus & Computer; General Science, Biology; History-U. S. and D. C.; Remedial Reading & Math.

Athletics: Req. (2 yrs. high school). Basketball, Soccer, Softball.

Plant: Modern 3-story classroom building, an historic mansion, a carriage house, and an occupational therapy annex. Media Center with extensive tape and cassette library of books. Library, 6,000 vol.

Admission: Registration fee $50, Educational, Neurological, Psychological Tests; Interview : child visits school for half day. Child must be of average to superior intelligence with specific learning disabilities (i.e., dyslexia, attention deficit) that impede academic success.

Tuition: (1995-96) Age 5-12 $15,465 Jr. High $16,015 Sr. High $16,565. **Financial Aid**: Tuition funded through D. C. & MD if approved by the public school system.

Summer Program: 6 weeks of Arts, Recreation, Remedial Instruction and Study Skills, mid-June through July. Scholarships available.

LAKE SHORE CHRISTIAN ACADEMY..........(410) 437-3529

860 Swift Road, Pasadena, MD. 21122
Head: Bill Natzer

Grades: K4-12   **Enrollment**: 70 Co-ed.

Special Features: ACE Program.

Tuition: (1995-96) Call for information

LANDON SCHOOL...........(301) 320-3200   FAX (301) 320-2787

6101 Wilson Lane, Bethesda, MD. 20817
Founded 1929. **Head**: Damon F. Bradley

Grades: 3-12. **Enrollment** 642 Boys; Enrollment increases 4 through 9.
Faculty: 72 full-, 8 part-time. **Average Class Size**: 8.5/1.

Special Courses: French , Latin, Spanish all 7-12. Math through Calculus, Computer. Science: General Science, Biology, Chemistry, Physics. History- Geography, Ancient, Modern World, Modern Soviet, Contemporary World Issues, Term Courses. Art-History, Design, Appreciation and Studio, Pottery, Ceramics. Photography. Music- History and Theory, Harmony, Choir, Glee

94

Club, Jazz, Band. Drama, Film making. AP.: Languages, Calculus, Biology, Physics, Modern European and U. S. History, English, Music. Cross registration with Holton Arms School (nearby Girls School) for AP. courses.

Athletics: Req. 3-12. Intramural & Interscholastic: Football, Cross Country, Track, Basketball, Wrestling, Soccer, Baseball, Tennis, Lacrosse, Riflery. **Clubs**: Community Service, Music and Drama, School Service, and numerous special interest clubs. **Publications**: Yearbook, Newspaper, Literary Magazine. **Community Involvement**: State and nationally recognized community service projects. Recommended by the Governor of Maryland as a model program for other schools.

Plant: Library 25,000 vol./ Language Lab, 5 Science Labs, 2 Art Studios, 2 Gyms, Auditorium 5 Playing Fields, 12 Tennis Courts, Performing Arts Center, All-weather track, Rifle Range, Green House, Ropes Course, 2 Computer Labs, 3 Traveling Computer Labs, Media Center..

Admission: Interviews; Entrance Tests in January; Application fee $50, covers testing.

Tuition: (1995-96) Grades 3 -6, $10,500; Grades 7 - 12, $11,200. **Lunch**: $580. **Books**: $200 **Transportation**: Available *Dress Code*: Jacket, shirt & tie req. grades 7-12. **Financial Aid**: 70-80 recipients.

Summer Program: Summer Sessions: Computer, study skills, enrichment, math courses. **Day Camp**: boys 6-11. 4-8 weeks. Tutoring available; Outside Education and speed Strength Training; Lacrosse. Baseball, Soccer, Basketball Tennis Camps.

LANGLEY SCHOOL..........(703) 356-1920

1411 Balls Hill Road, McLean, VA. 22101
Founded 1942 (parent owned co-op). **Head:** Mrs. Betty J. Brown.

Grades: N-8. **Enrollment**: 450 Co-ed. **Faculty**: 28 full-, 25 part-time. **Average Class Size**: 18-22.

Special Courses: French & Spanish K-8; Gen'l Science, Earth Science, Physical Science, Life Science; History-Middle Ages & Renaissance, U. S., 20th century U.S. with emphasis on Geography, Current Events. Typing, Band, Drama, Film-making. **Extended Day**: until 6 p.m.

Athletics: Intramural & Interscholastic. Basketball, Soccer, Softball, Track & Cross Country. **Publications**: Yearbook, weekly Memo, Literary Magazine, Quarterly Parent Magazine. **Community Involvement**: Service Projects.

Plant: New Library, 13,000 vol.; Computer Lab, AV Room. Science Labs, Greenhouse, Art Studio, Gym, Auditorium, Playing Fields, Jr. High Complex

Admission: Apply Sept.-Jan.; Parent Tour & Interview, child Visit & Testing; Transcripts & Recommendations . Application fee $30-$50;

Tuition: (1995-96) $5,460- $9,590 includes <u>Books.</u> **Transportation**: $940 one way, $1,725 both ways. *Dress Code*: Clean & neat. **Financial Aid**: Available.

Summer Program: Ages 3 - 16. 5 week program with variety of courses: Washington Art Program, Foreign Language-Spanish & French, Keyboard skills, Enrichment & Remedial Math & Reading, Study Skills. **Extended Day** Program.

LANHAM CHRISTIAN SCHOOL..........(301) 552-1156

8400 Good Luck Road, Lanham, MD. 20706
Head: Gene Pinkard

Grades: K- 12   **Enrollment**: 350 Co-ed

Special Features: Traditional program K-6; ACE curriculum 7 & 8; College Preparatory Program 9-12; Individualized Christian education for select students. Students advance at own pace with teacher/supervisor. **Extended Day**: 7 a.m.-5:30 p.m.

Tuition: (1995-96) $3,040 (Reduction for siblings).

LAUREL BAPTIST ACADEMY..........(301) 498-5060

7th & Montgomery Streets, Laurel, MD 20707
Head: Clyde Dowell

Grades: K-12   **Enrollment**: 50 Co-ed

Special Program: ACE Program.   **Extended Day**: to 6 p.m.

Tuition: (1995-96) K, $2,000; 1-12, $2,800. Reduction for siblings.

LEARY SCHOOL..........(703) 573-5400

6349 Lincolnia Road, Alexandria, VA 22312
Founded 1964   **Head** President, Albert Leary, Jr.   **Director**: Eugene Meale

Ungraded: 5-22 yrs.

Special Program: The Leary School is a private, day, co-educational, special education facility which serves students who have learning, emotional, and behavioral problems. Each child's identified learning styles, strengths, and weaknesses suggest the preferred methods of educational intervention.

An individualized educational program is formulated for each child in consultation with public school personnel, parents, and, when appropriate, the child. Psychological services, Counseling, and when needed, Career Development programs are all an intrinsic part of the Leary School program.

Admission: Most children are referred by their local public school system

Tuition Placement in the school through a public agency pays the full tuition and transportation fees.

LEESBURG CHRISTIAN SCHOOL..........(703) 777-4220

Route 1, P.O. Box 252 B, Leesburg, VA. 22075
Non-denominational 1969. **Head**: Mr. Terry Overstreet

Grades: Pre K-12. **Enrollment**: 175 Co-ed. **Faculty**: 15 full-, 2 part-time.
Average Class Size: 20.

Special Courses: German, Spanish.. Computer Literacy 1-12. General Science, World History, Remedial Reading & Math. Art, Music, Chorus. Religious studies req. Bob Jones Program.

Athletics: P.E. Req.; Interscholastic: Soccer, Baseball, Softball, Basketball.

Admission: Interview parents & child. Testing (depending on age).

Tuition: (1995-96) K, $2,300; 1-5 $2,450; 6-8, $2,600; 9-12, $2,750
Books & **Transportation**: Extra **Lunch**: Bring. *Dress Code*: Good grooming stressed; no jeans or T-shirts.

Summer Program: Academic Enrichment & Fine Arts Program featuring painting, drawing & music.

LEONARD HALL JUNIOR NAVAL ACADEMY..........(301) 475-8029

P.O. Box 507, Leonardtown, MD. 20650
Catholic 1909. **Head**: David Tibbs

Grades: 4-12. **Enrollment**: 65 Co-ed (52 Boys, 13 Girls) **Faculty**: 4 full-, 5 part-time.
Average Class Size: 15.

Special Courses: English, Math, Science, Social Studies. Computer; Numerous Electives. Remedial Reading. Religious Studies. Drill Team, Marching Units.

Athletics: Middle School Interscholastic Basketball and Soccer. Other sports offered: Volleyball, Softball, Kickball. **Publications**: Newspaper **Community Involvement**: Participate in local and state parades.

Plant : Library, Science Lab, Computer Lab, Drill Hall

Admission: Entrance Test by appointment, Fee $25.

Tuition: (1995-96) $2,975 . Lunch: Bring. Books: $130 **Transportation**: Available *Dress Code*: Uniform req. **Financial Aid** : Available

Future Plans : To expand to full elementary

LEXINGTON PARK CHRISTIAN SCHOOL...........(301) 862-4355

100 South Shangri-La Drive, Lexington Park, MD 20653
Head: Mrs. Sarah T.Patterson, Administrator

Grades: 1-9 **Enrollment**: 200 Co-ed   **Faculty**: 8 full-, 6 part-time. **Average Class Size** :20

Special Courses : Academic acceleration and remediation available. Band, Ensemble, Keyboard Piano, Orchestral instruments.

Athletics: Track,Basketball

Admission : Interview; Entrance Testing

Tuition: (1995-96) $2,450; Second child, $1,750 **Financial Aid** :Available

LINDEN HALL SCHOOL..........(717) 626-8512   FAX (717) 627-1384

212 East Main Street, Lititz, PA 17543 (near Lancaster, PA)
Moravian, 1746; America's oldest Boarding School for Girls.   **Head**: David J. Devey

Grades: 6-12, PG   **Enrollment**: 100 Girls (65 Boarding; Boarding begins 7th grade)
Faculty: 20 full-, 4 part-time. **Average Class Size**: 10

Special Courses: College preparatory with special emphasis on study skills and academic achievement. ESL-Gifted ED.- LD; Vocal/Instumental Music, Art, Dance, Photography.

Athletics: Field Hockey, Volleyball, Basketball, Softball, Soccer, Riding. **Community Service**: Students participate in various projects.

Plant: Located in small historic district; Self- contained campus on 46 acres;
Library 10,000 vol.; Gym, Swimming Pool, Outdoor Riding Rink, Stable for 22 horses; Stage. Dormitories with single rooms.

Admission: Application fee; Transcript, 2 Recommendations; Campus visit required.
Note Rolling admissions until all spaces are filled

Tuition: (1995-96) 7 Day Boarder, $18,000; 5 Day Boarder, $16,400;
Day Student, $7,000-$7,400. **Financial Aid**: Some Available

Summer Program: ESL; Riding, Basketball.

LINTON HALL..........(703) 368-3157 FAX (703) 368-3036

9535 Linton Hall Road., Bristow, VA. 22013
Catholic 1922. **Head**: Sister Glenna Smith, OSB

Grades: K-8. **Enrollment**: 163 Co-ed (91 Boys, 72 Girls) **Faculty**: 12 full-, 11 part-time. **Average Class Size**: 15.

Special Courses: Standard academic classes as well as instruction in Spanish, Art, Music, Drama, Outdoor Studies, Computer;   Religion req.; **Extended Day**: 6:30 a.m.-6:30 p.m.

Athletics: Interscholastic (Basketball, Soccer); Orienteering, **Clubs**: Leo. **Publications**: Yearbook.

Plant: Library 5,500 vol.; Learning Center, Science Lab, Gym/Auditorium, Playing Fields, Tennis Courts, Swimming Pool.

Admission: Personal Interview, Physical exam, Conduct recommendation from Principal, Transcript, Registration fee $50.

Tuition: (1995-96) $4,250 *Dress Code*: Uniform req. **Financial Aid**: Some available.

Future Plans: Increase student enrollment, Expand Computer Program

Summer Program: Sports, Recreation, and Enrichment Programs for ages 7-12; Summer Day Camp.

LITTLE PEOPLE'S PARADISE SCHOOL....,,......(202) 543-2618

308 15th Street, S.E., Washington, D.C. 20003
Head: Mrs. Dolores Conrad.

Grades: N-6 (N, Ages 2-4). **Enrollment**: 150 Co-ed. **Extended Day** : 6:30 a.m.-6:30 p.m.

Tuition: (1995-96) N, $75/wk. includes breakfast, lunch and snack, and **Extended Day**. Grades 1-6, $320/mo.

Summer Program: Year-round program for enrolled students.

LONE OAK MONTESSORI SCHOOL..........(301) 469-4888

10100 Old Georgetown Road, Bethesda, MD. 20814 (ages 3-6)
7108 Bradley Boulevard., Bethesda, MD. 20817 (ages18 mo.-12)

Head: Patricia Swann

Ungraded: Ages 18 mo.- 12   **Enrollment** : 170 Co-ed

Special Feature: Montessori Program. **Extended Day** : 7:45 a.m.- 5:30 p.m.

Tuition: (1995-96) $1,900-$5,200 **Extended Day** Extra

LOUDOUN COUNTRY DAY SCHOOL..........(703) 777-3841 FAX (703) 771-1346

237 Fairview Street, Leesburg, VA. 22075
Founded 1953. **Head**: Dr. Randy Hollister

Grades: Pre K-8. **Enrollment**: 159 Co-ed. **Faculty**: 18 full, 2 part-time.
Average Class Size: 18.

Special Courses: Latin 6-8, French and Spanish, K-8; Algebra, Computer as a scheduled class 6-8, other grades with classroom teacher. Gen'l Science 4-8; Hands on Science, K-5 . Civics, American History. Remedial Reading and Math. Note: Resource teacher for LD students. Art & Music. **Extended Day**: 7 a.m.-6:30 p.m.

Athletics: Required all grades. Intramural & Interscholastic: Soccer, Field Hockey, Basketball. Lacrosse, Track. Tennis also available. **Clubs**: Elective courses in photography, computer, jewelry making, chorus, etc. **Community Involvement**: Provide a complete Christmas (includes tree, gifts, and food) for the residents of the Loudoun Abused Women's Shelter.

Plant: Library 9,000 vol., Science Lab, Computer Lab, Playing Fields, Art Studio, Gym, Auditorium.

Admission: Interview, Testing, School Visit, Transcript, Recommendations; $60 Application & Testing fee.

Tuition: (1995-96) Pre-K, $5,100;   K- grade 5, $7,750; 6-8: $8,250. **Transportation**: varies, $400-$1,600. *Dress Code*: No jeans or T-shirts; other restrictions involve styles, and colors of dress. **Financial Aid**: Some Available .

Future Plans: School-wide network & technology integration.

LOVE OF LEARNING MONTESSORI SCHOOL..........(301) 596-4412

10840 Little Patuxent Parkway, Columbia, MD 21044
Head C. Awilda Torres

Ungraded : N2-age 12 **Enrollment**: Co-ed

Special Programs: Spanish K4-grade 6; Reading specialist on staff. **Extended Day**: 7 a.m. 4 p.m.

Tuition: (1995-96) Call for information.

Summer Program : Age 2-12. **Extended Day** : 7 a.m.-6 p.m.

LOWELL SCHOOL..... (202) 726-9153   FAX (202) 723-8469

16th & Kennedy Streets, N.W., Washington, D.C. 20011 (Pre Primary only)
4715 16th Street N.W., Washington, D. C. 20011 (Primary)
Founded 1965   **Head**: Abigail B. Wiebenson

Grades: N3- grade 3.   **Enrollment**: 200 Co-ed   **Faculty**: 21 full-, 6 part-time.
Average Class Size: 9-15

Special Programs: Mini courses for ages 5-8; field trips. **Extended Day**: ages 5-9, only: 3:00 p.m.-6:00 p.m.

Plant: 2 campuses, Library, 3,000 vol.; Science Lab, Art Workshop, Outdoor recreation area.

Admission: Individual Interview, Tour; Child visits, No formal testing.

Tuition : (1995-96) $6,000-$9,100 depending on program. Bring Lunch.
Financial Aid : Available

Summer Program : Programs for both Primary and Pre-primary. For ages 5-8, program includes field trips to area sites, woodworking & puppetry, and Spanish immersion. Extended Day.

MacARTHUR SCHOOL...........(202) 965-8700

4460 MacArthur Blvd. N.W, Washington, D. C. 20007
Developmental School Foundation 1975 **Head**: Denese Lombardi, M.A.

Grades : 1-12 (Day School, grades 5-12 only)   **Enrollment**: 115 Co-ed: Mostly Boarding at Psychiatric Institute of Washington.

MADEIRA SCHOOL..........(703) 556-8200

8328 Georgetown Pike, McLean, VA. 22102
Founded 1906. **Head**: Dr. Elisabeth Griffith.

Grades: 9-12. **Enrollment**: 300 Girls (135 day, 165 Boarding). **Faculty**: 29 full-, 16 part-time.
Average Class Size: 16

Special Courses: Curriculum: Full college-preparatory program in English, Math, Science, History, Foreign Language, the Visual and Performing Arts, and Computers. AP Courses in all subjects . A sample of History and English electives include: Comparative Women's History, African History, Latin American History, and History of the Middle East, 24 Frames Per Second: The Art of Film, A Decade in Depth: The 1960s.

Co-Curriculum Program   Grade 9 participates in a wilderness adventure program as well as classes in ethics, public speaking, and the arts. Grades 10-12 volunteer at government, business, and social service internships in the nation's capital..

Athletics: Req. 9-12. Intramural & Interscholastic: Aerobics, Basketball, Cross Country, Field Hockey, Gymnastics, Lacrosse, Life Saving, Modern Dance, Riding, Soccer, Softball, Squash, Swimming, Tennis, Volleyball, Weight Training.. **Clubs**: Thespian, Model U.N., Asian, French, Latin, Spanish, Debate. Math, Science, Student Council, Athletic Assn., Madrigals, Singers.. **Publications**: Yearbook, Newspaper, Literary Magazine. **Community Involvement:** (See Co-Curriculum under Special Courses).

Plant: Library 20,000 vol., Internet Access, Authomated catalogue; 6 Dormitories, 3 Science Labs, Health Center, Art Studio, Gym, Auditorium, Stables, Playing Fields, Indoor Pools, Tennis Courts, Indoor Riding Ring, Note: 400 acre campus with new 28,000 sq. ft. sports center.

Admission: SSAT, Interview, Personal Essays, Teacher & Principal Recommendation, Transcript. Application fee $40. First choice plan application, due December 15.

Tuition: (1995-96) Day $12,300; Boarding $21,620. Lunch included. Books: $350. *Dress Code*: Clean, appropriate clothing. **Financial Aid**: Available

Summer Program: Day camp - Coed ages 6-14; tennis, swimming, crafts, outdoor adventure.

MAHARISHI SCHOOL OF THE AGE OF ENLIGHTENMENT..........(301) 949-8350

12210 Georgia Avenue, Wheaton, MD 20902
Founded 1982 **Head**: Celeste Schindler, Principal.

Grades: 2 yrs. to grade 6. **Enrollment**: 60 Co-ed **Faculty**: 5 full-, 7 part-time. **Average Class Size**: 12

Special Programs: Art, Music,Transcendental Meditation; Science of Creative Intelligence. **Extended Day**: Available on premises by independent provider.

Athletics: P.E. Note: Additional after school activities organized by parents include Karate and ice skating.

Plant: Library, Playing Field, all purpose room.

Admission: $25 Application fee; Liberal admissions policy. Admission based on Application Review, Interview, and Transcripts: School must determine that the applicant's need can be met.

Tuition: (1995-96) Age 2-K, $1,000- $5,000 (depending on number of days and hours)plus activities fees ($25-$75 per semester); grades 1-6, $5,225, plus $50 per semester for Books and Material fee. *Dress Code*: Uniform req.

MANOR MONTESSORI SCHOOL.........(301) 299-7400   FAX (301) 299-7400

10500 Oaklyn Drive, Potomac, MD. 20854
11200 Old Georgetown Road, Rockville, MD. 20852 (N & K only)
Founded 1962. **Head**: Katherine Damico

Ungraded: Ages 2-1/2-9 (N-3rd). **Enrollment**: 185 Co-ed. **Faculty**: 17 full-, 10 part-time. **Average Class Size**: 28

Special Features: Montessori method , ungraded classes; Math, Language, Geography, Sensorial, Prac.Life, and Computer, French, Gifted Children's Program, Physical Education, Music & Art. **Extended Day**: 7:30 a.m.- 6 p.m.

Extra-Curricular Program: Soccer

Main Plant: 3 1/2 acres in Potomac, Air-Conditioned Building, All-purpose Room, Playgrounds.

Admission: Informal Interview with Directress. $50 Registration fee. Primary class -ages 2 1/2-6; Elementary class, ages 6-9.

Tuition: (1995-96) Half- day $4,050; N-PreK All-day, $5,200; K & 1st. $5,600.   Elementary (1st-3rd) $5,900 **Extended Day**: Nursery $6,900; K-3rd, $7,200. **Transportation**: $1,500, one way; $2,000, both ways. **Scholarship Aid**: Available.

Future Plans: To offer after-school programs including tennis and ice-skating.

Summer Program: Ages 18 months- 7 yrs.;   arts & crafts, swimming lessons, nature hikes. field trips, Spanish, Computer, P. E., Cooking. Hours: 7:30 a.m.-6 p.m.(minimum one week) or 9 a.m.-noon, 9 a.m.-3 p.m.; Call for information on New Toddler Program.

MARET SCHOOL ....(202) 939-8800   FAX (202) 939-8884

3000 Cathedral Avenue, N.W., Washington, D.C. 20008
Founded 1911. **Head**: Mrs. Marjo Talbott

Grades: K-12. **Enrollment**: 500 Co-ed. Enrollment increases 4, 7, 9. **Faculty**: 74 full-4 part-time.   **Average Class Size**: 12.

Special Courses: Languages: Latin 5-12, French & Spanish K-12; Math: Geometry, Advanced Geometry, Algebra I & II, Trig; Topics in Finite Math; Elementary Functions, Statistics; Precalculus; Science: Biology, Chemistry, Physics, Environmental Science, Chemistry in the

Community; Subtropical Ecology. Computer: Literarcy, Pascal, Graphics and Digital Imaging. Humanities: Modern Peoples; U.S History; Civil Liberties; History and the Aesthetics of Film; Race, Gender and Religions; American Literature; Creative Writing; Expository Writing; Faulkner, Fitgerald, Hemingway; Modern Drama; Psychological Themes in Literature; Style in Literature. Art: Ceramics, Woodworking, Painting, Mixed Media, Sculpture, Computer Graphic and Video, Photography. Music: Chorus, Band, Chamber Choir; Advanced Music Theory and Composition.
AP.: Latin. French, Spanish; Biology, Chemistry, Physics AB & BC; Calculus AB & BC; U.S. History, British Literature.
Note Faculty members work with juniors and seniors interested in developing an independent study course (i.e.. Advanced Music Theory and History) as a tutorial in a specific discipline or a sr. option course (i.e., teaching Spanish in a bilingual neighborhood school); takes place outside the traditional curriculum.   Intensive Study Week: 1 week program   in Feb., opportunity for students/teachers to propose different topics, create new classes. Senior Project Last 2 weeks, sr.year; students work with teachers in particular field of their interest.
Extended Day: to 6 p.m.

Athletics: Req. K-12. Intramural & Interscholastic: Football, Soccer, Basketball, Volleyball, Softball, Baseball, Weight Training,, Aerobics, Self-defense, Wrestling, Tennis, Lacrosse, Track & Field, Cross-Country. **Clubs**: Engineering Team, It's Academic; Grades 5-12, Musical; Amnesty International; Peer facilitators. SADD. Model U.N., etc. **Publications**: Yearbook, Literary and Visual Arts Magazine, Newspaper. **Community Involvement**: 70% of Upper School students do volunteer work on regular or ad hoc basis throughout the year.

Plant: 2 Libraries (12,000 vol.), 6 Science Labs, Field, 2 Gyms, Auditorium, 5 Art Studios, Math Lab, Music Room, 2 Computer Rooms with 40 computers, all housed in 6 buildings.

Admission: Tour/Interview; child Visits for full day; Recommendations & Transcript; SSAT for grades 6-11. Some Testing K-5.

Tuition: (1995-96) $10,935- $12.820.   Lunch: $450. Books: $100-$450. *Dress Code*: Neat and appropriate. **Financial Aid** : Available

Future Plans: Renovation of historic Woodley House.

Summer Program: Credit, Remedial & Enrichment programs for grades 5-12,(full, half-day); **Summer Camp** ages 4-9, full and half-day. **Summer Study**: Florida, France, and Spain..

MARTIN BARR ADVENTIST SCHOOL............(301) 261-0078

2365 Bell Branch Road, Gambrills, MD. 21054
Seventh Day Adventist   **Head**: Joni Woodruff

Grades: K-8 **Enrollment**: 32 Co-ed

Tuition: (1995-96) $145-$280/mo. Note: discount for siblings and church members. Registration fee $100

MATER AMORIS MONTESSORI SCHOOLS.........(301) 774-7468 or (202)362-3279

18501 Mink Hollow Road, P.O. Box 97, Ashton, MD. 20861
36th & Ellicott Streets, N.W., Washington, D.C. 20008
Founded 1968. **Head**: Charlotte Kovach Shea

Ungraded: age 2-l/2 -12. **Enrollment**: 40 (D.C.); 110 (MD) Co-ed. **Faculty**: 11 AMI (Association Montessori International) trained teachers. **Average Class Size**: 25.

Special Courses: Art, Music, General Science, Biology, History, Dance, Drama.
Extended Day: 7:30 a.m.-6 p.m.

Athletics: Softball, Kickball, Field Hockey, Basketball, Soccer, Volleyball.

Plant: Library, Science Lab, Auditorium, Playing Fields, Stables, 13 acre farm in Ashton, Md.

Admission: Parent Visit & Interview, child Visits class.

Tuition: (1995-96) Ages 2-l/2-5, Half- day $3,400; K, $4,700;   Ages 6-12, $5,300- $ 5,600.
Note: Transportation between campuses.   **Financial Aid**: Some Available.

MATER DEI SCHOOL..........(301) 365-2700

9600 Seven Locks Road, Bethesda, MD. 20817
Catholic 1960. **Head**: Christopher Abell

Grades: 1-8. **Enrollment**: 220 Boys. **Faculty**: 14 full-,6 part-time. **Average Class Size**: 20.

Special Courses: Latin 8, Art, Music. Substantial Reading requirement. Religious studies req., Computer.

Athletics: Req.; Intramural & Interscholastic 5-8; All sports offered. **Publications**: Newspaper.

Plant: Library 6,000 vol., Chapel, Gym, Art Studio, Swimming Pool, Playing Fields.

Admission: Testing in February, Parent Interview required,

Tuition: (1995-96) $5,750. Bring Lunch. Books: Extra. *Dress Code*: Uniform req.

Summer Program: Day camp for boys, ages 5-12.

McDONOGH SCHOOL..........(410) 363-0600

Pikesville, MD. 21117-0380

Founded 1873. **Head**: Dr. William C. Mules.

Grades: Pre l-12. **Enrollment**: 1,172 Co-ed Day & Boarding (5 day Boarding begins 9).

McLEAN SCHOOL OF MARYLAND............(301) 299-8277

8224 Lochinver Lane, Potomac, MD. 20854
Founded 1952. **Head**: Donald H. Grace

Grades: K-9. **Enrollment**: 330 Co-ed. **Faculty**: 54 full-, 11part-time
Average Class Size: 15

Special Program: Basic Traditional, challenging curriculum. Unique Dual Program for
Mainstream Students and those with individual learning styles. **Special Courses**: Spanish 7-9,
Art, Music, Drama, Computers/Keyboarding, and Leadership.

Athletics: P.E. classes daily. Interscholastic: Soccer, Softball, Basketball, Field Hockey,
Lacrosse. **Publications**: Newspaper, Literary Magazine, Yearbook.
Community Involvement: Ninth Grade Service at Our Lord's Table Soup Kitchen, Recycling
Program, Retirement Home and Community Music Programs.

Plant: Library 10,155 vol., Science Lab, Computer Labs, Art Studio, All Purpose Room/Gym,
Playing Fields.

Admission: Weekly Open House; Parent Interview; Student Visits Classroom; Transcript & Test
scores, WISC 3, Achievement Testing andTeacher Recommendations. Application fee.

Tuition: (1995-96) $8,500-$11,200   Books: $200-$300. **Transportation**: Available.
Dress Code: Uniform required **Financial Aid**: Available

MERCERSBURG ACADEMY.........(717) 328-6173   FAX (717) 328-9072

300 East Seminary Street
Mercersburg, PA. 17236
United Church of Christ 1836. **Head**: Walter H. Burgin, Jr.

Grades: 9-12, P.G. **Enrollment**: 380 (212 Boys, 168 Girls), 318 Boarding, 62 Day. **Faculty**:
59 full-time. **Average Class Size**: 12-14

Special Courses: Latin, French, Spanish, German,-all 9-12. Math through 2nd yr. Calculus,
Computer, Discreet Math. Science: Physical Science, Biology, Chemistry, Physics; term courses
in Botany, Genetics, Psychology, Behavioral Science, Anthropology. History - Intro. to World
History (9), Introd. to Western Civilization (10), U.S. & European; term courses in Latin
America, Sub- Saharan Africa, China & Japan. Economics. Religious Studies-Req.; Art:
Drawing, Painting, Sculpture, Art History. Music History, Theory. AP. courses in all academic
areas, Art History, and Studio Art. School Year Abroad;-English-Speaking Union; School Farm

Trek (Outward Bound Program).

Athletics: Intramural Softball. Interscholastic: Football, Cross Country, Field Hockey, Basketball, Swimming, Diving, Wrestling, Squash, Baseball, Tennis, Golf, Track & Field, Lacrosse, Soccer, Softball, & Volleyball. **Clubs**: 4 Music groups, 4 Choral groups; Student Council, Drama, Languages, Photography, Debate, Amnesty International, Ecology. **Publications**: Weekly Newspaper, Literary Magazine, Yearbook. **Community Involvement**: Tutoring at local elementary school, Youth Club; Helping Senior Citizens; Soup Kitchen.

Plant: New Library/Classroom Bldg. 48,000 vol.; 7 English classrooms, Major new classroom building 5 Science Labs, Gym, Auditorium, 8 Playing Fields, Swimming Pool, 17 Tennis Courts, All-weather quarter-mile Track, Indoor Track, Outdoor Volleyball court; School Farm, Chapel.

Admission: SSAT, PSAT; Interview, if geographically possible. Recommendations from 3 teachers; Transcripts for the previous 3 years.

Tuition: (1995-96) Boarding, $19,100; Day, $12,650 **Books**: $500. *Dress Code*: At evening meal: Coat & Tie for boys, skirt for girls. **Financial Aid**: 33% of student body.

Summer Program: Individual Camp offerings in June, July, & August. Numerous sports camps including tennis, field hockey, karate, swimming, & soccer camps. Ecology camp 1 week in mid June.

MONTESSORI CHILDREN'S HOUSE (Bowie)..........(301) 262-3566

5004 Randonstone Lane, Bowie, MD. 20715
Founded 1967. **Head**: Anne Riley.

Ungraded: Ages 2 1/2 -14. **Enrollment**: 170 Co-ed. **Faculty**: 5 full-, 4 part-time.
Average Class Size: 30

Special Courses: Montessori method used; Exposure to Music, Art, Dance, Drama (private lessons in art, music, ballet available). Remedial Reading and Math. 22 acre campus used to familiarize children with erosion, forestry, environment and care of animals. Limited **Day Care** 7 a.m.-6 p.m.

Plant: Library 5000 vol., Audio Visual Lab, Stables, Playing Fields, Tennis Courts, Outdoor Amphitheater, 22 acre rustic campus.

Admission: Parent & child Interview. Limited acceptances for children beyond age 5 if not previously enrolled in Montessori program. Special remedial & high aptitude applicants accepted. Those with limited handicaps includes deaf with cued speech and reading disabilities.

Tuition: (1995-96) $3,280-$4,100 **Day Care**: Extra, (depends on age). Books: $15-$50

Summer Program: Rustic Woods Day Camp - (Remedial instruction by special request). Arts & crafts, ecology, primitive construction, riding, sports, swimming, campouts, etc.

Continuation of Montessori philosophy for children 6-12 using the out of doors. Late June to late August.

MONTESSORI INTERNATIONAL CHILDREN'S HOUSE.........(410) 757-7789

1641 Winchester Road, Annapolis, MD. 21401
Founded 1977. **Head**: Jean Burgess

Ungraded: Ages 18 mo-11 yr.(5th grade) **Enrollment**: 140 Co-ed. **Faculty**: 6 full-, 5 Montessori Aides. **Average Class Size**: 20.

Special Courses: Montessori method. French conversation taught, Music, Art, Creative Dramatics, Creative Movements, Cooking. (Infant & Toddlers program) P.E.
Extended Day: 7:30 a.m.-6 p.m.

Plant: Library, new modern facility designed specifically for Montessori Primary & Elementary programs in country setting.

Admission: Interview with parent & child, Testing for Elementary. $25 Application fee.

Tuition: (1995-96) Toddler, $1,907; K Half-day $3,119; K Full-day, $4,445; Elementary $4,757 -$4,862 (Day Care: Extra) Bring Lunch.

Summer Program: 6 weeks, Montessori program for ages 2 1/2-6

MONTESSORI SCHOOL OF ALEXANDRIA ....(703) 960-3498

6300 Florence Lane, Alexandria, VA. 22310
Founded 1970. **Head**: Jean Adolphi

Ungraded: Ages 2-1/2-12. **Enrollment**: 96 Co-ed. **Faculty**: 10 full-, 9 part-time.
Average Class Size: 25.

Special Features: Montessori method, ungraded classes. Art, Music, French, Ballet, Gymnastics, Tap, Jazz, Karate **Extended Day** : 7:30 a.m.-6 p.m.

Admission: Child must be between ages 2 1/1 and 3-1/2 unless previously enrolled in Montessori school. Interview.

Tuition: (1995-96) Primary (Age 2 1/2-5) $3,650;   Age 5-6, $4,250;   Age 6-12 $4,850.
Dress Code: Uniform Req.

Summer Program: 10 weeks, includes swimming, karate, sports, gymnastics, nature study, arts & crafts daily; ages 5-12.   Montessori School Program Half-day for ages 2 1/2-4 : arts & crafts, nature study, music (afternoons) $120 half-day, $150 all day.

MONTESSORI SCHOOL OF HOLMES RUN.........(703) 573-4652

3527 Gallows Road, Falls Church, VA 22042
Head: Judith Clarke
Ungraded: Ages 2 1/2-12   **Enrollment**: 60 Co-ed

Special Programs: Montessori program

Tuition: (1995-96) Half-day, (3 & 4 yrs) $2,750; K Full-day $3,150; 1-6, $3,750. Reduction for siblings. **Transportation**: one way, $90/mo; both ways, $180/mo.

MONTESSORI SCHOOL OF McLEAN.........(703) 790-1049 FAX (703)790-1962

1711 Kirby Road, McLean, VA. 22101
Founded 1973. **Head**: Joan Marie Parasine.

Ungraded: Ages 2 yrs. 9 mo.-12 yr. **Enrollment**: 165 Co-ed. **Faculty**: 7 full-, 6 part-time. **Average Class Size**: 28.

Special Courses: Ungraded classes. French or Spanish (Elem.); Computers all levels; Art, Dance, and Drama (elem)   Music & P.E. at all levels. **Clubs** : Bluebirds or Girl Scouts (if parent leader available)

Plant: Library, 5,500 vol.; Art Studio, Playing Fields

Admission: Interview, Application fee $85.

Tuition: (1995-96) $4.200-$4,800. Books: $110. **Transportation**: $1,200 one way; $1,500 both ways. **Dress Code**: Neat attire, no jeans in Pre-school; Uniform required in Elementary grades.

Summer Program: Academic program, Montessori curriculum; Summer Camp program: cooking, songs, games, field trips, gardening, Ages 2 1/2-5..

MONTESSORI SCHOOL OF NORTHERN VIRGINIA.........(703) 256-9577

6820 Pacific Lane, Annandale, VA. 22003
Founded 1962. **Head**: Betsy Mitchell.

Ungraded: Ages 2-9. **Enrollment**: 130 Co-ed. **Faculty**: 6 full-, 8 part-time. **Average Class Size**: 25

Special Courses: Montessori method, French, Orff music program. Art, P.E.; Emphasis on cultural studies; Creative Dramatics Computer instruction. **Extended Day**: 7 a.m. - 6 p.m.

Plant: Library, Spacious bright classrooms that open to the outside; shady, park-like playground.

Admission: Parents Visit & Observe; Interview. Application and $50 fee by Feb. 15 for fall admission; Mid-year admission from waiting list.

Tuition: (1995-96) $1,990-$5,050 includes <u>Books</u>   *Dress Code*: Comfortable clothing. **Financial Aid** Limited.

Summer Program: 4 - 6 weeks, ages 2 1/2-7. Wide range of activities including Montessori academic, arts & crafts, outdoor play, food preparation, nature study.

MONTROSE CHRISTIAN SCHOOL........... (301) 770-5337

5100 Randolph Road, Rockville, MD 20852
Southern Baptist 1977. **Head**: Kenneth Coley

Grades: K-12. **Enrollment**: 650 Co-ed. **Faculty**: 36 full-time. **Average Class Size**: 15-20.

Special Courses: Spanish; Computer. Gen'l Science, Biology, Chemistry, Physics. World History, Civics, Geography. Bible study req. Remedial Reading and Math. Mechanical Drawing, Typing. AP.: English and History. **Extended Day**: 7 a.m.-6 p.m.

Athletics: Req; Soccer, Basketball, Volleyball, Softball, Track. **Clubs**: Student Government. **Publications**: Yearbook. **Community Involvement**: Christmas Baskets.

Plant: Library, Gym, Auditorium, Science Lab.

Admission: Formal Application, Interview, standardized Testing. (Must be able to work at grade level).

Tuition: (1995-96) K, $2,130; 1-6 $2,940; 7-12 $3,250. **Extended Day**: Extra.

MOUNT CALVARY SCHOOL...........................(301) 735-5262

6704 Marlboro Pike, Forestville, MD 20747
Catholic **Head**: Mr. William J. Clancy, Jr.

Grades: K-8   **Extended Day**: Available

Tuition: (1995-96) $1,650 Reduction for siblings.

MUSLIM COMMUNITY SCHOOL, INC.............(301) 340-6713

7917 Montrose Road, Potomac, MD. 20854
Islamic, Non-Sectarian-Multinational 1980 **Head**: Salahuddiin A. Kareem

Grades: Pre K-9 **Enrollment**: 150 Co-ed **Faculty**: 16 full-, 2 part-time.

Average Class Size: 13

Special Courses: Arabic, K-9. Algebra and Computer. General Science. History- World, Islamic, Modern U.S.; Religious Studies, req.; ESOL. Note: All classes except Arabic are taught in English. Art, Science Fairs, Zuramic Competitions, Spelling Bees-annually.

Athletics: Girls: Gymnastics, Volleyball. Boys: Soccer, Martial Arts. **Publications**: Yearbook, Literary Magazine.

Plant: Library, 9,100 vol.; Language Lab, Science Lab, Auditorium, Playing Fields, Tot Lot- Playing Ground, Basketball Court.

Admission: Pre registration June 15th, $50 fee. Transcripts, Personal Interview with Family. Note: Boys and Girls separated at grade 5.

Tuition: (1995-96) $250- $350/mo.; Reduction for siblings. **Books**: $35. **Transportation**: $120/mo. *Dress Code*: Uniform req. **Financial Aid**: Some Available.

NANNIE HELEN BURROUGHS SCHOOL, INC.........(202) 398-5266

601 50th Street, N.E., Washington, D.C. 20019
Baptist 1909. **Head**: Mrs. Shirley Hayes

Grades: N-6. **Enrollment**: 160 Co-ed. **Faculty**: 9 full-, 5 part-time. **Average Class Size**: 20.

Special Courses: Spanish, Music, Science includes Aerospace and Computer Science; Bible Classes 5 & 6. After school program in cultural arts. Emphasis on Leadership Training. **Extended Day**: 7 a.m.- 5:30 p.m.

Athletics: P.E. Req. - includes kickball. **Publications**: Quarterly newsgram. **Community Involvement**: Share assemblies with public school.

Plant: Library, Auditorium, Gym, Playing Fields.

Admission: Interview (parent & child), Tests. Registration fee $100.

Tuition: (1995-96) $324-$351/ mo. includes **Extended Day** Extra, $50/mo.

Summer Program: Enrichment program.

NATIONAL CATHEDRAL SCHOOL.........(202) 537-6300   FAX (202) 537-5625

Mount St. Alban, Washington, D.C. 20016-5000
Episcopal 1900. **Head**: Agnes C. Underwood.

Grades: 4-12. **Enrollment**: 550 Girls, class expands at grade 7. **Faculty**: 72full-, 13 part-time

Average Class Size: 15-18.

Special Courses: Latin 7-12; Spanish & French 4-12; German 10-12; Greek / Russian/ German/Chinese/Japanese consortium with Sidwell Friends & St. Albans (upper school). English. Math thru Calculus, Computer. Science: Biology, Chemistry, Physics; History-American Gov't; American History, Soviet Union, Japan, Modern European, Developing World Politics, Middle East, World, Geography. Economics. Religion Courses req.(grades 4-8 and 2 semesters grades 9-12). Studio Art, Art History. Music - Orchestra & Band; Drama. Some co-ordinate courses & activities with St. Albans. AP.: English, Languages, Calculus, Computer, Science, History, Economics, Art History . **Extended Day**: Available for grades 4-8, until 6 p.m.

Athletics: Req.(except for one season grade 12) Intramural & Interscholastic: Field Hockey, Soccer, Basketball, Volleyball, Tennis, Dance, Gymnastics, Track & Field, Lacrosse, Softball, Swimming, Diving, Cross Country, Aerobics, Weight Training, Rock Climbing, Kayaking, **Clubs**: Over 25, including: Foreign Language, Government, Debate, Drama, Madrigals, Chorale White Chapel Guild, Black Student Union, Environmental Awareness, Mock Trial, School Gov't, Service Board, Planning Board, Vestry. **Publications**: Newspaper, Yearbook, Literary magazine. **Community Involvement**: 60 hrs. req. grades 9-12.

Plant: 2 Libraries 21,000 vol., (students also have electronic access to the libraries at St. Albans School); Language Lab, 7 Science Labs, Art Studio, 2 Gyms, 2 Auditoriums, Playing Fields, 8 Tennis Courts, Theater (used jointly with St. Albans) and Experimental Theater, Computer Center Swimming Pool at St. Albans.

Admission: $60 Application fee, SSAT for grades 6-11, NCS Test for grades 4, 5. English test for grade 7. Interview/Visit. Process should begin in the fall; applicant file must be completed by Feb 15 for consideration in first group of applicants

Tuition: (1995-96) $13,500 includes Lunch & Fees; Books: $125-$355 *Uniform*: req. grades 4-6; *Dress Code* gr. 7-12. **Financial Aid**: Full and partial grants available.

Summer Program: Problem-Solving and technology; co-ed, students entering grades 4-6. Two three week sessions, 9 a.m.-3 p.m. plus Extended Day.

NATIONAL CHRISTIAN ACADEMY ....(301) 567-9507

6700 Bock Road, Ft. Washington, MD 20744
Pentecost, 1981 **Head**: Dr. Fred Snowden

Grades: N3-grade 12. **Enrollment**: 506 Co-ed (160 Boys, 250 Girls) **Faculty**: 23 full, 12 part-time aides. **Average Class Size** : 23

Special Courses: Spanish, Gen'l Science, Biology, Chemistry. History- U.S., Gov't, World, and Bible. Computer. Religious Studies req. Typing, Driver's Ed, Band, Drama. **Extended Day**: 6:30 a.m.-6:30 p.m.

Athletics: Girls & Boys Basketball & Volleyball Teams (Jr, & Sr. High)

Plant: Gym, Auditorium, Playing Fields, Science Lab, Computer Lab. Cafeteria, Chapel.

Admission: $50 Registration fee; Parent/Principal Interview; Transcript.

Tuition: (1995-96) N3-N4, $100/wk; K-6, $290/mo; 7-12, $305/mo.Reduction for siblings. Books: Extra. **Transportation**: Available, fees based on distance and numbers of children. *Dress Code*: Uniform req. K5-grade 12.

Summer Program: Day Camp; Call for information.

NATIONAL PRESBYTERIAN SCHOOL...(202) 537-7500   FAX 202-537-7568

4121 Nebraska Avenue, N.W., Washington, D.C. 20016
Presbyterian 1969. **Head**: Mrs. Jane Harter.

Grades: N3-grade 6. **Enrollment**: 215 Co-ed. **Faculty**: 27 full-, 8 part-time. Note: Reading & Language Specialists and Math Specialist on staff. **Average Class Size**: 24, with 2 classroom teachers.

Special Courses: French, Science Lab, Religious Studies, Drama, Art, Music, Handbells, P.E.. **Extended Day**: until 6 p.m.

Athletics: Req. K-6. Intramural Non-competitive program of body movement, skills, and games. Member of Sports League-grades 5 & 6 **Clubs**: Karate, Computer, After-school Sports, Drama, Art, Science, French, Math, Newspaper, Literary Magazine **Publications**: Newsletter, Yearbook

Plant: Computerized Library 11,000 vol.; computers in classrooms. Science Lab, Art Studio, Gym/Auditorium. School shares 12.5 acre campus with the National Presbyterian Church & Center and shares some of the facilities of the church.

Admission: Parent Visits school; Application and non-refundable application fee; Upon completion of application, child spends day at school; Tests, Transcripts, Recommendations from previous schools; Admissions Committee makes decision and candidate notified after March 1.

Tuition: (1995-96) N & Pre K, $5,500; K-6. $9,200   **Finacial Aid** : Available.

Future Plans: Acquisition of additional playing fields.

Summer Camp Program: Early June to early September, variety of summer programs; Ages 4-11; Staff includes professional teachers. Swimming at American University. **Extended Day** Available..

NATIONHOUSE WATOTO SCHOOL........... (202) 291-5600   FAX (202) 726-5681

770 Park Road, N.W., Washington, D. C. 20010

Head: Mr. Agyei Akoto

Grades: N (age 2 1/2) -12   Enrollment: 85 Co-ed

Special Programs : French, Swahili; African Youth Organization and Dance. Drill Team; Computer Club. Adult Education Programs. Extended Day: 7:30 a.m.-6 p.m.

Tuition: (1995-96) Pre-Primary, $310/mo; Grade 1-12. $275/mo.

Summer Program: Academic & Recreational; 8 a.m.-6 p.m.

NATIVITY CATHOLIC ACADEMY.........(202) 723-3322

6008 Georgia Avenue, N.W., Washington, D.C. 20011
Catholic 1925. Head: Mrs. Valeri M. Smith.

Grades: PreK-8. Enrollment: 260 Co-ed. Faculty: Departmentalized small group instruction.

Special Programs: Religion, Reading, Math, Spanish, Language Arts, Social Studies, Science, Music and Art. Education for the whole child: spiritual, intellectual, social and physical; growth in the knowledge and experience of Jesus as personal Lord, Savior and Brother. Nativity School Band 4-8. Extended Day: 7 a.m.-6 p.m.

Athletics: P.E. Girls & boys basketball teams competition (CYO League). Clubs: Student Council, Band. Publications: Newspaper.

Plant: Library (with large audio/visual sections), Auditorium, Gym, Math Lab, Chapel (at church).

Tuition: (1995-96) $1,950-$2,200   Registration $30 Books: $100 Extended Day Extra

Summer Program: Summer camp for students ages 4-14.

NAYLOR ROAD SCHOOL.........(202) 584-5114

2403 Naylor Road, S.E., Washington, D.C. 20020
Founded 1939. Head: Mrs. Patricia Ward.

Grades: N3-grade 6. Enrollment: 200 Co-ed. Faculty: 22. Average Class Size: 18.

Special Courses: Spanish N-6, Art, Music, Shop, Individual Science Program 1-6; Traditional Classes stressing Reading & Language Development. Small groups, individualized instruction. Extended Day   6:45 a.m.-6 p.m.

Plant: Library 3,000 vol.; Language Lab, Science Lab, Shop.

114

Admission: Applications accepted in Feb., Testing l-6.

Tuition: (1995-96) N, $3,050; Pre-K, $3,150.; K, $3,300.; 1-6 $3,600-$4,000; (varied payment plans available). **Lunch**: Bring. **Books**: Extra. *Dress Code*: K-6, Uniforms.

NEW CITY MONTESSORI SCHOOL..........(301) 559-8488

3120 Nicholson Street, Hyattsville, MD. 20782-3108
Founded 1968. **Head**: Shirley Windsor, Administrator.

Ungraded: Ages 2 1/2 - 9. **Enrollment**: 80 Coed. **Faculty**: 5 full-, 6 part-time.
Average Class Size: 20

Special courses: Montessori method, ungraded. Computers; Spanish; Art.
Extended Day: 7:30 a.m..-6 p.m.

Admission: Application form and $25 fee; Informal Interview with parent & child.

Tuition: (1995-96) $2,730-$3,955. **Extended Day** : Extra; depends on age and number of hours.

NEW HOPE ACADEMY..........(301) 459-7311

7009 Varnum Street, Landover Hills, MD 20784
Non-Denominational Christian **Head** Joy Morrow

Grades: N2-grade 8 **Enrollment**: 165 Co-ed

Special Programs: Korean Lanuage, 1- 8. Optional after school Dance Program includes Ballet and Ethnic Dance. **Extended Day**: 7:30 a.m.-6 p.m.

Tuition: (1995-96) $2,040-$4,200; discount for siblings.

NEW LIFE CHRISTIAN SCHOOL ....(301) 663-8418 FAX (301 698-1583

5913 Jefferson Pike, Frederick, MD 21702
Head: Paul Kemp

Grades: K-12 **Enrollment**: 225 Co-ed

Special Courses: ABEKA and Bob Jones Program; Spanish & French

Plant: Classroom Building and Gym

Tuition : (1995-96) Half-day K, $1,400; 1-12 $2,200 -$2,600; Reduction for siblings.

Future Plans : Proposed pre-school for 3-4 yr. olds.

 NEWPORT SCHOOLS............(301) 942-4550

11311 Newport Mill Road, Kensington, MD. 20895
Founded 1930   **Head**: Andrew A. Zvara

Grades: PreK-12 (Note; Town & Country Day School, N-8; Newport Preparatory School, 9-12.) **Enrollment** : 270 Co-ed **Faculty**: 45 full & part-time. **Average Class Size**: 15

Special Courses: Latin & French, 7-12; Spanish PreK-12. Science: Biology, Chemistry, Physics, History & Philosophy of Science. History- World, American. Political Theory, Government, Economics. Studio Art & Fundamentals; Fundamentals of Music, Choir, Bell Choir Drama, Photography. AP.: Biology, Calculus, Computer Science, American History, English Literature & Composition. **Extended Day:** 7 a.m.-6 p.m.

Athletics: P.E. req.; Intramural, Interscholastic. Soccer, Basketball, Tennis, Softball. **Clubs**: Chess; Variety depending on interest. **Publications**: Year-book, Literary Magazine **Community Involvement:** Grades 9-12, Community Service.

Plant: Library 11,000 vol., 4 Science Labs, Art Studio, Auditorium/Gym, Playing Fields, Tennis Courts, Weight Room. Computer Lab.

Admission: Rolling Admissions. Pre-school (Interview); K - 11, Tests. Application Fee $35. Student visit.

Tuition: (1995-96) PreK, $7,050; K-grade 4, $8,235; grade 5-12, $9,120   Lunch $450 Books Extra   Uniform: req. grades 1-8; *Dress code* for 9-12. **Financial Aid**: Available for grade 1 and up.

Summer Program: Recreational: designed for children 4 yrs. and up; Activities range from Red Cross swimming lessons, sports, academic enrichment, applied arts, and Science exploration. Computer technology is used across the activities to enhance the program. Call for more information.

 The NEW SCHOOL OF NORTHERN VIRGINIA..........(703) 691-3040   FAX (703) 691-3041

9431 Silver King Court, Fairfax, VA 22031
Founded 1989   **Head**: John Potter

Grades: K-12 **Enrollment Capacity**: 130 co-ed **Faculty**: 13 **Average Class Size**: 7-12

Special Courses: A motivating, safe, small school community that encourages students to take responsibility for their eduaction and to flourish academically. Multi-age classes, college prep. high school. Flexibility based on respect for students' unique sensitivities and interests, recognition of multiple intelligences. Atmosphere that engenders confidence, citizenship, mutual respect, strong sense of self. Independent projects and courses encouraged and supported.

Curriculum Highlights: Multi-sensory curriculum enhanced by day-long to multi-week field trips, locally, nationally, and abroad. Art departmnet includes traditional disciplines plus video production, animation, digital photography and computer art graphics using state-of-the-art software and hardware. At all levels the Math program incorporates NCTM standards and most recent research on Math Education; approaches Math from an applications perspective. Emphasis is on the use of Drama as a teaching tool.

Athletics: Physical Fitness important. **Community Involvement**: Internships req. each year in High School.

Plant: Wooded play area; Basketball Court & Volleyball court..

Admission: Interview & Student Visist req. Application fee, $60; Tuition deposit, $400.

Tuition: (1995-96) $6,900-$9,900 **Transportation**: Limited routes; $150/mo. **Financial Aid**: Limited.

Summer Program: Academic summer school for high school; computer camp, and drama camp.

NORWOOD SCHOOL..........(301) 365-2595 FAX (301) 365-4912

8821 River Road, Bethesda, MD. 20817
Founded 1952. **Head**: Richard Ewing, Jr.

Grades: K-6. **Enrollment**: 325 Co-ed. **Faculty**: 41 full-, 6 part-time. **Class Size Ranges from:** 6-13 students.

Special Courses: Computer at all grade levels. Aural/oral French 1-6; Art, Music, Drama, Dance. Variety of after-school enrichment courses include Piano, String instruments. Science, Gymnastics. **Extended Day** : 4-5:45 p.m.

Athletics: P.E. Req. all grades; Skills taught for Hockey, Lacrosse, Basketball, & Soccer. **Clubs**: Brownies, Girl Scouts. **Publications**: Newsletter **Community Involvement**: Each class participates in an outreach project approved by the administration which parents help organize and implement. There are 3 school-wide charity drives sponsored by the Parents Association.

Plant: Library 15,000 vol.: 3 Science Classrooms, Computer Centers with 12-16 computers each; 2 Art Classrooms, Gym, Playing Fields, Music/Arts/Drama Bldg.

Admission: Applications taken Sept.-Feb. 1 for following year. Parental Visit req.; Student Visit req. grade 1-5; Testing for 1-5. Transcript and Teacher Recommendations. For K and grade 1, if student tested elsewhere, then visit to school for informal evaluation by K Director. Notification by Mid-March.

Tuition: (1995-96) $9,770-$10,190. *Dress Code*: Simple, serviceable clothes.

Financial Aid.: Available

Summer Program: "Summer at Norwood" 3 two-week sessions featuring art, music, science, computers, sports & games; Keyboarding, "mad about math".Note: Program available for PreK also.

NOTRE DAME ACADEMY..........(703) 687-5581   FAX (703) 687-3103

35321 Notre Dame Lane
Route l, Box 197, Middleburg, VA. 22117
Catholic 1965. **Head**: Sister Cecilia Liberatore, SND

Grades: 9-12. **Enrollment**: 155 Co-ed **Faculty**: 12 full-, 3 part-time. **Average Class Size**: 15.

Special Courses: French & Spanish , 9-12; History: World, Russian, U.S., Virginia, Latin American. Sociology, Economics, World Issues, American Gov't.; Science: Psychology, Gen'l Science, Chemistry, Biology, and Physics. Computer Science, Keyboarding. Religious studies req.; Drama, Art-Drawing, Design, Studio Ceramics, Graphics (one credit in Fine Arts Req.) Music- Choral, Instrumental, Orchestra; Photography, AP.: English, Biology, Calculus, American History. Note: Senior Career Internship; Independent Study, Dual enrollment-Shenandoah University.

Athletics: Req. to grade 10; Interscholastic: Volleyball, Soccer, Cross-Country, Basketball, Baseball, Tennis, Field Hockey, Lacrosse.. **Clubs**: French, Spanish, Campus Ministry, Admissions Aides, Peer Ministry, Athletic Assn., Choral, Drama. **Publications**: Newspaper, Yearbook. **Community Involvement**: 20 hrs. of Volunteer Service req. each year; Food & Clothing Assistance, Senior Citizens Day; Students may volunteer to teach religion to children in local parish.

Plant: Library 10,000 vol.; 200+ acre campus; Science Labs, Auditorium, Gym, Playing Fields, Tennis Courts, Art Studio. Meeting & Publications Building.

Admission: Interview req.; Application fee $30. Records, Transcripts, References, Applicant must write auto-biography.

Tuition: (1995-96) Day: Catholic $6,300; Non-Catholic $6,750. **Lunch**: Extra *Dress Code*: Uniform req. **Transportation**: Car pools- vans. **Financial Aid**: Available..

Summer Program: Art, Adventure Bound

NYSMITH SCHOOL FOR THE GIFTED..........(703) 713-3332   FAX (703) 713-3332

13525 Dulles Technology Drive, Herndon, VA 22071
Founded 1983   **Head:** Carole Nysmith

Grades: N-8 **Enrollment**: 450 Co-ed **Faculty**: 58 full-, 20 part-time.

Average Class Size :   18:2

Special Courses: Individualized Math/Reading; Counseling weekly (K-8). Use of 4 Computer Labs daily. French and Science Labs daily; Poetry; History; American/ Ancient History; Earth/Physical Science; Art.   **Extended Day**: 6:30 a.m.-6:30 p.m.

Athletics: req.;   **Clubs**: Student Council; Art; Poetry; Math; Karate; Fencing. **Publications**: Yearbook, Literary Magazine, Newsletters

Admission: Interview, School visit, Teacher Recommendations. IQ 130 on any standardized intelligence test.

Tuition: (1995-96) $6,220-$10,800 includes Books, & supplies. **Extended Care**: Available Lunch: Catered or Bring; (milk available). **Transportation**: Available. **Financial Aid**: Some Available

Future Plans : New building

Summer Camp: Sports, cooking, crafts, karate, fencing, computers, tennis and daily swimming.

OAKCREST SCHOOL..........(202) 686-9736 or 686-5057   FAX (202) 686 -5920

4101 Yuma Street, N.W., Washington, D.C. 20016
Founded 1976. **Head**: Barbara Falk

Grades: 7-12. **Enrollment**: 130 girls. **Faculty**: 9 full-, 9 part-time.
Average Class Size: 20.

Special Courses: College Preparatory Program. Latin, French I-IV, Spanish I-V; Science: Biology, Chemistry, Physics, Physical Science, Earth & Life Science. History: U.S/Government, Ancient, Medieval and European, 20th Century, World Geography, Philosophy of Man & Society; Math: Algebra I & II, Geometry, Trig, pre-Calculus and Calculus. Theology: Philosophical Foundations of Theology; Metaphysics : The spiritual doctrinal formation at Oakcrest is entrusted to Opus Dei, a personal prelature of the Catholic Church.   Studio Art, Food Technology. AP.: English, Spanish, Calculus. Note: Each student meets regularly with her faculty advisor who provides academic and personal guidance. Special emphasis on character development: the faculty work closely with the parents who are recognized as primary educators of their children.

Athletics: P.E.;   PVAC Soccer, Basketball, Softball, Tennis. **Clubs**: Junior & National Honor Society, Service Club, Speech, Right to Life, Performing Arts. **Publications**: Yearbook, Literary Magazine, Newsletter. **Community Involvement**: Help with programs and visits to the Washington Home for the elderly.

Plant: Library, Science Lab, Art Studio, Tennis Court, Basketball Court, Chapel.

Admission: Verbal and Math Aptitude Tests, sample of Writing. $25 fee. Interview, Transcript, Recommendations; Rolling Admission.

Tuition: (1995-96)   grades 7-8, $5,400; 9-12, $6,200. **Books**: Extra. **Lunch**: Students bring. *Dress Code*: Uniform req. **Financial Aid**: Some partial available.

OAKLAND SCHOOL..........(804) 293-9059

Oakland Farm, Boyd Tavern, VA. 22947 (Near Charlottesville).
Founded 1950. **Head**: Judith Edwards

Ungraded : Ages 8-16 (8-14 for admittance) **Enrollment** : 85 Co-ed; Boarding 65, Day 20.
Faculty : Residential 13 , Part-time -1; Teaching Staff, 18. **Average Class Size**: 4-5

Special Features: Ungraded - for children of normal or better intelligence who have not succeeded in regular classroom - many children with learning disabilities. Note: Curriculum through grade 9. Teaching of Reading and Study Skills a specialty; Word Processing taught.

Athletics: Interscholastic Soccer, Baseball, Basketball. Horseback Riding. **Clubs**:
Physical Fitness, Jogging, Rocket models, Cooking, etc. **Community Involvement**:
Participate in special community events.

Plant: Library, Large farm, Swimming Pool, Tennis Courts, Horseback Riding Trails & Ring, Gymnasium and Recreation Building. New Dining Room and Kitchen. Note: Computers: one for every three students.

Admission: Application, Transcripts including Educational & Psychological Evaluations; Interview with Visit to school.

Tuition: (1995-96) Day, $11,250; Boarding, $22,500; includes Books and all school materials.

Summer Program: 7 week summer camp & school. Academic Reading, Math, and English for ◄ hrs.daily during week;   Recreational instruction includes horseback riding, swimming, tennis, golf, archery, arts & crafts, and nature.

OAKWOOD SCHOOL..........(703) 941-5788 FAX (703) 941-4186

7210 Braddock Road, Annandale, VA. 22003
Founded 1971. **Head**: Robert C. McIntyre.

Grades: K-9. **Enrollment**: 100 Co-ed. **Faculty**: 30 full-time. **Average Class Size**: 10-12

Special Courses: General Science, Biology, Earth Science; History - U.S. and World; Geography. Reading/Language arts; Math. Music Appreciation; Perception Art; P.E. (regular adaptive) Speech/Language Therapy. Occupational Therapy. All subjects taught remedially for the bright learning disabled child as needed.

Athletics Req.; Volleyball, Football, Softball, Soccer, Hockey, Gymnastics, Weights,

Trampoline. All taught as part of the Physical Education program for all students.

Plant: Library 5,000 vol.; Large bright class rooms; Science & Math Labs; Computer Lab; Reading Lab, Speech/Language Therapy Clinic; P.E. Room; Weight room; Athletic field, custom designed playground.

Admission: Interview with parents or referring professional. Parents complete confidential history . Transcripts of other evaluations and school records. Oakwood "short form" educational evaluation. Conference with parents at which placement recommendation is made. Students who are LD, Gifted LD, Speech/ Language Disfunctions-mild to moderate range of disabilities. Oakwood is not appropriate for MR, ED, seriously physically handicapped.

Tuition: (1995-96) $ 12,600   **Transportation**: Privately arranged. *Dress Code*: Appropriate, modest, and clean. **Financial Aid** : Partial grants available based exclusively on need.

ODENTON CHRISTIAN SCHOOL.......... (410) 674-5625 or (301) 621-9469

8410 Piney Orchard Parkway, Odenton, MD. 21113
Head: Mr. T.E. Pike

Grades: K3-grade 12. **Enrollment**: 700 Co-ed   **Faculty**: 45 full-time.

Special Program: Music, Art, Gym, Computers and Foreign Languages. ABEKA Curriculum Open year 'round, including summer school program. DIFFERENT ON PURPOSE: Different in "purpose, belief, goals, discipline, emphasis, academics, and results." **Extended Day**: 6 a.m.-6 p.m.

Plant : New gym

Admission: Test(s) and Interview. Admit qualified students of any race, color, national or ethnic origin.

Tuition: (1995-96) $1,800. Books & Activity Fees: K, $220; 1-12, $240. Registration $75, Testing $35. *Dress Code*: Uniform req.

Future Plans: Expand Music program, Band, Art, Computer, Athletic and Foreign Language Programs.

OLDFIELDS SCHOOL...(410) 472-4800   FAX (410) 472-3141

1500 Glencoe Road, Glencoe, MD. 21152
Founded 1867. **Head**: Hawley Rogers.

Grades: 8-12. **Enrollment**: 186 Girls (38 Day, 148 Boarding). **Faculty**: 37 full-, 13 part-time. **Average Class Size**: 10; Student/Teacher ratio, 5:1.

Special Courses: Latin, French, Spanish, 8-12; Math thru Calculus, Computer. Science: General Science, Biology, Chemistry, Physics, Astronomy, Human Physiology; Electives in Psychology and in Child Development. History- Ancient History, Western Civilization, American History (req.), Holocaust/WWII, Comparative Systems, America and the World, Women in Modern America, Civil Rights Movement & the Vietnam War, Life on the Frontier. Art: Studio, Portfolio, Photography, Ceramics, Art History (Modern Art 1800-1980 & American Art), Performing Arts: Acting, Stagecraft, Introd. to Musical Theatre, Advanced Dance, Music Theory, Singers. Note: Small ESL program; Tutoring and extensive teacher help available but no LD program per se. AP.: In all disciplines.

Athletics: Req.; Interscholastic & Intramural: Field Hockey, Basketball, Tennis, Lacrosse, Softball, Soccer, Volleyball, Cross-Country, Badminton, Riding, Dance: Jazz, Ballet, Pointe, Tap; Aerobics, Weight Training. **Clubs**: Art, Current Issues Forum, Dance Co., Dubious Dozen, Environmental Awareness, Focus, International, Outing, Tour Guides, Volunteer Action. **Publications**: Literary Magazine, Yearbook, Newspaper. **Community Involvement**: Volunteer program-projects include Day Care & Nursing Home Visits, Shelters, etc.

Plant: Library 10,000 vol., Science Labs, New Fine Arts Wing (includes studios for Graphics, Sculpture, Drawing & Painting; Library extension for expanded Art History collection). Gym, Computer Center; 7 Dorms, 3 Photography Dark Rooms, Choral Arts Center with 4 practice rooms; Playing Fields, Tennis Courts, Outdoor Pool, Stables, Indoor Riding Arena, Outdoor Riding Rings, David Niven Theater, Dance Studio.

Admission: Application fee $35; SSAT or WISC, Interview, 2 Teacher Evaluations, Transcripts Early decision: Dec. l; Regular decision March 10.

Tuition: (1995-96) $12,650, Day; $21,900 Boarding, Books: $400 per semester. *Dress Code* No jeans, T-shirts or sweatshirts; otherwise, clothing in good repair. **Financial Aid**: Available

OLD MILL CHRISTIAN ACADEMY.......... (410) 987-4744

649 Old Mill Boulevard., Millersville, MD 21108
Christian non-denominational 1979 **Head**; Rev. Darryl Hare
(Formerly Calvary Temple Christian) Principal: Mary E. Rodgers

Grades: PreK-12 **Enrollment**: 100 Co-ed **Faculty**: 6 full-, 3 part-time. **Average Class Size**: 15-20

Special Courses; Video Spanish 9-12. Computer Basics and Basic Programming. General Science, Biology, Chemistry. U.S. and World History, Constitutional History, Geography. Remedial Reading and Math. Religious Studies req. Typing, Home Ec., Auto Mechanics. Music, Chorus. P.E. req.

Plant: Library , Multi-purpose Room, Sanctuary

Admission: Testing throughout the year.

Tuition: (1995-96) K-12, $170-$180/mo..; Note; all rates are for church members. **Books**: Extra **Lunch**: Bring   *Dress Code*: No blue jeans, no tennis shoes; some rules relating to color of clothing.

ONENESS-FAMILY SCHOOL..........(301) 652-7751

6701 Wisconsin Avenue, Chevy Chase, MD 20815
Founded 1988   **Head**: Andrew Kutt

Grades: PreK3- grade 6.   **Enrollment**: 50 Co-ed   **Faculty**: 5 full-, 5 part-time
Average Class Size: 18

Special Courses: Spanish, French, Pre K-6. Keyboard,Computer. General Science. History-Creation Stories, Earth History, Ancient History to Present including American. Human Values Education, Health, World Religions, World Cultures. Art, Music, Drama, Creative Movement, Yoga.   Note: Pre-school can be 3 full or 5 half days. **Extended Day** : 7:30 a.m.-6 p.m.

Athletics: Not Required. Intramural: Soccer, Basketball, Running; Many non- competitive and cooperative games. **Clubs**: Ecology, Peace. **Publications**: Newspaper. **Community Involvement**: Performances at Nursing homes and at cultural events which fosters international harmony and communication. Cleaning local parks and streams; Recycling and Conservation.

Plant: Library 3,500 Vol., Language Lab, Science Lab, Art Studio, Auditorium. Use Norwood Park for many activities.

Admission: Application, $50 fee; Interview and Visit, Recommendations. March 15th deadline; other spaces open on an individual basis and occasionally open up during school year.

Tuition: (1995-96) $6,200- $6,900 includes Books. Bring Lunch **Transportation**: one way, $750; both ways, $1,200. **Extended Day** : Extra **Financial Aid**: Some Available

Summer Program: Camp-5 sessions: Swimming, outdoor activities; Peace studies, creative arts, environmental science.

OPEN DOOR CHRISTIAN SCHOOL..........(410) 859-5100

7300 Ridge Road, Hanover, MD 21076-1417
Head: Jack Constable

Grades: N3-grade 7   **Enrollment**: 130 Co-ed

Special Program: Quality traditional education. ABEKA Program.
Extended Day : 6:15 a.m.-6 p.m.

Tuition : (1995-96) Call for information. *Dress Code*: Uniform req. **Extended Day**: Extra

Summer Program: All day program available.

OUR LADY OF PERPETUAL HELP..........(202)678-0211;   K-4, (202)889-1662

1409 V Street, S. E., Washington, D. C. 20020 (K-4)
1604 Morris Road, S. E., Washington, D. C. 20020 (5-8)
Catholic   **Head**: Sister Mary Elizabeth Semmelmayer, SSND (Upper School)

Grades: K4-8   **Enrollment**: 275 Co-ed

Special Programs: Spanish, K-8; Freedom Youth Academy, independent program after school at Morris Road until 6 p.m.   **Extended Day** 6:30 a.m.-6 p.m., at V Street;

Tuition: (1995-96) $1,870   **Financial Aid** : Available

OUR LADY OF SORROWS SCHOOL..........(301) 891-2555

1010 Larch Avenue, Takoma Park, MD 20912
Catholic   **Head**: Mrs. Gail Ruffin

Grades : K4-8   **Enrollment** : Co-ed

Special Programs: Spanish 6-8; Computers, K-8; Performing Arts program with emphasis on drama and dance. **Extended Day** : 7 a.m.-6 p.m.

Tuition: (1995-96) $2,100-$2,200

OUR LADY OF VICTORY SCHOOL...........(202) 337-1421

4755 Whitehaven Parkway, N.W., Washington, D.C. 20007
Catholic 1954. **Head**: Miss Susan Milloy, Principal

Grades: N-grade 8. **Enrollment**: 130 Co-ed. **Faculty**: 10 full-, 6 part-time.
Average Class Size: 16

Special Courses: Spanish, Computer, Art, Study Skills, Library Skills, Algebra, General Science. Band, Choir. **Extended Day**: 7:30 a.m.- 6 p.m.

Athletics: P.E.: After school, Soccer, Softball, Basketball, T-Ball.

Plant: Library, Computer Lab, Auditorium.

Admission: Interview with Principal; Visit school for day; Placement test.

Tuition: (1995-96) $3,200, in parish; $4,200 out of parish. **Books**: $180. **Lunch**: Bring. *Dress Code*: Uniform req.

Summer Program : Re-enforcement programs for Math and Language Arts.

OUR LADY QUEEN OF PEACE SCHOOL..........(202) 584-4278

3740 Ely Place S. E., Washington, D. C. 20019
Catholic **Head**: Sister Ellen Marie Hagar, DC

Grades: PreK-8   **Enrollment**: Co-ed

Special Programs: Learning Disabled program. **Extended Day**: 6:30 a.m.-6 p.m.

Tuition: In Parish, $1,200; Out of Parish, $1,950 **Extended Day** Extra

OUR SAVIOR LUTHERAN SCHOOL..........(703) 892-4846

825 South Taylor Street, Arlington, VA. 22204
Lutheran 1953. **Head**: Charles Fischer.

Grades: K-8. **Enrollment**: 150 Co-ed. **Faculty**: 6 full-, 3 part-time.
Average Class Size: 20.

Special Courses: Gen'l Science K-8.   Christian Education, strong phonics program, self-contained classrooms. Religious Studies req.; Outdoor camping trip in Spring for upper grades; Music, Band. **Extended Day**: 7 a.m.-6 p.m.

Plant: Library 2,400 vol.

Admission: Interview, Testing if needed. $100 Registration fee.

Tuition: (1996-96) $2,495. **Limited** **Transportation**: $800. (contact school for further fee schedules.) *Dress Code*: Traditional school clothes.

OUR SAVIORS' SCHOOL................(301) 420-5076

3111 Forestville Road, Forestville, MD 20747
Head: Susan Janes

Grades: N-6

Tuition: (1995-96) Call for information

OWL SCHOOLS..........(202) 462-4034

1328 16th Street, N.W., Washington, D.C. 20036
Founded 1971. **Head**: Margaret Harris.

Grades: N-6. **Enrollment**: 115 Co-ed. **Faculty**: 6 full-, 4 part-time.
Average Class Size: 12.

Special Courses: French N-6, Remedial Reading. Math, Art, Music, P.E. **Note**: Special classes for advanced students, Reading Enrichment. **Extended Day**: 7:45 a.m.-6 p.m.

Community Involvement: Foster grandparent program at Rock Creek Manor Nursing Home.

Plant: Library, Gym/Auditorium

Admission: Child Visits school for a day; Placement Tests. Application Fee $60.

Tuition: (1995-96) $5,150 **Fees** $150 **Extended Day** $1,350 **Development Fund Fee** $250

Summer Program: All day Camp Program: Academic program in morning, afternoon focus is on arts & crafts, recreational, swimming, etc. **Note**: Summer Program in France for grades 3-6.

PAINT BRANCH MONTESSORI SCHOOL..........(301) 937-2244

3215 Powder Mill Road, Adelphi, MD. 20783
Head: Patricia Barshay/Sandra Thomas

Ungraded: Ages 2-12. **Enrollment**: 100 Co-ed. **Faculty**: 8 full-, 5 part-time. **Average Class Size**: 17

Special Features: Sign Language; Art & Music; full day for age 3; Before and After School, Students attend Fairland Athletic Complex for P.E. **Note**: Ages 9-12 do Community Service, **Extended Day**: 8 a.m.-5 p.m.

Admission: School Visit

Tuition: (1995-1996) Half-Day, $2,920; Full Day, $4,566- $4,760.
Before & After School, $170 /mo.

PARKMONT SCHOOL..........(202) 726-0740 FAX (202) 726-0748

4842 16th Street N.W., Washington, D. C. 20011
Founded 1972. **Head**: Ron McClain.

Grades: 6-8, Middle School; 9-12 Upper School(ungraded). **Enrollment**: 65 Co-ed.

Faculty: 11 full-, 6 part-time.   **Average Class Size**: 7-12.

Special Courses: Innovative small school dedicated to fostering individual growth and enthusiasm for learning. Unique academic structure of short, intensive courses and challenging, high interest curriculum. We are committed to experiential learning and make considerable use of the city and its resources. Individual attention and close adult-student relationships provide support when needed, build a strong sense of community and enable our students to thrive.
Internships in the areas of Community Service and other areas of interest.

Athletics: Complete Soccer Program, Marathon Training, Tennis, Volleyball, Softball, Canoeing and Camping, Climbing, Dance. Note: Participate in WSSA Athletic League.

Plant: Science Lab, Art Room, All Purpose Room, Ceramics Studio, Photo Lab. New Hampshire Campus.

Admission: Parent Interview with Director followed by a full-day student visit. $50 Application fee; Rolling admission.

Tuition: (1995-96) $10,950 **Financial Aid**: Available

Summer Program: Summer School..

PAUL VI HIGH SCHOOL........... (703) 352-0925   FAX (703) 273-9845

10675 Lee Highway, Fairfax, VA 22030
Catholic   **Head**: Fr. Robert Mulligan, O.S.F.S., Principal

Grades: 9-12   **Enrollment**: 1,052 Co-ed **Faculty**: 74 full-, 6 part-time.
Average Class Size: 22

Special Courses : Broad Computer curriculum; Honors, AP and Special Education Services..

Athletics: Full sports program for boys and girls. Several Clubs and activities; Campus ministry program.

Admission: Incoming freshmen take placement test in December of 8th grade.

Tuition: (1995-96) In parish, $4, 435; Non-parish $4,860;   Non-Catholic $5,735
Transportation: $750-$850 **Financial Aid** : Available

Summer Program: Introduction to High School, Study Skills.

PHELPS SCHOOL..........(610) 644-1754 FAX (610) 644-6679

583 Sugartown Road, P.O. Box 476, Malvern, PA 19355 (22 miles west of Philadelphia)
Founded 1946   **Head**: Norman T. Phelps, Jr.

127

Grades: 7-12, PG. **Enrollment**: 140 Boys, all Boarding **Faculty**: 24 full-. 5 part-time. **Average Class Size**: 8

Special Courses: Strong program for underachievers; LD, ADD, ESL; Remedial and Developmental Reading Computers. Instrumental Music, Art & Ceramics, Photography, Woodworking.

Athletics: Soccer, Cross-Country, Basketball, Baseball, Lacrosse, Riding, Golf, Tennis, Wrestling, Power Lifting, Karate.

Plant: 110 acre campus; Library, Science Lab, Computer Lab, Student Center, Dark Room, Music Studio, Gym, Auditorium with Stage, 4 all-weather Tennis Courts, Indoor and Outdoor Equestrian facilities, 8 Dormitories.

Admission: Application, Interview, Recommendations, Transcript & Available Testing..

Tuition: (1995-96) $16,000. **Financial Aid**:   Some Available

Future Plans: New Dormitory, Library & Academic support program center under construction.

Summer Program: 5 week, Remedial: Reading, Language Arts, Math & Study Skills.

PINECREST SCHOOL..........(703) 354-3446

4015 Annandale Road, Annandale, VA. 22003
Founded 1957. **Head**: Mrs. Elaine Alger

Grades: N-3. **Enrollment**: 90 Co-ed. **Faculty**: 8 full-, 3 part-time. **Average Class Size**: 12.
Special Courses: French, Music, P.E.

Plant: Library

Admission: Interview, Registration fee $50

Tuition: (1995-1996) Pre-school $3,090; K 1/2 day $3,410; K & 1, $4,773; 2-3, $4,990.
Transportation: Additional   **Financial Aid**: Available

Future Plans: To add extended hours.

POTOMAC HEIGHTS CHRISTIAN ACADEMY..........(301) 753-9350

37 Glymont Road, (P.O.Box 149) Indian Head, MD. 20640
Head: Gilbert Bailey.

Grades: K3-grade 8. **Enrollment**: 165 Co-ed.

Special Courses: ABEKA curriculum. **Extended Day**: 6:30 a.m.-6 p.m.

Tuition (1995-96) 3 days Half-day K, $924; 5 Half- days, K, $1,355; 1-8, $2,218
Extended Day : Extra.

POTOMAC SCHOOL..........(703) 356-4101

1301 Potomac School Road, McLean, VA. 22101
Founded 1904. **Head**: Brian R. Wright, Ph. D.

Grades: Pre K-12. **Enrollment**: 875 Co-ed. **Faculty**: 130 full-, 25 part-time.
Average Class Size: 16-18.

Special Courses: Latin, French, Japanese, Spanish, 7-12. **Math** thru Advanced Calculus,
Computer (3 Labs). **Science**: General Science, Biology, Chemistry, Physics, Astronomy.
History: Ancient & Medieval, Modern Western, U.S., American Gov't, Russian, Chinese,
Japanese; Art, Music, Drama. **AP**.: American History, French, Latin, Spanish, Biology,
Chemistry, Physics, Art History, Computer Science and Calculus.
Note: Ethics Course, grade 10; Month long Senior Project.

Athletics: Req.; Intramural & Interscholastic. Football, Cross Country, Soccer, Baseball,
Lacrosse, Track, Field Hockey, Basketball, Golf, Wrestling, Softball, Swimming, Self-Defense.
Clubs: Chorus, Madrigal Singing group, Band, Student Gov't, Math team, Chess, Environmental,
Model Senate, Model U.N., Peer Support Group. **Publications**: Newspaper, Yearbook, Literary
Magazine of the Arts. **Community Involvement**: Community Service Program PreK-12.

Plant: 3 Libraries, 32,000 vol.; 11 Science Labs, 5 Art Studios, 2 Gyms, Auditorium, Playing
Fields, Nature Trails, Swimming Pool, Tennis Courts; 75 acre campus.

Admission: Applications by Jan. 15, Fee $60; Testing in Jan. & Feb.; Acceptance March. Visits
by parents requested. School seeks broad ethnic, geographic and socio-economic student body.

Tuition: (1995-96) $7,050-$12,740   Lunch Bring, PreK-grade 8; $610, grade 9-12.
Books: Extra   **Transportation**: $750 one way; $1,340 both ways. Uniform: Req. grade 4-8
only; *Dress Code*, Grades 9- 12. **Financial Aid**: Available.

Summer Program: Academic: Co-ed, Grades 7-12. Writing Workshop, French, Spanish,
Algebra, Geometry, Physics, Biology, Chemistry, Study Skills, Computer Skills. Camp for age
3-17, Co-ed: Computer, Weight Training, Wilderness Adventure, Counselor Apprentice,
Theater. Discovery Camp, Science Camp, Out for Fun Camp, Day Camp, Jr. Day Camp,

POWHATAN SCHOOL.......... (703) 837-1009   FAX (703) 837-2558

Route 1, P.O. Box 177A, Boyce VA.22620
Founded 1948   **Head**: John G. Lathrop

Grades: K-8   **Enrollment**: 170 Co-ed   **Faculty**: 18 full-,7 part-time.   **Average Class Size** : 19

Special Courses: Spanish 7-8, French K-3, 7-8; Algebra, Geometry, Computer. General Science, Biology. History- U.S., American. Remedial Reading and Math. Art, Music.
Extended Day: 3:30-6 p.m.

Athletics: Req.; Soccer, Field Hockey, Lacrosse, Basketball, Track, Skiing, Climbing Wall, Gymnastics. **Community Involvement**: Nursing Home Project; African Literacy Project; Salvation Army Food Drive; Adopt a Family at Christmas & Thanksgiving; Foster Child Project.

Plant: Library 10,000 vol., Science Lab & Art Studio; Auditorium, Gym, Playing Fields, Music and Dance Facility.

Admission: $50 Registration fee. Testing in Spring. Classroom visits encouraged.

Tuition: (1995-96) K,full day: $6,660; grades: 1-3, $7,330;   4-5, $7.825; 6-8, $7,970
Books & Supplies: $175-$250 . **Transportation**: $320-$690 depending on distance
Dress Code : yes   **Financial Aid** : Available.

Summer Program: Summer Sports Camp/ General Summer Camp.

THE PRIMARY DAY SCHOOL..........(301) 365-4355   FAX (301) 469-8611

7300 River Road, Bethesda, MD. 20817
Founded 1944. **Head**: Mrs. Carter-Anne Nadonley.

Grades: Pre K-2. **Enrollment**: 175 Co-ed   **Faculty**: 20 full-, 7 part-time.
Average Class Size: 20 - 24

Special Courses: Curriculum includes all subjects appropriate to well-rounded primary program. The Phonovisual Method, a multi-sensory phonics based system, is the foundation for the language arts subjects. Resource teachers, working with small groups, allow for individual attention. Weekly assembly programs, presented by the students, help develop poise and self-confidence in appearing before an audience. In addition to literature, art, music, and physical activities included in the curriculum, children may pursue extra classes in these subjects. Second Graders enjoy hands-on science, computers, a special course in Creative Writing, and French..

Community Involvement: Children participate in MS Readathon, UNICEF, Christmas gifts to children in the Handicapped Children's ward at D.C. General Hospital.

Plant: Library, 5,500 vol., Auditorium, Playing Fields, Science Room, Art Room.

Admission: Parent and child Interview in Jan. & Feb. for following fall. Age, maturity level, & average intelligence are criteria for admission & placement. $50 fee.

Tuition: (1995-96) $4,900-$7,300, includes books. Lunch: Brown bag. **Financial Aid**: Available.

Future Plans: Presently building new wing with Music Room, Computer, Math Lab, and Language Arts Room.

PURITAN CHRISTIAN SCHOOL..........(301) 253-4357

6325 Griffith Road, (P.O. Box 5039) Laytonsville, MD. 20882
Orthodox Presbyterian 1977 **Head**: Dr. Barry M. Whitcomb

Grades: N3-grade 12 **Enrollment**: 150 Co-ed. **Faculty**: 11 full-, 3 part-time.
Average Class Size: 15.

Special Courses: French 7-8, Spanish, Latin, & Greek, all 9-12. Computer K-12; Math includes Trig & Calculus. General Science, Biology, Chemistry, Physics. Various History and Social Science Courses. Religious Studies required. Art & Music K-8.

Athletics: P.E. req. all grades; Basketball, Soccer, Volleyball. **Publications**: Yearbook

Plant: Science Lab, Playing Fields.

Admission: Fee $60; Interview, Recommendations, Standardized Test Scores, Transcript.

Tuition: (1995-96) Half day N &K, $1,500; 1-8, $3,105; 9-12, $3,300; Reduced rate for siblings. **Transportation**: $890 round trip,. *Dress Code*: Uniform req.

QUEEN ANNE SCHOOL..........(301) 249-5000   FAX (301) 249-3838

14111 Oak Grove Road, Upper Marlboro, MD. 20772
Episcopal 1965. **Head**: J. Temple Blackwood

Grades: 6-12. **Enrollment**: 240 Co-ed. **Faculty**: 17 full-, 9 part-time.
Average Class Size: 15.

Special Courses: French & Spanish, 8-12; Math includes Calculus & Computer. Science: General Science, Biology, Chemistry, Physics, Ecology, Biology of Chesapeake Bay, Physiology; History- Geography, U.S., American Gov't, World, Contemporary Issues, Gov't & Politics, American History and Culture. Introduction to the Principle of Economics, Psychology. Religious studies req. Studio Art, Art History. Chorus, Madrigal Singers, Symphonic Band, MS Band. Beginning & Advanced Acting. AP.: Calculus, Biology, Chemistry, English, French, Spanish, Art, History. **Extended Day** 3:30-5 p.m.

Athletics: Req. through Grade 10. Intramural & Inter-scholastic: Soccer, Lacrosse, Basketball, Softball, Track & Field, Baseball, Tennis. **Clubs**: Minority Awareness, SADD, Spirit.
Publications: Yearbook, Literary Magazine, Newspaper. **Community Involvement**: Nursing home volunteers, Community outreach.

Plant: Library 10,000 vol., 3 Science Labs, Art Studio, Auditorium, Gym, Playing Fields, Tennis

Courts, Computer Lab.

Admission: Student & Parent Interview, Tests(ERB), Application fee $25; Recommendations, Transcript. Full or half-day Visit by student (optional). Writing sample.

Tuition: (1995-96) 6- 8, $7,900; 9-12, $8,900. **Transportation**: Available. Books: 6-8, Leased, , 9-12, purchase text Books. *Dress Code*: Moderate **Financial Aid**: Based on need

Summer Program: "EXCEL 2000" intensive science and math curriculum. Summer classes offered are Language Skills; Mathematics- Basic Math & Algebra; English-Creative Writing. Study Skills, Tutoring. Art, Photography. Soccer & Basketball camps.

RANDOLPH MACON ACADEMY....(703) 636-5200 or 1-800-272-1172

Front Royal, VA 22630
Methodist 1892   **Head**: Col. Trevor D. Turner, USA Ret.

Grades: 7-12, PG **Enrollment**: 370 Co-ed, Mostly Boarding.

RESTON MONTESSORI SCHOOL..........(703) 481-2922

1928 Issac Newton Square West. Reston, VA 22090
Head: Kathleen Lanfear

Grades: N 2 1/2- grade 3 **Enrollment**: 99 Co-ed   **Average Class Size**: 25

Special Programs: Bilingual French program for grades 1-3 (all subjects taught in English and French) Computers for grades 1-3. Note: Sign Language, Spanish, Dance, Gymnastics extra curicular offerings   **Extended Day** 7 a.m.-6:30 p.m.

Plant: Library, 2 Activity Rooms; Spacious classroom building.

Admission: Call for brochure and appointment; Visit

Tuition: (1995-96) N & K, $6,100-$6,700; 1 - 3, $6,600;   **Extended Day** $260/mo
Financial Aid: Some available after 1st year of enrollment.

Summer Program: Ages 2 1/2-10; swimming optional; arts & crafts. Relaxed academic program

RIVENDELL SCHOOL.........(703) 525-3860

1031 North Vermont Street, Arlington, VA 22201
Non-Denominational, Christ Centered 1989   **Head**: Mr. Steve Larson

Grades: K-8 **Enrollment**: 110 Co-ed **Faculty**: 7 full-, 2 part-time.

<u>Average Class Size</u>: 15

<u>Special Courses</u>: All academic subjects areas are taught within 4-8 week unit themes.   Art & Music K-8. French, Spanish & German in different grades. Paedeia seminar discussions are conducted weekly at all grade levels.

<u>Athletics</u>: P.E. req. 1-8. Instruction in Hockey, Soccer, Volleyball, Basketball, Softball, Fitness. <u>Publications</u>: Weekly newspaper. <u>Community Involvement</u>: Students visit Nursing Homes, assist in Salvation Army feeding and toy distribution programs. Sponsored fund raising for children with cancer.

<u>Plant</u>: Library, 5,000 vol.; Computer Room, Music Room, Art Room, Chapel, Auditorium, Playing Field, Playground.

<u>Admission</u>: Applications accepted all year, Fee $25. March notification date for following year admission. Possible Testing. Students are admitted on basis of Transcript, Recommendation Form, and Family Interview.

<u>Tuition</u>: (1995-96) K, $3,250; 1-8, $4,200 includes <u>Books, Fees, Activities, Field Trips, and $100 Uniform allowance.</u> Bring <u>Lunch</u>. *Dress Code*: Uniform req., <u>Financial Aid</u>: 20% of school's operating budget is used to provide aid (based on need).

<u>Future Plans</u>: To add a class a year (15 students) until school has student body of 120-150, grades K-8.

RIVERDALE BAPTIST SCHOOL..........(301) 249-7000

1133 Largo Road, Upper Marlboro, MD. 20772
Baptist 1971. <u>Head</u>: Dr. Richard J. Stashevsky

<u>Grades</u>: K4-12. <u>Enrollment</u>: 1,000 Co-ed. <u>Faculty</u>: 52 full-time. <u>Average Class Size</u>: 26.

<u>Special Courses</u>: Spanish grades K5-12; <u>Math</u>: Algebra, Geometry, Trig & Calculus, Math Analysis, Accounting. <u>Computer</u>: College Keyboard, Basic Computing, Cobol/Pascal; <u>Science</u> : General Science, Physical Science, Anatomy, Enviornmental Science, Biology, Chemistry, Physics, Psychology. <u>History</u>: Geography, U.S., World, Modern, European, American Government. <u>English</u>: includes Creative Writing, Journalism. <u>Fine Arts:</u> Art, Mechanical Drawing, Choir, Band (grades 5-12).Speech, Drama. Driver's Ed. <u>Extended Day</u>: 7 a.m.-6 p.m.

<u>Athletics</u>: Not required. Interscholastic: <u>Boys</u> Football, Wrestling, Soccer, Basketball, Tennis, Baseball, Track. <u>Girls</u> Volleyball, Soccer, Basketball, Softball. Cheerleading, Track, Tennis.. <u>Clubs</u>: Nat'l Honor Society, Student Council. <u>Publications</u>: Yearbook.

<u>Plant</u>: Library 15,000 vol.; Computer Lab, Science Lab, Gym, Auditorium, Playing Fields.

<u>Admission</u>: Achievement Test Scores; Transcript; Personal Evaluation Form, Interview.

Tuition: (1995-96) $3,539-$4,265. Books: $80-$225. **Transportation** : $781-$1,727 one way, $1,177-$2,585 both. *Dress Code*: Uniform req. **Financial Aid**: By application

Summer Program: Camp for Elementary Grades

ROCK CREEK INTERNATIONAL SCHOOL...........(202) 387-7254

2200 California Street, N.W., Washington, D.C. 20008
Founded 1988 **Head**: J. Daniel Hollinger, Ph.D.

Grades: N-4 **Enrollment**: 135 Co-ed **Faculty** : 20 full, 2 part-time
Average Class Size: 15

Special Programs: Beginning in Kindergarten, students take a core curriculum of Language Arts and Math in two languages. Other subjects of Science, World Studies, Music, Art, Computer, and Theatrical Arts are taught in English, French or Spanish. Instrumental Music, Sewing, and Cooking.   Note: After school programs: Dutch, Arabic, or Swedish, as well as Enrichment courses which may include French Cooking, Dance, Soccer, etc. (Extra fee)
Extended Day: after school to 6 p.m.

Athletics: P.E.; Soccer, Dance. **Clubs**: Science

Plant: Science Lab, Art Studio, Gym, Auditorium, Playing Fields.

Admission: Parent Visit, Child Visit and Assesment; Transcript, Recommendations.

Tuition: (1995-96) Pre-School $8,520;   K-4, $9,400 includes Books.   Lunch, Bring.
Extended Day: Extra. **Transportation**: $1,140 one way, $1,590 both. **Financial Aid:** Some

Future Plans: To add: grade 5 by 1996-97 academic year; middle school by the year 2,000

Summer Program: Merry-Go-Round the World Summer Camp: Dual language in English and French or Spanish and immersion in French or Spanish.

ROOTS ACTIVITY LEARNING CENTER.........(202) 882-5155

6222 N. Capitol Street, N.W., Washington, D.C. 20011
Founded 1977. **Head**: Bernida Thompson.

Grades: N(6 wks) - grade 8. **Enrollment**: 160 Co-ed. **Average Class Size**: 15.

Special Courses: Spanish & French; Full academic curriculum, Computer. Specialize in African-American History & Culture. P.E. **Extended Day**: 7 a.m.-6 p.m.

Admission: Interview with parent, $10 Application fee.

Tuition: (1995-96) Infant: $603/mo; Age 3-5, $381/mo.; grade 1-4, $333/mo.; grade 5-8 $313/mo.; **Extended Day,** Breakfast & Lunch Extra.

Summer Program: Day Camp 7 a.m.-6 p.m. Swimming, arts & crafts, field trips. Academic program for grades 1-8.

SACRED HEART SCHOOL..........(202) 265-4828

1625 Park Road, N. W., Washington, D. C. 20010
Catholic **Head** : Reynaldo Almeida

Grades : Pre K-grade 8 **Enrollment**: 223 Co-ed **Extended Day** : 3-6 p.m.

Tuition: (1995-96) Registration fee, $175. K-8, $1795 in parish; $1,885 out of parish Reduction for siblings. **Extended Day**: Extra.

ST. AGNES SCHOOL......(See St. Stephen's School)

ST. ALBANS SCHOOL..........(202) 537-6435 FAX (202) 537-5613

Wisconsin & Massachusetts Avenues, N.W., Washington., D.C. 20016
Episcopalian 1909. **Head**: The Rev. Mark H. Mullin.

Grades: 4-12. **Enrollment**: 550 Boys (25 Boarding). Boarding begins 9th grade.
Faculty: 65 full-, 8 part-time. **Average Class Size**: 15.

Special Courses: Latin, French, Spanish: all 8-12; Russian, Japanese, 9-12; Chinese & Greek. Math thru Calculus. Science Biology, Chemistry, Physics, Earth Science. History- Ancient Rome, Ancient Greece, Omnibus-American & European History, History & Culture of Islam. Fine Arts Painting and Drawing, Graphics, 3-Dimensional Art, Studio; Music-Survey of Western Music, Music Theory, Instrumental-Orchestra. Computer. Religious studies req.; The Bible, Question of God. Drama, Film-Making. AP: English, Languages, Math, Computer, History Science.
Note: Coordinate classes with National Cathedral School for Girls; Boys in both the Boys Choir and the Men's Choir at the Cathedral often attend St. Albans. Student Exchange program with Russia & Japan. **Extended Day** ; Grades 4-8 only, 3:30 p.m.-6 p.m.

Athletics: Req.; Intramural & Interscholastic (13 Varsity Sports): Basketball, Soccer, Swimming, Wrestling, Track, Lacrosse, Weight Training, Football, Baseball, Tennis, Cross Country, Golf, Rock Climbing, Kayaking. **Clubs**: Glee, Madrigals, Orchestra, Press, Drama, Service, Government, Art, Band.. **Publications**: Newspaper, Yearbook, Literary Magazine. **Community Involvement:** 60 hours of Social Service prior to senior year are required for graduation.

Plant: Library 24,000 vol., (A computer system now links the libraries of St. Albans with those at National Cathedral School for Girls.) 3 Science Labs, 3 Art Studios, 2 Gyms, Auditorium, Playing Fields, Swimming Pool, 8 Tennis Courts, Computers, Music Room.

Admission: SSAT Nov.-Dec.; Interview, Transcript, teacher Recommendations. Fee $60. Lower School (4-8) has own testing in January.

Tuition: (1995-96) Day $12,499; Boarding $18,856 **Books**: Extra. **Lunch** : $823 (Day students) *Dress Code*: Coat & tie. **Scholarship Aid**: Both full and partial available.

Summer Program: Academic. **Summer Camp**: Tennis, Soccer, Basketball, Baseball, Sports Clinics; Early June Program; Late afternoon program 3 -6 p.m., ages 6 -12.

ST. AMBROSE SCHOOL.............(301) 773-0223

6310 Jason Street, Cheverly, MD 20785
Catholic   **Head**: Sister Aedan Butler, OSB

Grades: K-8   **Extended Day**: Available

Tuition: (1995-96) $2,440; Reduction for siblings.

ST. ANDREW'S SCHOOL...........(410) 266-0952

4 Wallace Manor Road, Edgewater, MD 21037
Methodist 1985   **Head**: Kristine Angelis

Grades: N- grade 5 **Enrollment**: 125 Co-ed   **Faculty**: 10 full, 9 part-time
Average Class Size: 12

Special Programs: Spanish, Computer, Art. Music, Religion, P.E.
Extended Day: 6:30 -8 a.m. and 3:30-6:30 p.m.

Extra-Curricular, Athletic Programs: Dance, Karate, Baseball; Computer Club
Admission: Schedule Interview, Test.

Tuition: (1995-96) N, $3,687; K-5, $3914 **Financial Aid**: Available **Extended Day** Extra

Summer Camp: N-grade 5, 7 a.m.-6 p.m.

ST. ANDREW'S EPISCOPAL SCHOOL..........(301) 530-4900 FAX (301) 493-0370

8935 Bradmoor Drive, Bethesda, MD.20817
Episcopal 1978. **Head**: Dr. James M. Cantwell

Grades: 6-12. **Enrollment**: 360 Co-ed. **Faculty**: 55 full-, 3 part-time **Average Class Size** 15

Special Features: Latin, French, & Spanish, all 7- 12; Spanish for native speakers. Math thru Calculus; Computer-Basic, Pascal, C-Language. Science: Earth Science, Life Science, Physical Science, Biology, Chemistry I & II, Physics I & II, Molecular Biology.. History: World and American, Africa's History, Geography-Area Studies, Modern Oppression & Resistance, History Consortia (Middle Eastern Studies & Modern Day Issues/Science & Technology). Religious Studies: one trimester req. each year. Visual Art: one tri-mester per year of Painting, Film Making, Sculpture; Performing Arts: Music, Drama, Public Speaking, Dance, one trimester req. each year AP: English, Biology, Math, Latin, French, Spanish, History.

Athletics: Req. Interscholastic. Soccer, Basketball, Volleyball, Tennis, Baseball, Softball, Lacross e, Weight Lifting, Wrestling, Track & Field, Cross Country. **Clubs**: Outing, Hiking, Camping, Chorus, SADD, Model U.N., International Club, Band. **Publications**: Yearbook, Literary Magazine, Newspaper. **Community Involvement**: Grades 9-11, 20 hrs. a year req.; Grade 12, 60 hrs.

Plant: Library 12,000 vol.; Language Lab, 5 Science Labs, 4 Art Studios, Gym, Auditorium, Playing Fields, 4 Tennis Courts, 3 Computer Labs.

Admission: $50 Application fee; Interview, student and parent; SSAT, 2 teacher Recommendations, Transcript, Writing sample. Feb. 15 deadline for application, Rolling Admission after deadline if space available.

Tuition: (1995-96) $11,440-11,865   Books: extra   Lunch: Cafeteria service or bring from home.   *Dress Code*: Neat and tidy.   **Financial Aid**:   41 partial

Summer Program: Word Processing, Study Skills, Typing.

ST. ANN'S ACADEMY..........(202) 363-4460

4404 Wisconsin Avenue, N. W., Washington, D. C. 20016
Catholic   **Head** : Mrs. Murray Greenwall

Grades: N3-8   **Enrollment**: 275 Co-ed

Special Programs: Spanish, 1-8; Art, Music. Computers K-8. P.E. **Extended Day**: 7 a.m.- 6 p.m.

Tuition : (1995-96) Half-day N (3 & 4) $1,200; K-8, $2,805. Reduction for siblings.
Extended Day : Extra

ST. ANNE'S-BELFIELD SCHOOL............(804) 296-5106   FAX (804) 979- 1486

2132 Ivy Road, Charlottesville, VA 22903
Episcopal 1910, merged 1970 **Head**: The Reverend Dr. George E. Conway

Grades: PreK-12   **Enrollment**: 827 Co-ed (26 Boarding; 5 day Boarding begins 7th grade)
Faculty: 92 full-, 8 part-time.   **Average Class Size**: 15

Special Courses: Latin 7-12, French & Spanish 8-12. Math includes AP Calculus, Computer.
Science: Biology, Chemistry, Physics, Honors Chemistry, Honors Physics. History- World, U.S.,
American Gov't, History of Russia & USSR, Global Change: The Developing World. Economics,
Humanities, Public Speaking. Religion-History of the Early Church. Art History, Ceramics,
Studio Art; Drama, Theatre History, Photography. AP: English, Calculus, U.S. History,
Biology, Latin, French, Spanish.

Athletics: req. all grades. Intramural: Tennis. Interscholastic: Field Hockey, Lacrosse,
Volleyball, Cross Country, Football, Basketball, Golf, Tennis, Soccer, Wrestling. Also offered:
Weight Lifting, Aerobics.   **Clubs**: Student Gov't, Ski, Drama, Video Update, Pop Quiz Team,
Science Quiz Bowl Team,Yearbook, Newspaper, Foreign Language Clubs, Art Forum, Gold Key
Society. **Publications**: Newspaper, Literary Magazine, Yearbook. **Community Service**: 60 hrs.
req. for graduation.

Plant: Library 10,000 vol., with CD/Rom and Internet capabilities. 6 Science labs, Art Studios,
Gym, 2 Auditoriums, 5 Playing Fields, 5 Tennis Courts, Weight & Aerobics Rooms, New Student
Union & Fine Arts facility, IBM & Apple Computer Lab.

Admission: Application fee $30. Required: Interview, Teacher Recommendations, Transcript,
SSAT, ERB, or ISEE Test. Rolling admissions begin Jan. 1.

Tuition: (1995-96) Day $4,900-$8,830; Boarding $15,300-$16,450. **Lunch**: $1.50-$2.00 daily
Books: $200-$250 *Dress Code*: Shirts must have collars & tucked in, no T-shirts or cut- offs.
Financial Aid : Available

Summer Program: Academic: 6 weeks : Algebra and pre-Algebra, Basic English Writing
Skills, Computer Skills/Typing, SAT Preparatory (2 wk), Spanish Review, Upper Level Writing
Competency. Summer Camp: ages 2 1/2-5 or ages 5-12, 9 one week sessions.
Adventure Camp: grades 1-8; Camp Counselors Apprentice Program, grades 7-9. Summer Stock
Theater, grades 2-6. One week camps: Boys' Lacrosse, Girls' Lacrosse & Field Hockey; Boys',
Girls'Basketball Camp , Boys' & Girls' Soccer Camp..

ST. ANSELM'S ABBEY SCHOOL..........(202) 269-2350

4501 S. Dakota Avenue, N.E., Washington, D.C. 20017
Catholic 1942. **Head**: Rev. Peter Weigand, OSB, M.T.S.

Grades: 6-12. **Enrollment**: 198 Boys. **Faculty**: 22 full-, 16 part-time.
Average Class Size: 15.

Special Courses: Latin 7-12, French & Spanish, 8-12, German, 10-12, Greek 11-12. Math
includes Calculus and Computer. Gen'l Science, Biology, Chemistry, Physics. History- U.S.,
Western Civilization, Economics. Religious Studies, req.; Art, Music. AP. English Literature,
Composition, American Literature, Latin, French Literature & Conversation, Physics, Chemistry,

Biology, U.S. History, European History, Comparative Governments, U.S. Politics and Government, and Calculus.

Athletics: Req. thru grade 10: All students 6-10 are req. to participate weekly in intramural sports; Basketball, Softball, Soccer, Volleyball, Stickball. Note: Students in grades 11-12, req. to participate in a sport; optional co-ed recreational program offered 9-12. Interscholastic: Soccer, Basketball, Baseball, Tennis, Cross-Country, Wrestling **Clubs**: Newman, Forensic, Priory Players, Latin Bowl, Cultural Student Organization, Math Counts, Knowledge Master, "It's Academic," Theater, Film, Science. **Publications**: Yearbook, Newspaper, Literary Magazine. **Community Involvement**: 2 1/2 hours a week of community service to various off-campus agencies in the metro area req. for all students in grades 11-12.

Plant: Library 12,500 vol., 3 Science Labs, Art Studio, Gym, Auditorium, Green House, 2 Playing Fields, 4 Tennis Courts, Chapel, 35 acres of land.

Admission: Rolling Admission, Tests in Jan. & Feb. or until classes filled. Interview follows testing. Limited openings for transfer into gr. 8, 10, 11. $35 Application & Testing fee.

Tuition: (1995-96) grade 6, $8,600; 7 & 8, $8,800; 9-12, $9,100; plus fees ($400-$650). **Transportation**: school accessible by Red & Green Metro lines. *Dress Code*: Jacket & tie, no jeans or athletic shoes. **Scholarship Aid**: 40 partial.

Future Plans: New gym, new Library; expand athletic program & facilities.

Summer Program: Remedial courses in Math, Languages; Enrichment courses in Science Math, English, Study skills.

ST. ANTHONY SCHOOL..........(202) 526-4657

12th & Lawrence Streets N.E., Washington, D. C. 20017
Catholic   **Head**: Mrs. Luray Greenwell

Grades: Pre K-8   **Enrollment**: 260 Co-ed   **Extended Day** : 7:15 a.m.- 6 p.m.

Tuition: (1995-96) In parish, $1,705; Out of parish, $2,353; Reduction for siblings. Books: $75

ST. AUGUSTINE SCHOOL..........(202) 667-2608

1421 V Street, N. W., Washington, D. C. 20009
Catholic   **Head**: Ms. Adela Acosta

Grades: PreK-8 **Enrollment**: 220 Co-ed **Extended Day**: 7 a.m.-6 p.m.

Tuition: (1995-96) $1,970; Reduction for siblings. **Extended Day**: Extra.

ST. BARTHOLOMEW'S SCHOOL...........(301) 229-5586

6900 River Road, Bethesda, MD 20817
Catholic 1962   **Head**: Mr. Daniel Shaheen, Principal

Grades: K-8 **Enrollment**: 215 Co-ed **Faculty**: 15 full-, 5 part-time.
Average Class Size: 20

Special Courses: Spanish. Algebra, Computer. General Science. U.S. & World History,
World Regions, U.S. Geography, Civics. Religious Studies req.; Ability Grouping in Reading &
Math which allows acceleration in both disciplines. Art, Music. **Extended Day**: 3 p.m.- 6 p.m.

Athletics: Req.; CYO Basketball, Baseball, Soccer. **Clubs**: Yearbook, Newspaper.
Publications: Newspaper, Yearbook. **Community Involvement**:
Students are encouraged to participate in service projects.

Plant: Library, 3,000 vol.; Science Lab, Playing Fields, Church Hall Auditorium.

Admission: Testing (fee) Math, Reading ; Transcript; School Visit

Tuition: (1995-96) In parish, $2,625 (reduction for siblings) Out of parish, $ 4,450
Tuition charges includes <u>Books</u> & Extra Fees. *Dress Code*: Uniform req
Financial Aid: Limited.

Summer Program: Academic Enrichment.

ST. BENEDICT THE MOOR SCHOOL..........(202) 397-3897

330 Twenty-first Street N. E., Washington, D. C. 20002
Catholic   **Head**: Sister Brenda Cherry, OSP

Grades: PreK-8 **Enrollment**: 240 Co-ed

Special Programs: Remedial Reading & Math; P.E., Art, Music, Choir. Computer
Extended Day: 7 a.m.-6 p.m.

Tuition: (1995-96) $1,825; Reduction for siblings. **Extended Day** Extra

ST. BERNARD'S SCHOOL.......................(301) 864-3801

5811 Riverdale Road, Riverdale, MD 20737
Catholic   **Head**: Sister Elizabeth Raffo, CSC

Grades: K-8 **Extended Day**: After school only

Tuition: (1995-96) $1,290

ST. CATHERINE'S SCHOOL.........(804) 288-2804   FAX (804) 285-8169

6001 Grove Avenue, Richmond, VA 23226
Episcopal, 1890 **Head** : Auguste J. Bannard

Grades: Jr.K-12 **Enrollment**: 720 Girls (Boarding, 80, begins grade 9)
Faculty: 76 full-28 part-time. **Average Class Size**: 15-17

Special Courses: 20 credits required for graduation: English 4; Foreign Language 3
(Languages offered include Mandarin Chinese and Russian); History 3; Math 3;   Lab Science 2;
Religion 1 1/3; Fine Arts 1; Computer Literacy and P.E.; Co-ed Classes with St. Christopher's at
all levels. Tri-mesters. AFS ; Mini-mester (2 wk. mid-winter program) Concentrated study in
specific areas encourages internships, travel-study trips. Honors and AP Courses.
Extended Day: 7 a.m.-6 p.m., year round for Jr.K-7, including holidays.

Athletics: P.E. all levels; 24 Teams in 12 Sports, JV and Varsity; Horseback Riding, Tennis,
Wilderness Program, Waterman Program (Camping, Canoeing, etc.) **Clubs and extra-
curricular activities**: Choir, Band, String Ensembles, Performing Dance Groups, Drama Group,
Student Council, Altar Guild, Multicultural Awareness Group; **Publications**: Newspaper,
Yearbook, Literary Magazine.

Plant: 16 acre campus; 2 Libraries.; Science, Fine Art, Music, and Theater Buildings;
Gym, Tennis Courts, Playing fields.

Admission: $25 fee; Transcript; SSAT Math & English; Recommendations; Rolling
Admission.

Tuition: (1995-96) Upper School: Day, $8,870; Boarding, $18,950 **Financial Aid**: Available

Future Plans: Library, Chapel, and Student Center renovations; Plan to increase boarding
enrollment.

Summer Program: Creative Arts Program for ages 3-12.

ST. CHARLES ELEMENTARY SCHOOL....................(703) 527-0608

3299 N. Fairfax Drive, Arlington, VA 22201
Catholic 1922   **Head**: Sister Benedict Kesock, O.S.B., Principal

Grades: K-8 **Enrollment**: 250 (109 Boys, 141 Girls) **Faculty**: 14 full-, 4 part-time
Average Class Size: 20-25

Special Courses: Spanish (K-5, once a week); French (6-8, once a week)
Extended Day: 7- 8 a.m. and 2:45- 6 p.m.

Athletics: Jr. High Boy's and Girl's Basketball

Plant: Mobile Science Labs, Cafeteria, Library, Computers in each classroom.

Admission: Visit school; Copy of Birth Certificate, Baptismal Record (req. if Catholic), Transcript, Health records. Registration fee $50

Tuition: In Parish, $1,500; Catholic, Non-parish $1,670; Non-Catholic $2,360; (Reduction for Siblings); Tuition may be paid in 10 equal monthly installments. **Books, Various Supply Fees:** Extra. *Dress Code*: Uniform req. grades 1-8. **Financial Aid**: Available to "In Parish" families.

ST. FRANCIS EPISCOPAL DAY SCHOOL...........(301) 365-2642 FAX (301) 365-7500

10033 River Road, Potomac, MD 20854
Episcopal 1988 **Head**: Carol R. Shabe, Director

Grades: Preschool-grade 5. **Enrollment**: 225 Co-ed. **Faculty**: 25 full-, 13 part-time.
Average Class Size: Preschool, ratio 6:1; Elementary, 10: 1.

Special Courses: All grade levels: Computer, Art. Music, Science Lab, Cultural
Arts Enrichment Program, Creative Writing, Library Skills; Curriculum related field trips.
Instrumental Music, St. Francis Singers Choral group, grades 3-5 Nuturing, self-esteem building
environment and challenging appropriate curriculum in all subject areas. Chapel program..
Note: Spanish, grades 1-5. **Extended Day**: Available.

Athletics: req. Sports Skills program. **Note**: Pre-school, Creative Movement. **Clubs**: Scouts,
After School Programs. **Publications** : Literary Magazine, Newsletter, Yearbook. **Community
Involvement**: Community Outreach Programs

Plant: Library, Multi-purpose room, Creative Playground. Art and Bookbinding Rooom,
Computer Lab, Science Lab, Classroom Libraries

Admission: Application Fee, $40, Apply Sept. through Jan. Children, applying for Pre-school
participate in play-session evaluations. Elementary grades spend a day at school, Assessment
Testing, Transcript, Teacher Recommendations. Parents tour school, Visit classroom, Meet with
Director.

Tuition: (1995-96) $2,350-$7,150. Activity fee. **Lunch**: Bring **Financial Aid** : Available

Future Plans : Summer Program.

ST. FRANCIS deSALES SCHOOL.........(202) 529-5394

2019 Rhode Island Avenue, N. E., Washington, D. C. 20018
Catholic   **Head**: Sister Vicki Staub, SSJ

Grades : PreK4-8 **Enrollment**: 230 Co-ed **Extended Day**: 7 a.m.-6 p.m.

Tuition: (1995-96) In parish, $1,820; Out of parish, $1,930; Reduction for siblings. Registration fee $80. Books $90 PreK supplies. $150. **Extended Day** $44/wk;, Reduction for siblings.

ST. FRANCIS XAVIER SCHOOL..........(202) 581-2010

2700 O Street. S. E., Washington, D. C. 20020
Catholic **Head**: Mrs. Therese Leeke

Grades: K-8 **Enrollment** 250 Co-ed

Special Courses: Spanish, Computer, Music, Art, P.E. **Extended Day**: 6:30 a.m.-6 p.m.

Tuition (1995-96) $2,160. Reduction for siblings. **Extended Day**: Extra

ST. GABRIEL'S SCHOOL..........(202) 726-9212

510 Webster Street. N. W., Washington, D. C. 20011
Catholic **Head**: Sister Janet Stolba, RJM

Grades : K-8 **Enrollment** : 250 Co-ed **Extended Day**: until 6 p.m.

Tuition (1995-96) $1,985. Reduction for siblings.

ST. HUGH'S SCHOOL..........................(301) 474-4071

145 Crescent Road, Greenbelt, MD 20770
Catholic **Head**: Mr. Philip Robey

Grades: K-8

Tuition: (1995-96 $1,600

ST. JAMES SCHOOL ....(301) 733-9330 Fax (301) 739 1310

St. James, MD. 21781
Episcopal 1842. **Head**: Rev. D. Stuart Dunnan, Ph. D.

Grades: 7-12. **Enrollment**: 163 Co-ed, (114 Boys, 49 Girls) Boarding 82, Boarding begins 7th. **Faculty**: 25 full-, 1 part-time. **Average Class Size**: 12.

Special Courses: French & Spanish 9-12, Latin 7&8; ESL; Math thru Calculus; Science Biology, Chemistry, Physics; History: English, American, Modern European, Ancient, Russian. Geography. Religion, Philosophy, Economics. Word Processing, Drama, Art, Music, Study

Skills. AP.: Calculus, American History, Biology, Chemistry, Physics.

Athletics: Req.; Interscholastic:(Member of ISSACS) Football, Baseball, Basketball, Soccer, Track, Tennis, Cross Country, Squash, Aerobics, Wrestling, Field Hockey, Golf, Weight Lifting, Lacrosse. **Clubs**:Ski, Chess, Irving Society(literary), Mummers Society (Drama), Orpheus Society (Music),Library Committee, Varsity Club, Photography, Choir. **Publications**: Yearbook, Newspaper, Literary Magazine.

Plant: Library 18,000 vol., 3 Science Labs, Art Studio, Large Field House, 6 Playing Fields, 10 Tennis Courts (4 indoor), 3 Squash Courts, Pottery Studio, Chapel, 8 Dormitories, Computer Lab, Fine Arts Center.

Admission: SSAT or SCAT (latter administered on campus during visit) Interview/campus tour; $35 Application fee; Transcript, Recommendations.

Tuition: (1995-96) Day $9,500; Boarding $16,500. <u>Books:</u> $200. *Dress Code*: Boys: coat & tie; Girls: Skirt or Dress, & Blazer. **Financial Aid**: Available.

Future Plans: Renovation of Student Center; Build New Library & New Girls Dorm.

Summer Program: Day Sports Camp

ST. JOHN'S COLLEGE HIGH SCHOOL..........(202) 363-2316

2607 Military Road, N.W., Washington, D.C. 20015
Catholic 1851 **Head**: President, Brother Thomas Gerrow FSC

Grades: 7-12. **Enrollment**: 510 Co-ed **Faculty**: 50 full-, 4 part-time.
Average Class Size: 25

Special Courses: College Preparatory with AP and Honor Courses in all areas. Grades 9-12: required Leadership Development Program (JROTC or Lead).

Athletics: Athletic Program participates in all Girls and Boys Sports under the new Washington Catholic League. **Clubs**: Numerous. **Publications**: Yearbook, Newspaper.

Plant: Library 13,000 vol., 4 Science Labs, Computer Lab, Chapel, Auditorium, Gym, Football/Baseball Stadium, Soccer/Lacrosse Field, Softball Field, 4 Tennis Courts, Rifle Range- 27 acre campus.

Admission: Archdiocese Admission Tests; Interview, Transcript, Recommendations; $25 Application fee.

Tuition: (1995-96) 7 & 8, $5,700; 9-12, $6,290 <u>Books:</u> $200. *Dress Code*: "JROTC"or "Lead" Catholic School Uniform, girls-skirts/blazer; boys- pants, tie, blazer. **Financial Aid:** Available. **Transportation**: Bus from Montgomery and Prince Georges Mall.

Summer Program: Review & makeup courses in most major subjects. Enrichment courses in Writing and Computer Literacy. Reviews of elementary Math, English, Reading, Study Skills, and Keyboarding.

ST. JOHN'S EPISCOPAL SCHOOL..........(301) 774-6804

3427 Olney-Laytonsville Road, Olney, MD. 20832
Episcopal 1961. **Head**: Mr. John H. Zurn

Grades: K-8. **Enrollment**: 165 Co-ed. **Faculty**: 8 full-, 14 part-time.
Average Class Size: 17, max. 18

Special Courses: Spanish K-8, Latin 7-8, Algebra, General Science. Religious studies req.;
Art, Music, Drama. **Extended Day**: 7- 8:15 a.m.; 3:15 p.m.- 6 p.m.

Athletics: Req.; Intramural: Field Hockey, Soccer, Lacrosse, Track, Volleyball, Gymnastics, Wrestling, Aerobics, Basketball. **Publications**: Yearbook, Literary Magazine. **Community Involvement**: Visit nursing home, food & clothing collections; Thanksgiving baskets for needy;, MS Read-a-Thon; Work at soup kitchen;

Plant: Library 6,000 vol., Science Lab, Art Studio, Playing Fields.

Admission: Parent Interview, Classroom Visits; Application Fee $50. Students may be admitted during school year, if space available.

Tuition: (1995-96) $5,550. **Lunch**: Bring. **Books**: Approx. $100. *Dress Code*:
Uniform req. **Financial Aid**: Available..

Summer Program: Reading, Math, Science, Computer & Art; Enrichment program; Soccer Camp.

ST. JOHN'S LITERARY INSTITUTION AT PROSPECT HALL..........(301) 662-4210
FAX (301) 662-5166

889 Butterfly Lane, Frederick, MD. 21702
Roman Catholic 1829. **Head**: To be announced

Grades: 9-12. **Enrollment**: 220 Co-ed (130 Boys, (90 Girls) **Faculty**: 18 full and part-time.
Average Class Size: 24

Special Courses: French, Spanish; Math through Calculus; Science includes Physics. Epochs in History & Philosophy, Religion req. ; Art, Computer Science. Note: Honors Courses 9-12 with children placed according to testing. In connection with the county, courses are offered for the gifted child in Art & Music or any specific subject.

Athletics: Intramural & Interscholastic. Soccer, Volleyball, Basketball, Baseball, Softball, Golf, Tennis, Cross-Country. **Clubs**: Ski, Cheerleaders, Science, Nat'l Honor Societies, Student

Council, Afro-American, Drama, Mock Trial, SADD. **Publications**: Yearbook, Student-Alumni Newsletter. **Community Involvement**: Nursing Home; Soup Kitchen in Washington monthly; Each grade involved in on-going projects.

Plant: Main Bldg. nominated to Nat'l Historic Trust. Library, Computer Lab, Chapel, Gym, Playing Fields, Science Labs, Tennis (nearby). Also, some portable classrooms.

Admission: Placement Testing, Transcript. Recommendations.

Tuition: (1995-96) $4,291. Lunch: Cafeteria optional. Activity Fee: $125. Books: Extra. **Transportation**: Available to Montgomery County, $95/mo. *Dress Code*: Uniform req. **Financial Aid**: Available

Summer Program: Stu Vetter's Basketball Camp; Baseball program.

ST. JOHN THE EVANGELIST SCHOOL..........(410) 647-2283

669 Ritchie Highway, Severna Park, MD. 21146
Catholic **Head**: Sister Linda Larsen

Grades: K3-8. **Enrollment**: 445 Co-ed **Extended Day**: 7-8 a.m., 3-6 p.m.

Tuition: (1995-96) Half-day K $2,205; K-8 $3,150; Reduction for siblings and in parish member.

ST. JOSEPH'S SCHOOL..........(301) 937-7154

11011 Montgomery Road, Beltsville, MD 20705
Catholic **Head** : Mr. Thomas F. Moran

Grades: K-8 **Enrollment** : 280 Co-ed

Special Courses: Religion req.; Language Arts, Science, Social Studies, Art, Computer 1-8. Remedial Reading. Advanced Math 7 & 8. Extensive vocal and instrumental music program. **Extended Day** : until 6 p.m.

Athletics: Basketball, Softball, Soccer, Baseball, T-ball, etc. **Clubs**: Altar Service, Safety Patrol, Brownies, Girl Scouts, Boy Scouts, Band.

Tuition: (1995-96) In parish, $1,950; Out of parish, $2,725. **Extended Day**: Extra **Financial Aid**: Available

ST. LUKE'S CATHOLIC SCHOOL.........(703) 356-1508

7005 Georgetown Pike, McLean, VA 22101
Catholic   **Head:** Margaret Cahill

Grades: K-8   **Enrollment**: 236 Co-ed

Special Programs: Seton Center for Learning Disabled. Computer, French, Art, Music, P.E.
Religious Studies are an integral part of academic program. **Extended Day**: to 6 p.m.

Tuition: (1995-96) In Parish, $2,500; Out of Parish, $3,600; **Extended Day**: Extra

ST. MARGARET'S SCHOOL.........(804) 443-3357

P.O. Box 158, Tappahanock, VA. 22560
Episcopal 1921 **Head**: Margaret R. Broad

Grades: 8-12   **Enrollment**: 130 Girls (95 Boarding)

ST. MARIA GORETTI REGIONAL HIGH SCHOOL.........(301) 739-4266 FAX (301) 739-4261

1535 Oak Hill Avenue, Hagerstown, MD. 21742-2980
Catholic 1930. **Head**: Sr. Susan Albert, SSND

Grades: 9-12. **Enrollment**: 211 Co-ed. **Faculty**: 14 full-, 2 part-time.
Average Class Size: 18

Special Courses: French I-IV, Spanish I-IV, Latin. Math-5 yr., Computer Science, Key
boarding. Science: Biology, Chemistry, Physics, Psychology. History: World Cultures, U.S.
History. Shakespeare. Religious studies req.;

Athletics: Req. 9-12. Intramural & Interscholastic. Soccer, Tennis, Swimming, Golf,
Volleyball, Basketball, Baseball, Softball. **Clubs**: Drama, Folk Music, Cheerleading,
Enviornmental. **Publications**: Yearbook, Newspaper, Literary Magazine. **Community
Involvement**: Tutoring elementary pupils, and helping handicapped and elderly in nursing
homes.

Plant: Library, 2 Science Labs, Art Studio, Gym/Auditorium, Playing Fields.

Admission: Admission is open. Interviews conducted.

Tuition: (1995-96) $4,092 includes lab fees. **Books & Fees**: $200- 300 *Dress Code*:
Uniform req. **Financial Aid**: Some partial tuition assistance available.

Summer Camp: Basketball, Soccer, Volleyball for boys & girls.

147

ST. MARTIN'S LUTHERAN SCHOOL.........(410) 280-2024   FAX (410)280-2024

1120 Spa Road, Annapolis, MD. 21403
Founded 1965. **Head**: Margaret Wolfe

Grades: Pre K-grade 8. **Enrollment**: 195 Co-ed. **Faculty**: 8 full-, 10 part-time.
Average Class Size: 22.

Special Courses: Music, Art, Library, Computer Program. Religion req., Remedial Reading
& Math. P.E. req. **Extended Day**: 7-8:30 a.m.; 3-6 p.m.

Plant: Library/Computer Lab, Gym, Science Lab, All-Purpose room.

Admission: Interview parent/child. Testing K-8. Registration fee.

Tuition: (1995-96) PreK, $988-$1,482; K, $2, 469 (half-day); grades l-5, $3,580; grades 6-8.
$4,580 **Lunch**: Hot lunch 3 days, Bring 2 days/wk; fee for milk

ST. MARY'S RYKEN HIGH SCHOOL.........(301) 475-2814, or 932-4422

Camp Calvert Road, Leonardtown, MD. 20650
Catholic 1981. Sponsored by Xaverian Bros. **Head**: Mr. Harry L. Swaney

Grades: 9-12. **Enrollment**: 500 Co-ed. **Faculty**: 26 full-time **Average Class Size**: 25.

Special Courses: Latin, French, & Spanish all 9-12. Computer. Science Physical Science,
Biology, Chemistry, Physics, Earth Science, Physiology, Psychology, Child Development;
Electronics. History: World & U.S. History, Contemporary Issues, World Geography, World
Cultures - Third World, Russia Since 1917, The Civil War. Religious Studies: req. Art, Music,
Typing, Orchestra, Band, Mechanical Drawing, Drama.   Remedial Reading & Math. All students
take a Life Skills Program. AP.: English, History, Chemistry, Math, Music, Art.

Athletics: Not req. Interscholastic. Basketball, Baseball, Cross County, Soccer, Track,
Wrestling, Field Hockey, Softball, Golf, Tennis, Cheerleading. **Clubs**: Science, Forensics,
Foreign Language, Religious Activities. **Publications:** Newspaper, Yearbook, **Community
Involvement**: 30 hrs. of community service req. for graduation.

Plant: Library 20,000 vol., Science Labs, Art Studio, Gym, Playing Fields, 110 acre campus.

Admission: 8th grade, Entrance/Placement Test - others submit Transcript.

Tuition: (1995-96) $3,975 and fees. Books: $150. Lunch: purchase **Transportation**: Some
Available - extra charge *Dress Code*: specific regulations.

ST. MARY'S SCHOOL..........(410) 263-3294 (H.S.) (410) 263-2869 (Lower)

Duke of Glouster St., Annapolis, MD. 21401-2599
Catholic. **Head**: Sr. Phyllis McNally (H.S.) Timothy Lynch (Lower)

Grades: K-12. **Enrollment**: Co-ed: High School, 540; Lower School, 900.

Special Features: **Extended Day** in Lower School: until 5:30 p.m.

Tuition: (1995-96) Half-day K, $1,850-$2,150; Full- day K, $2,900-$3,200 ; grades 1-8, $2,445-$2,945; High School, $3,880-$4,380. Note: Lower tuition for in parish family.

ST. MARY'S STAR OF THE SEA SCHOOL..........(301) 283-6151

6485 Indianhead Highway, Indianhead, MD 20640-9727.
Head: Bill Eager

Grades: K-8 **Enrollment**: 250 Co-ed **Extended Day**: 6:30 a.m.-6:30 p.m.

Tuition: (1995-96) K, $1,090; 1-8,$1,925 Reduced fees for siblings.

ST. PATRICK'S EPISCOPAL DAY SCHOOL..........(202) 342-2805 FAX (202) 342-2802

4700 Whitehaven Parkway, N.W., Washington, D.C. 20007
Episcopal 1956. **Head**: Peter A. Barrett

Grades: N-6. **Enrollment**: 415 Co-ed. **Faculty**: 42 full-, 17 part-time.
Average Class Ratio: 1:8

Special Courses: Computer, French/Spanish, Video-Production, Science, Art Music, Religion, Choir, Handbell choir, Recorder Consort. Note: After school programs include cooking, science, computer. **Extended Day**: to 6 p.m.(contract students only)

Athletics: P.E. Req. Note: Varied after-school sports programs, including gymnastics
Publications: Yearbook. **Community Service** : Grate Patrol, Martha's Table, etc.

Plant: Library 15,000 vol., CD-ROM, computerized card catalog; Technology Center (computer/video production), Amphitheater, 2 Science Labs, Art Studio, 2 Music/Rehersal Rooms ,Gym,/Auditorium, 2 acre Playing field, 4 Playgrounds..

Admission: Beg. in Sept. for following year: Parent Interview, Student Visit; Application fee $40. Ethnic, cultural, racial, religious, economic diversity sought. Preference given to siblings and children of parishioners.

<u>Tuition</u>: (1995-96) N Half-Day $5,750; N 2 afternoons & 1 Full Day $7,490; Full Day $8,98 Elementary $9,800. includes <u>Books</u>.   Bring <u>Lunch.</u> *Dress Code*: Conservative. **Financial Aid**: Available

<u>Summer Program</u>: Day Camp, Ages 3-12; Swimming, sports, arts, drama and video. Outdoor Adventure Camp, ages 8-12: overnight, week-long camps based in the Outer Banks (first session) and the Blue Ridge Mountains (second session)

ST. PETER'S CATHOLIC SCHOOL...........(301) 774-9112

2900 Sandy Spring Road, Olney, MD 20832
<u>Head</u>: Carol A. Mikone

<u>Grades</u>: K -8 <u>Enrollment</u>: 300 Co-ed

<u>Special Features</u>: Spanish 1-8. <u>Extended Day </u>: until 6 p.m.

<u>Tuition</u>: (1995-96) Call for information   <u>Extended Day</u>:Extra *Dress Code:* Uniform req. <u>Transportation</u>: Limited

<u>Summer Program</u>: Call for information.

ST. PETER'S INTERPARISH SCHOOL..........(202) 544-1618

422 Third Street, S. E., Washington, D. C. 20003
Catholic <u>Head</u>: Mrs. Mary M. Randolph

<u>Grades</u>: Pre K4 - grade 8   <u>Enrollment</u>: Co-ed

<u>Special Courses</u>: French 1-8, Computer, Art, Music, P.E. <u>Extended Day</u>: 7:30 a.m.-6 p.m.

<u>Tuition</u>: (1995-96) In Parish, $2,610; Out of Parish, Catholic, $3,240; Non-Catholic, $3,340 Reduction for siblings. <u>Extended Day</u>: Extra

ST. STEPHEN'S & ST. AGNES SCHOOL...(703) 549-3542 (K-8)
(703) 751-2700 (9-12)

400 Fontaine Street, Alexandria, VA. 22302 (K-5)
4401 W. Braddock Rd., Alexandria, VA 22304 (6-8)
1000 St. Stephen's Road, Alexandria, VA. 22304 (9-12)

Episcopal, St. Agnes 1924, St. Stephens 1944.   <u>Head</u>: Joan G. Ogilvy Holden

<u>Grades</u>: K-12. <u>Enrollment</u>: 1035 Co-ed <u>Faculty</u>: 120 full-, 13 part-time. <u>Average Class Size</u>: 15.

Special Courses: Latin 6-12, French & Spanish 4-12; Math Algebra I-III, Geometry, Trig., Calculus, Finite Math; Computer Science, K-12. Science General Science K-9, Biology, Chemistry, Physics, Field Studies. History: 9-12 Ages of Humanity-(4 yrs. req.) Interdisciplinary, Multicultural History course; Medieval History (gr.6), Twentieth Century World History (gr.7) Interdisciplinary Science/Geography (gr.8). Religious Studies req.; Studio Art; Music: K-6 Orff Music Program, 7-12 Chorus, Band, Orchestra, Guitar, Chamber Music, Jazz Band. Photography, Drama, Dance. AP.: English, Calculus AB, Calculus BC, Art, Pascal, Latin, Spanish, French, History, Biology, Chemistry, Physics. **Extended Day**: 7 a.m.-6 p.m.

Athletics: Req. to grade 11. Intramural & Interscholastic. Basketball, Football, Softball, Baseball, Tennis, Field Hockey, Soccer, Lacrosse, Track & Field, Wrestling, Volleyball, Cross Country. **Clubs**: In Middle School, generated by student; Upper School: Language, Debate, Model O.A.S. & U.N., Library, SADD, Service Unity. **Publications**: Yearbook, Newspaper, Literary Magazines. **Community Involvement**: Service Projects at all grade levels. Required Service Project, 40 hrs. for Upper School students.

Plant: 3 Libraries, Language Lab, 4 Computer Labs, Media Center, 14 Science Labs, 7 Art Studios, 3 Gyms, 6 Playing Fields, 6 Tennis Courts, Large Multi-purpose Room, 6 Performing Arts Rooms.

Admission: Tour & Interview & Campus Visit. Testing- SSAT 6-12. Transcripts, Essay, 2 Teacher Recommendations. $50 Application & Testing Fee. Students generally fall into above average to superior range of ability.

Tuition: (1995-96) K- 8, $10,480. 9-12, $11,650. Lunch: $538-$718. Books: $170-$530. **Transportation**: $950-$1,200 round trip. *Dress Code*: Appropriate attire expected at all times-specific rules for Lower, Middle & Upper School. **Financial Aid**: Available.

Future Plans: Expansion and renovation on Upper School campus.

Summer Program: Courses for credit & enrichment for all grades. Classes daily early June - early August. Also SAT Prep. Course. Note: For rising Seniors: Internships in area businesses, Oxford Study Program in England.

Summer Camp: Day Camp early June - early August, Co-ed, Ages 3-11: Sports, computer, swimming, arts & crafts, music/drama, field trips. All Sports Camps: Boys & Girls: Lacrosse, Soccer, Basketball, Softball, Tennis, Football, Weight Training; In addition: World Cultures, Adventures in Spanish, Flight Camp, Music Academy, Computer Camp.

ST. TIMOTHY'S SCHOOL..........(410) 486-7400   FAX (410) 484-5910

Stevenson, MD. 21153
Episcopal 1882. **Head**: Deborah Cook.

Grades: 9-12. **Enrollment**: 83 Girls (57 Boarding) **Faculty**: 14 full-, 6 part-time.
Average Class Size: 7

Special Courses: French I-V, Latin I-II, Spanish I-IV; Science: Physical Science, Biology, Chemistry, Physics. History: World History I & II, American.   Religious Studies (req. one year)--Intro. to World Religion. Studio Art, Photography, Music Theory, Piano, Modern Dance, Ballet, Drama. AP & Honors Courses.: English, French, Calculus, History of Art, Biology. Note: Special Programs such as English as a Foreign Language. English Speaking Union; Independent Senior Project. Capital Connections (with Washington, D. C., Baltimore, and Annapolis) Accademic Resource Center.

Athletics: Req.; Intramural & Interscholastic. Field Hockey, Cross-Country, Lacrosse, Soccer, Tennis, Aerobic Dance, Basketball, Riding, Badminton   **Clubs**: Choir, Handbell Choir, Madrigals, Dramatics, Social Activities, Current Events, EAC.   **Publications**: Yearbook, Literary Magazine. **Community Involvement**: Social Service,   Tutoring, Special Games Day

Plant: Library 20,000 vol.; Academic Resource Center, 3 Science Labs, Art Studio, Gym, Auditorium, Theater, Stables & Indoor Riding Arena, Cross Country Equestrian Course, Playing Fields, Swimming Pool, 10 Tennis Courts, Music & Dance Studios, Chapel, Dormitories, Infirmary, Faculty Homes, Darkroom.

Admission: $30 fee; Transcript, Interview, SSAT, English, Math; Applicant Essay; Principal and Personal Recommendations. Notification: Rolling with reply by April 10.

Tuition: (1995-96) Day $11,600;   Boarding $21,300. Books: $400-$500   *Dress Code*: Uniform req. for classes. **Financial Aid**: Available.

ST. THOMAS MORE CATHOLIC SCHOOL..........(202) 561-1189

4265 Fourth Street, S. E., Washington, D.C. 20032
Catholic   **Head**: Ms. Roberta Taylor

Grades : K4-8   **Enrollment**: 250 Co-ed

Special Programs: Spanish K-8, Computer K-8; Art. Music, P.E. **Extended Day** : 6:30 a.m. -6 p.m.

Tuition: (1995-96) Out of parish $190/mo; Reduced rate for in parish students and siblings. **Extended Day**: Extra

ST. VINCENT PALLOTTI HIGH SCHOOL..........(301) 725-3228   FAX (301) 776-4343

113 St. Mary's Place, Laurel, MD. 20707
Catholic 1921 **Principal**: Mr. Paul Leonarczyk

Grades : 9-12. **Enrollment**: 450 Co-ed. **Faculty**: 30 full-, 11 part-time.
Average Class Size: 19.

Special Programs : Academic Honors Program, Student Exchange with Foreign Countries; Required Christian Service Projects.

Special Courses: Chorus, Sculpture, Marine Biology, Mechanical Drawing, Photography, Quattro, Cable TV, Shakespeare, Economics; <u>AP</u>: Courses in Math, Science, History, English, and Foreign Languages.

Athletics: Pom Pons, Cheerleading, Football, Basketball, Baseball, Track, Swimming, Soccer, Lacrosse. Tennis, Softball, Volleyball. **Clubs**: Language, Computer, Ski, Photography, Mock Trial, Odyssey of the Mind, Multi-cultural, Art, Drama. **Publications**: Yearbook, Literary Magazine, Newspaper. **Community Involvement**: Christian Service Class, Partnership with Laurel-Regional Hospital and Nursing Home.

Plant: Library 10,000 vol., 2 Science Labs, 2 Computer Labs, Playing Fields, Gym, Cafeteria, 2 Resource Center.

Admission: Application (fee)and form with Student Essay, Recommendations, Standardized Testing, $150 Tuition deposit.

Tuition: (1995-96) $5,050; <u>Also</u> $100 Activities Fee and $100 graduation fee for seniors. *Dress Code*: Uniform req. **Financial Aid**: Available

Future Plans: Building expansion due to increased enrollment.

Summer Program: Accademic credit given in most subjects.

SANDY SPRING FRIENDS SCHOOL..........(301) 774-7455 FAX (301) 924-1115

16923 Norwood Road, Sandy Spring, MD. 20860
Quaker 1961. **Head**: Stephen Gessner, Ph.D.

Grades: PreK-12. (Note: July, 1993, Friends Elementary merged with Sandy Spring Friends) **Enrollment**: 435 Co-ed; 45 Boarding (begins at 9th grade); **Faculty**: 53 full-, 5 part-time. **Average Class Size**: 16.

Special Courses: Spanish PreK-12, French, 6-12 ESL. <u>Math</u> thru Calculus; <u>Science:</u> Gen'l Science, Biology I and II, Chemistry, Physics; <u>English</u> Literature Survey Courses, Writing, English Electives; <u>History</u>: World History, 20th Century Courses; Visual Arts & Performing Arts at all levels. 9th Grade Experience with Outdoor Exploration Program and Activities in community building, Community Service and Drama; Weekly meeting for worship-period emphasizing reflection and values; Intersession (one week experimental learning). <u>AP:</u>Courses Available. **Extended Day**: 7:15 a.m.-6 p.m.

Athletics: Req.; Intramural & Interscholastic: Tennis, Cross Country, Ultimate Frisbee, Gym Games, Soccer, Lacrosse, Basketball, Gymnastics, Jogging, Hiking, Biking. **Clubs**: Multi-Cultural Committee, Yearbook, Ecology, Amnesty Internat'l, Recycling, Computer. **Publications**: Literary Magazine, Weekly Newspaper, Yearbook. **Community Involvement**:

Required at all levels.

Plant: Library 17,000 vol.; Gym ; New Elementary facility, Renovated Middle School, New state of the art Science Center with Greenhouse and Observatory, Photography Lab, 3 Art Studios,, Theater, Woodshop, 6 Classroom Buildings, Dormitory, Print Shop, 4 Soccer and Lacrosse Fields, Tennis Courts.

Admission: Interview and Visit; Application, $50 fee; Suggest applying by Feb. 15th for consideration in first round of decisions. References, Transcript. SSAT, Middle School placement Test.

Tuition: (1995-96) Elementary, $6,500-$7,500; Middle, $8,250-$8,750; Upper, (Day) $10,750; 5 day Boarding $15,000; 7 day Boarding, $18,500. Deposit, $600. **Transportation**: Available, one way or round trip $1,100. *Dress Code*: Clean, neat, simple & appropriate. **Financial Aid**: Approximately 25% of the student body receives aid.

Summer Program: Summer Friends: Numerous academic programs, sports, arts, and trip camp available.

SETON JR. AND SR. HIGH SCHOOL............................(703) 368-3220 or 368-9450

9314 Maple Street, Manassas, VA 22110
Catholic **Head**: Anne Carroll

Grades: 7-12 **Enrollment**: 275

Tuition: (1995-96) grades 7 & 8, $2,000; 9-12, $2,400.

SEVERN SCHOOL..........(410) 647-7700

Water Street, Severna Park, MD. 21146
Founded 1914. **Head**: William J. Creeden

Grades: 6-12. **Enrollment**: 500 Co-ed. **Faculty**: 40 full-, 15 part-time.
Average Class Size: 15

Special Courses: Latin, French, & Spanish;. Study Skills, Art, Music, Math through Calculus; Computer through Paxel. Science: Biology, Chemistry, Physics, Ecology, Marine Biology. History: Third World Cultures, Ancient History, European Civilization, Sociology, Economics, American Philosophy, Local Government. Typing, Driver's Ed, Drama, Mechanical Drawing, Sculpture, Ceramics, Painting & Drawing, Music Appreciation Choir, Theater. AP.: English, History, Biology, Languages, Math, & Computer.

Athletics: Req.; Intramural 6-8, Interscholastic 8-12; Lacrosse, Football, Soccer, Tennis, Golf, Wrestling, Swimming, Basketball, Field Hockey, Baseball. **Clubs**: French, Latin, Spanish, Ecology, Sailing, SADD, etc. **Publications**: Yearbook, Newspaper, Literary Review.

Plant: Library 16,000 vol.; Language Labs, Science Labs, Art Studios, Gym, Playing Fields, Tennis Courts, Use of Golf Course & Swimming Pool.

Admission: Testing; Transcripts. Interview, Recommendations; $30 fee.

Tuition: (1995-96) $9,950. **Lunch**: Extra. **Books**: Approx. $200. **Transportation** $800 *Dress Code*: Uniform- Boys, shirt & tie; Girls, dresses or pants. **Financial Aid** : Available.

Summer Program.: Summer School; Day camp; Field Hockey, Lacrosse, & Soccer camps.

SHERIDAN SCHOOL..........(202) 362-7900 FAX (202) 244-9696

4400 36th Street, N. W., Washington, D. C. 20008
Founded 1927. **Head**: Hugh C. Riddleberger.

Grades: K-8. **Enrollment**: 213 Co-ed. **Faculty**: 26 full-, 3 part-time
Average Class Size: Student/teacher ratio, 8:1

Special Courses: Strong academic emphasis with much time also given to Art, Music, and Sports. French 4-8. Computers K-8. General Science; Unique Mountain Campus in Blue Ridge provides outdoor and environmental education including ropes course, rock-climbing and caving. History : includes Colonial, Greek, Medieval, and African American Studies; Anthropology. Spring Musical 6-8.   **Extended Day** and after school classes, 7:30 a.m.-6 p.m..

Athletics: Req.; Intramural Basketball; Interscholastic: Soccer, Basketball, Softball, Track. **Clubs**: Science, Computer, Photography, Art. **Publications**: Yearbook, Newspaper, Literary Magazine. **Community Involvement**: All classes participate in at least one community service project per year.

Plant: Library 8,400 vol.; 2 Science Labs, Art Studio, Auditorium/Gym, Playing Field, Mountain Campus - 130 acres in Luray, VA.

Admission: Parent Interview, Student Visits School; Tests for K-8. Fee $50. Notification mid-March.

Tuition: (1995-96) $10,050-$11,780, includes Lunch & Books *Dress Code*: Uniform req. Fridays only, grades 4-8 **Financial Aid**: Available.

Summer Program: Discovery Camp at Mountain Campus; City Campus: Creative Arts Camp plus one week camps for entire summer, ages 3-13.

SIDWELL FRIENDS SCHOOL..........(202) 537-8100

3825 Wisconsin Avenue, N.W., Washington, D.C. 20016
(Lower School: Pre K-grade 4, 5100 Edgemoor Lane, Bethesda, MD.)
Quaker 1883. **Head**: Earl Harrison, Jr.

Grades: Pre K-12. Enrollment: 1,053 Co-ed (increases K, 3, 5, 7, 9). Faculty: 105 full-, 35 part-time. Class Size: 15-24

Special Courses: Latin, French, Spanish - all 7-12; Chinese 9-12. (l yr. study in Art req.; 2 yrs. of Science) Environmental Science, Philosophy, Physical Science, Scientific Writing, Physics; Math thru Calculus. History - Global, Ancient, Medieval, Modern European, English, American; American & Chinese studies program. Typing, Drama, Outdoor Leadership, Technical Theater, Sculpture, Music. Note: Independent Studies, Seminars. AP.: Physics, Biology, Chemistry, Math, Languages and Computer Science. Extended Day: 3-6 p.m.

Athletics: P.E. Req. Intramural & Interscholastic: Baseball, Basketball, Cross Country, Field Hockey, Golf, Indoor Soccer, Lacrosse, Gymnastics, Soccer, Tennis, Track & Field, Volleyball, Swimming, Diving.. Clubs: Over 20 special interest - including Language, Debate, Chess, Computers, Model U.N. Community Service: Required.

Plant: Library 35,000 vol., Language Lab, Science Labs, Computer Labs, Auditorium, Gym, Playing Fields, 6 Lane Track, Tennis Courts, Arts Center, Quaker Meeting Room.

Admission: Applications, Sept.- Jan. 15, $50 + Testing fee.

Tuition: (1995-96) $11,180-$13,020 Lunch: included. Transportation: To grade 6, $700 one way; $1,500 both ways. Books: $400-$525. Dress Code: Cleanliness, neatness, simplicity. Financial Aid: Available.

Summer Program: Word Processing, Computer: Windows, Excel, Desk-top Publishing; Photography; Summer Day Camps: Basketball, Tennis, Art, Dance, Drama. Residential Summer Camp-Corsica: Summer studies-Math, English, Science, History, SAT review.

SILVER SPRING CHRISTIAN ACADEMY.......(301) 649-9747

1820 Franwall Avenue, Silver Spring, MD. 20902
Presbyterian 1986   Head: Mrs. Janice Adams, Administrator

Grades: 9-12   Enrollment: 17 Co-ed   Faculty: 12 part-time   Average Class Size: 8-10

Special Courses: German; Math thru Calculus; Computer. Biology, Chemistry, Physics. History: American, European, Ancient, Government. Religious Studies Req.; Art, Typing. AP:: Courses in Science, Math, History & Literature.

Athletics: req.; Intramural: Soccer, Basketball, Volleyball. Publications: Yearbook, Newspaper Community Involvement: Christian service projects req.

Plant: Library, 5,000 vol.; Science Lab, Auditorium; Basketball court outside.

Admission: Parent Application, Student Questionnaire, Transcript, Testing; Parent & Student Interview Note: Student and one or both parents should be members in good standing in an evangelical church OR Board approval for non-church applicants. Registration fee $100

Tuition: (1995-96) $3,500 Lunch: Bag *Dress Code:* Students are expected to dress with modesty and decency. **Financial Aid**: Available, Limited..

Future Plans: To expand school to 80 students at another Silver Spring location; curriculum to continue to be college preparatory.

SISTER CLARA MUHAMMAD ELEMENTARY SCHOOL...........(202) 610-1090

2313-15 Martin Luther King, Jr. Avenue, S.E., Washington, D. C. 20020
Islamic **Head**: Mrs. Zakiyyah Abdus-Salaam, Principal

Grades: N-9 (N ages 2-4) **Enrollment**: 85 Co-ed **Faculty**: 13 full-, 1 part-time
Average Class Size: 9

Special Courses: Islamic Studies, Arabic Language, Quranic recitation; discipline and moral conduct stressed. **Extended Day**: 7 a.m.-6 p.m.

Tuition: (1995-96) $200/mo; reduction for siblings. $25 Application fee.

Future Plans: To expand to grade 12.

SLIGO ADVENTIST ELEMENTARY SCHOOL..........(301) 434-1417

8300 Carroll Avenue, Takoma Park, MD. 20912
Seventh Day Adventist 1929. **Head**: Mr. William Ruby

Grades: N3-8. **Enrollment**: 400 Co-ed. **Faculty**: 23.

Special Courses: Remedial Reading, French, Art, Music, General Science; Bible req.
Extended Day : 7 a.m.-6 p.m. Note: Full Day Care program for 3 & 4 yr. olds, year-round 7 a.m.-7 p.m.

Athletics: Req. 5-8. **Clubs**: Drama, Pathfinders (church sponsored -like Scouts).
Publications: Weekly newspaper.

Plant: Library, Auditorium/Gym, Playing Fields.

Admission: Testing, Recommendations; Admission Board approves application.

Tuition: (1995-96) K-8, $3,550. Activity Fee $25 **Transportation**: $42-$127/mo. depending on zone. Books: $85-$100 *Dress Code*: Modest apparel. **Day Care** (3 & 4 yr. olds) $95/wk

SOUTHERN MARYLAND CHRISTIAN ACADEMY..........(301) 870 -2550,
934-3655, 753-8148

9805 Faith Baptist Church Road, White Plains, MD 20695

Head: Ted Knapp, Principal

Grades: K3-12   **Enrollment**: 250 Co-ed

Special Programs: Regular Academic Program; Foreign Language, Sign Language, Computers. Typing, Drafting; Music, Band, Art.   **Extended Day** 6 a.m.-6:30 p.m.

Athletics : P.E.; Jr. & Sr. High play sports in conference play league.

Tuition: (1995-96) $2,452; Reduced rate for siblings. High School Fee $300, Registration $150.

SPENCERVILLE JUNIOR ACADEMY..........(301) 421-9101 FAX (301) 421-0007

15930 Good Hope Road, Silver Spring, MD. 20905
Seventh Day Adventist 1946. **Head**: Harold Grosboll

Grades: K-10. **Enrollment**: 230 Co-ed. **Faculty**: 15 full-, 6 part-time.
Average Class Size: 19.

Special Courses: Algebra, Geometry, Earth Science, Biology, Keyboarding, Computer Programing; Band, Choir; Religious studies req.   **Extended Day**: Mon.-Thurs. 3-6 p.m.

Athletics: Req.; Intramural: Volleyball, Floor Hockey, Soccer, Softball, Basketball, Tennis, Flagball, Badminton. **Publications**: Yearbook.

Plant: Library 7,500 vol., Science Lab, Gym, Playing Fields, Lab.

Admission: Interview, Test, Registration fee.

Tuition: (1995-96) $1,750-$3,500 depending on grade level & whether student is member of sponsoring church, Adventist but non constituent, or non-Adventist. **Books**: Extra. **Lunch**: Bring. *Dress Code*: Neat, clean & modest.

SPRINGFIELD ACADEMY..........(703) 256-3773

5236 Backlick Road, Springfield, VA. 22151
Founded 1958. **Head**: Jack Merritt.

Grades: age 6 wks.-grade 3. **Enrollment**: 135 Co-ed. **Faculty**: 12 full-, 5 part-time.
 Average Class Size: (K-2) 15.

Special Courses: Remedial Reading & Math,; Ballet, Art, Music.
Extended Day: 6:30 a.m.-6:30 p.m.

Plant: Library 100+ vol., 5 acre campus.

Admission: Parent & child interviews; registration fee N and K $45, and lst & 2nd, $75.

Tuition : (1995-96) Infant & Toddler Care (6 wks-age 2), $125/wk.-$160 /wk; N-grade 3, $115/wk.includes **Extended Day & Lunch**. *Dress Code*: Moderate.

Summer Program: Camp 6:30 a.m.-6:30 p.m., arts & crafts, swimming, films, field trips, outdoor activities. Registration fee $25.

STONE RIDGE SCHOOL of the SACRED HEART.........(301) 657-4322   FAX (301) 657-2381

9101 Rockville Pike, Bethesda, MD. 20814
Catholic 1923. **Head**: Sister Anne Dyer, RSCJ

Grades: Jr.K-12. **Enrollment**: 638 Girls (13 Boys Jr.K-K only), Expands at grades l, 6, 9.
Faculty: 54 full-, 11 part-time. **Average Class Size**: 16-18. Student/teacher 9:1

Special Courses: College Preparatory. Advanced & accelerated preparation for AP exams in History, Biology, Chemistry, English, Art, French, Spanish; Math, and Computer Science. Independent Study; Career Internship. Exchange program through Network of Sacred Heart schools in U.S. and abroad. Middle School: Choice of French or Spanish, (5-8) Latin req. grade 8. Communications Lab provides training in effective leadership and group process skills. **Extended Day**: for JK-grade 8, 3-6 p.m.

Athletics: Req.; Intramural & Interscholastic: Field Hockey, Tennis, Basketball, Volleyball, Softball, Soccer, Lacrosse, Swimming, Diving, Cross Country, Track. **Clubs**: 20 including Model U.N., SADD, Ethnic Awareness, etc. **Publications**: Yearbook, Literary Magazine, Newspaper. **Community Involvement**: Jr.K-8: Develop. of social awareness. Grade 9: Training program for service in Education/Geriatrics/ Social Justice. Instruction in Proposal Writing. Grade 10-12: Community Service required.

Plant: Chapel, 3 Libraries, 2 Language Labs, 5 Science Labs, 3 Art Studios, Auditorium, 3 Gyms, 3 Playing Fields, 4 Tennis Courts, Photography Lab, Playgrounds..

Admission: $50 Application Testing fee Jr.K-12. Rolling admission. Applicants should apply by Feb. l. Test and Interview required.   Will accept SSAT, gr. 6-12, then application fee $35.

Tuition: (1995-96) Half- day Jr.K. & K, $5,400 ; full-day Jr.K-6, $8,950; grades 7-8, $9,695. grades 9-12, $10,295   Books: $150-$360. *Dress Code*: Uniform req. **Transportation**: Metro-Medical Center **Financial Aid**: Available.

Future Plans: New Upper school academic building 1996

Summer Programs: Art; Reading Skills, Math enrichment.

STUART HALL..........(703) 885-0356   FAX (703) 886-2273

P.O. Box 210, 235 West Frederick Street, Staunton, VA. 24402
Episcopal 1844. Head: Rev. J. Kevin Fox

Grades: 6-12. Enrollment: 108 (94 Girls; 14 Boys, middle school only); 50-60 Boarding, begins grade 8.   Faculty: 16 full-, 5 part-time. Average Class Size: 7

Special Courses: French, Spanish, 9-12. Math includes Pre-Algebra thru Calculus; Computer Processing. Science: Gen'l Science, Biology, Chemistry, Physics, Enviornmental Science, History- Non-Western World Cultures, World History, U.S./Government I & II. Philosophy and Religion, involves Ethics and Volunteer Work. Art: all media including Stained Glass and Ceramics. Music: Appreciation, Voice, Piano. Drama. Note: LRC-Learning Resource Center and ESL (English as a Second Language). AP. at Mary Baldwin College.

Athletics: P.E. Req. Intramural: Field Hockey, Volleyball, Aerobics, Tennis, Swimming. Interscholastic: Member Blue Ridge Conference: Volleyball, Soccer, Basketball, Tennis, Softball, and Riding (all year). Recreational Sports: Cross-Country, Cycling, Lacrosse, Skiing, Dance: Ballet, Tap, Modern. Clubs: Ecology, World Affairs, Student Gov't, Art. Drama, Pop Quiz Team. Publications: Literary Magazine, Newspaper, Yearbook. Community Involvement: All Seniors participate in Volunteer work: Tutoring at local elementary school; Hospitals, Ride with Pride; Special Olympics, Friendship Club.

Plant: Library, Gym 14,000 vol.; Science Labs, Art Studio, Gym, Auditorium, 3 Tennis Courts, Indoor Pool, Darkroom, Playing Fields, Riding at nearby stables.

Admission: Personal Interview; Rolling Admission. Note: Seek motivated college-bound individual who is an average to above average student.

Tuition: (1995-96) Day, $6,500; 5 Day Boarding, $15,150 (includes Lunch) 7 Day Boarding, $17,150. Books, Fees, etc.: $500. Dress Code: Class Dress- Skirts, Dresses, Bermuda Shorts, Dress Pants, Collared Shirts. Financial Aid: Available; 30% of student body receives need-based aid.

Future Plans: New Science Labs, Athletic Center and Gym by 1996-97.

Summer Program: Co-ed Summer School for new credit or enrichment work in ESL, English, Math, Science, History, French, Spanish, SAT prep.

SUMMIT SCHOOL..........(301) 952-0787   FAX (301 627-6699

664 Central Avenue, Edgewater, MD 21037
Founded 1989   Head: Dr. Jane Snider

Grades: 1-8 Enrollment 65 Co-ed Faculty: 17 Full-, 2 part- time. Average Class Size: 9-12

Special Courses: Algebra, Computer. Remedial Reading daily; Speech, Language, and Occupational Therapy. **Extended Day**: 3-5 p.m.

Athletics: Not req. **Clubs**: Pioneering, Canoeing, Drama, Newspaper, Chorus. **Publications**: Yearbook, Newspaper. **Community Involvement**: 8th grade class involved in service project..

Plant: Library, 5,000 vol., Auditorium, Soccer Field, Basketball Court, Reading Rooms.

Admission: Application fee $50. WISC and Achievement testing, followed by a Visit for a day..

Tuition: (1995-96) $14,900 **Lunch**: Bring *Dress Code*: Boys: solid color trousers and shirt; must have collar on shirt; navy/ Khaki camp shorts. Girls: solid shirts/ jumpers/ skirts/pants. Shorts same as Boys. **Financial Aid**: Available.

Future Plans: Gym and Theatre

Summer Program: Reading; Math, Creative Writing, Camping, Fishing, etc,

SYDENSTRICKER SCHOOL.........(703) 451-4141

7001 Sydenstricker Road, Springfield, VA. 22152
1965. **Head**: Mrs. Lore Araujo.

Grades: N-grade 2. **Enrollment**: 120 Co-ed. **Faculty**: 4 full-, 2 part-time. **Average Class Size**: 15.

Special Courses: German 1-2. Remedial Reading & Math, Developmental Reading, Study Skills; Computer. General Science. Music, Art, Dancing. Note: Program is designed to provide stimulating atmosphere in which child is relaxed, develops enthusiasm for learning and gains self-confidence, enabling him to make a smooth transition into other school systems. (Psychologist on call.) **Extended Day** : 7 a.m.-6 p.m.

Plant: Library 2000 vol., Computer Lab, Art Studio, 5 acres, Nature Trail.

Admission: Application, Interview, Transcript or Tests for K-2; Primary Mental Abilities test.

Tuition: (1995-96) Call for information. Depends on age and hours in school.

TAKOMA ACADEMY.........(301) 434-4700

8120 Carroll Avenue, Takoma Park, MD. 20912
Seventh Day Adventist 1904. **Head**: Larry Blackmer

Grades: 9-12. **Enrollment**: 336 Co-ed. **Faculty**: 19 full-, 2 part-time. **Average Class Size**: 21.

161

Special Courses: French I-II, Spanish I -III. Math includes honors courses in Algebra, Geometry, Trig, Calculus; Word Processing. Science includes honors courses in Biology and Chemistry; Physics. History: World, U.S., and American Government. Religious Studies req. Remedial Reading and Math; ESL program. Note: TALL-Takoma Academy Learning Laboratory is set up to help any student with study skills, gap learning, organization, etc. Art: Drawing & Design, Color & Methods. Music: Choir, Bell Choir, Orchestra, Sax Quartet. Drama. AP.: English, American Government.

Athletics: Req. 9-10; Intramural Basketball, Volleyball, Football, Softball; Interscholastic: Basketball, Cross-Country, Track. Clubs: Biota, TA Magazine. Publications: Newspaper, Yearbook. Community Involvement: TALK- program to adopt a kid at Christmas. Community Service Day: student body spends a day cleaning up regional parks and communities.

Plant: Library 16,000 vol., Science Lab, Art Room, Shop, Auditorium, Gym, Tennis Courts, Playing Fields. 400 meter track.

Admission: Application fee $10; Placement Test, Interview, Transcript Recommendations. Registration starts in July.

Tuition: (1995-96) $445/mo. Adventist; $505/mo., Non-Adventist. Lunch: Purchase Books: $150. *Dress Code:* Clean, tidy clothes which are modest.

TALENT HOUSE PRIVATE SCHOOL &
        CHILD CARE CENTER..........(703) 273-8000   FAX (703) 591-1431

9211 Arlington Boulevard., Fairfax, VA. 22031
Founded 1963. Head: Administrator- Lisa Turissini

Grades: N (6 weeks)-grade 8. Enrollment: 330 Co-ed. Faculty : 55 full-, 35 part-time. Average Class Size: 10-20.

Special Programs: French, Latin; Music, Computer ; Accelerated Math and Language. Values curriculum; International Studies; Intergenerational program; monthly Field Trips. Teen living, Chorus, Debate, Bible Studies, Drama. Cooking   Extended Day : 6:45 a.m.-6:30 p.m..

Athletics: P.E.; Karate, Gymnastics, Wrestling, Dance. Clubs: Boy/Girl Scouts;

Plant: Playing Field, Swimming Pool, Sport Court; 7 acre campus.

Admission: Transcript; Parent/child Interview,

Tuition: (1995-96) $90-$180 wkly. Lunch K-8, $2.50 daily Transportation : $20-$35 wkly within a five mile radius. Financial Aid : Available

Summer Program: Recreational - sports clinics, arts & crafts, swimming, field trips, picnics. tennis, archery, etc.

TARA-RESTON CHRISTIAN SCHOOL.........(703) 438-8444

10742 Sunset Hills Road, Reston, VA. 22090
Bible oriented, non-denominational 1972. **Head**: Mrs. Jane A. Rogers.

Grades: PreK- grade 8 **Enrollment**: 300 Co-ed. **Faculty**: 15 full-, 6 part-time.
Average Class Size: 26

Special Courses: French, PreK-3 and 7/8; Latin 4-8; Strong academic program, students generally 2 years ahead of average local school grade. Bible req.; ESL program and Federal Gov't approval for I-20 students.

Admission: Interview, Testing, grades 1-8.

Tuition: (1995-96) Pre K-6, $2,160; 7/8, $2,340. **Transportation**: Limited, $810

Summer Program : Academic summer school

TERESA HOME SCHOOL.........(703) 524-7677

813 N. Cleveland Street, Arlington, VA. 22201 (grade 1-5)
2401 N. Ninth Street, Arlington, VA. 22201 (age 2-6 yrs)
1835 N. Nash Street, Arlington, VA. 22209 (age 2-6 yrs.)
Christian 1928. **Head**: Pamela Lassell, Principal.

Grades: N-5 **Enrollment**: 65 (grades 1-5), Co-ed. **Faculty**: 6 full-, 1 part-time.
Average Class Size: 10-15.

Special Courses: Art, Music, Dance, Math, Computers, General Science; Advanced Reading Program. Informal Christian education offered, accelerated academic program for all grades. Piano lessons available. **Extended Day** 7 a.m.-6 p.m.

Athletics: Req. - Soccer available.

Plant: Library, Auditorium.

Admission: Parent/child interview; summer school may be req. Registration, fee $100 yearly.

Tuition: (1995-96) K-5, $425/mo. includes **Extended Day** (Nursery Day Care Extra)

Summer Program: Academic & camp programs include swimming, field trips, arts & crafts, and Bible School.

KATHERINE G. THOMAS SCHOOL.........(301) 424-5200

9975 Medical Center Drive, Rockville, MD 20850

Head: Judith Zangwill, Administrative Director

Grades: PreK- grade 5   **Enrollment**: Co-ed   **Average Class Size**: 7-9

Special Features: Program for pre-school and elementary school students of average or above average intellectual potential who have Learning and/or Language Disabilities. Speech/Language Therapy and Occupational Therapy are available on site and integrated with classroom learning. Curriculum is implemented through the study of themes which revolve around Social Studies topics and integrate activities in Language-Arts, Math, Science,Art, Music, and Physical Education.

Athletics: P.E., Team Sports, within the school

Admission: Rolling Admission; applicants should apply as early as possible and submit psycho-educational and other test reports. Interview, School Visit.

Tuition : (1995-96) Preschool, $11,000; K-grade 5, $16,750. **Financial Aid**: Tuition may be funded through a public school system, following due process procedures, if public school has no appropriate program for the child.

THORNTON FRIENDS SCHOOL..........(301) 384-0320

13925 New Hampshire Avenue, Silver Spring, MD. 20904
Quaker, 1973. **Head**: Douglas R. Price.

Grades: 6-12 & PG (somewhat ungraded). **Enrollment**: 84 Co-ed. **Faculty**: 8 full-time, 10 part-time. **Average Class Size**: 9

Special Courses: College Preparatory (95%); Communication skills emphasized (writing, listening, reading, speaking, thinking); Development of strong inner self taught/learned; Socratic teaching method.

Athletics: Not required. Interscholastic: Soccer, Basketball, Softball. **Publications**: Yearbook, Literary Magazine. **Clubs:** Drama. **Community Involvement**: 40 hrs. per year required per student.

Plant: Library 8000 vol., Science Labs, Auditorium, Tennis Court, Playing Field. Use of nearby Gym, Pool, Bowling,, Skating.

Admission: Transcript & Recommendations. Interview with parents & student - student may visit class. Rolling Admission. We are looking for students who are curious, alert, lively, interesting, persuasive, kind.

Tuition: (1995-96) $9,995   **Lunch**: Bring. **Books**: $400   *Dress Code*: Students dress may not advertise drugs, alcohol, smoking violence, or sex. **Financial Aid**: Available

TORAH SCHOOL OF GREATER WASHINGTON..............(301) 593-2318

919 University Boulevard West, Silver Spring, MD 20901
(Mailing) P.O. Box 2613, Silver Spring, MD 20915
Jewish, 1994   **Head**: Rabbi Yitzchak Charner

Grades : K-6   **Enrollment**: 100 Co-ed   **Average Class Size**: 15

Special Courses : Hebrew, Art, Music, Choir, P.E. **Extended Day**: 8 a.m.(K)- 6 p.m.

Admission: Registration, $150.

Tuition: (1995-96) K, $5,000; 1-6, $5,500. **Extended Day**: Extra

TOWN & COUNTRY SCHOOL OF VIENNA...(703) 759-3000

9525 Leesburg Pike, Vienna, VA. 22182
Founded 1970. **Head:** Patricia Haas

Grades: N-3. **Enrollment**: 200 Co-ed. **Faculty**: 13 full-, 10 part-time.

Special Courses: Spanish, Music, Art, Library, Computers. **Extended Day Care** 7 a.m.-6 p.m.

Plant: 6 acres, Swimming pool, Fields and Playground, Library.

Admission: Parent/child interview, transcripts, registration fee.

Tuition (1995-96) Half- day $340/mo.; Full day $620/mo. **Extended Day** : $100/mo.
Transportation: Available.

Summer Program: Day Camp - age 2-1/2-grade 5. Extended hours, **Day Care** available.
Swimming instruction, arts & crafts, sports, over-nights for older children, field trips.

TREE OF LIFE CHRISTIAN ACADEMY..........(410) 761-6102

1406 B Crain Highway, Suite 102, Glen Burnie, MD 21061
Head : Janet Giles

Grades: K-12   **Enrollment**: 47 Co-ed **Faculty**: 4 full-, 1 part-time. **Average Class Size**: 15.

Special Programs: ACE; Art, Music, P.E (limited); Computer Courses; Mini Classes for Math,
Science, and Literature.

Admission: Interview of Parents and child; Overview of previous academic achievement,etc.

Tuition: (1995-96) K-8, $160/mo.; 9-12, $185/mo. (12 mo.contracts)

165

Future Plans: Expansion of student body; add more computer courses.

TRINITY CHRISTIAN SCHOOL..........(703) 273-8787 FAX (703) 591-0737

10520 Main Street, Fairfax, VA 22030
Interdenominational, 1987 **Head**: Mr. James L. Beavers

Grades: 1-8 **Enrollment**: 179 Co-ed **Faculty**: 10 full-, 4 part-time.
Average Class Size: 18

Special Courses: Latin, French, Spanish, in a Language Survey course, Grades 6-8. Art, Music, weekly; Religious Studies, req.: Bible classes daily, all grades, Chapel twice monthly.

Clubs : Some Athletic Clubs. **Publications**: Yearbook, Newsletter, Literary Magazine.

Admission: Apply after mid February. Registration fee $75. Interview required; Assessment Testing; References.

Tuition: (1995-96) $3,200. **Books**: $250-$325. *Dress Code*: Uniform req. **Financial Aid**: Some available.

Future Plans: Long range plans include the addition of High School grades; Search is underway for expanded school site.

TRUTH FOR YOUTH SCHOOL.........(301) 733-0712

41 Bryan Circle, Hagerstown, MD. 21740
Church of God (Universal). **Head**: Miss Lucille Marquiss.

Grades: K-8. **Enrollment**: 60 Co-ed. **Faculty**: 5 full-, 3 part-time.

Special Program: Traditional curriculum

Tuition: (1995-96) K, $20/mo; 1-8, $50/mo. Reduction for siblings.

VIENNA JUNIOR ACADEMY.........(703) 938-6200

340 Courthouse Road, Vienna, VA. 22180
Seventh Day Adventist 1930. **Head**: Gary D. Wilson

Grades: K-11 **Enrollment**: 115 Co-ed. **Faculty**: 5 full-time.

Special Programs: English Handbells, Choir.

Athletics: Baseball

166

Tuition: (1995-96) K, $160/mo; 1-6, $230/mo; 7-8, $235/mo; 9-10, $245/mo.; grade 11 $300/mo.; Note: All levels add a registration fee per month; K-8, $165; 9-10, $185; grade 11, $300. (Reduction for siblings).

Future Plans: Add grade 12.

WAKEFIELD SCHOOL..........(703) 364-4111 FAX (703) 364-4176

P.O. Box 107, The Plains, VA 22171
Founded 1971. **Head**: Craig Channell

Grades: Pre K-PG. **Enrollment**: 250 Co-ed.
Faculty: 32 full-, 2 part-time. **Average Class Size**: 12.

Special Courses: 6th grade Language Exploratory; Latin 7-12, French 1-12, Spanish, German 7-12, & Homeric Greek 7-12.   Math thru Calculus, Computer. Science : General Science, Biology, Chemistry and Physics. History: British, U.S., World Civilizations, Philosophy of History, Geography, Political Science, Economics, Geopolitics. Studio Art, Art History; Music Theory & Literature, Instruments. Calligraphy. AP.: French, Spanish, German, Latin, English Composition and Literature, Calculus, Biology, Physics, Chemistry. Art   Note: Trips to foreign countries, JCL convention, Model U.N. & Harvard Model Congress participants; Hiking, Nature Study, Sightseeing, & Theater opportunities. Also note: K is full day, 9 a.m.- 4 p.m..

Athletics: Req. to grade 10. Intramural & Interscholastic: Volleyball, Soccer, Basketball, Field Hockey, Skiing, Tennis. **Clubs**: Harvard Model Congress, U. VA. Model U.N.; Enviornmental Club, Jr. Classical League (highly competitive in Certamens), Drama, Art, Foreign Language Club. **Publications**: Newspaper, Literary Magazine, Science Journal, Yearbook . **Community Involvement** : Scout Troops, Adopt a Highway Program; Provide food for needy at holidays; Work with elderly residents of assisted care facility; Environmental Club. Student mentorship program for at risk students.

Plant: Library 7,000 vol.; 2 Science Labs, Art Studio; Leased facilities include auditorium and gym, playing fields, tennis courts.

Admission: SSAT, Wakefield Placement Test (March, and as needed) Transcripts, Recommendations, Interview. Note: Will not accept students expelled from other schools or those with serious learning disabilities.

Tuition: (1995-96) Day $3,400-$5,950. . Lunch: Extra   Books: $100-$250. **Transportation**: $700.   *Dress Code* Uniform req. **Financial Aid**: Available

Future Plans: To be completed by Dec. '95 a new school facility on 50 acre site 45 miles outside of Washington to include 25 classrooms, 3 science labs, a gym, 2 athletic fields and a playground..

Summer Program: 6 weeks of sports, arts, computers, and field tripts.

WALDORF SEVENTH DAY ADVENTIST SCHOOL............(301) 645-8222

11245 Berry Road, Waldorf, MD 20603
Adventist **Head**: Becky Maxwell

Grades: 1-8 **Enrollment**: 20 Co-ed

Tuition: (1995-96) Church member, $190/mo; Adventistt but non-church member, $275/mo.;
Non-adventist, $250/mo.

WASHINGTON ACADEMY.........(202) 686-5617

4301 Connecticut Avenue, N. W. (Van Ness Center, Suite 147) Washington, D.C. 20008
Founded 1981. **Head**: Dr. David Martin;   Marcel Rocca(President)

Grades: 9-13. **Enrollment**: 30 Co-ed. **Faculty**: 5 full-, 10 part-time.
Average Class Size: 5-7.

Special Courses: Latin, Ancient Greek, French, Spanish, German, ESL; U.S., British, &
World Literature; Sciience: Gen'l Science, Biology, Chemistry, Physics, Ecology. Environmental
Science; Computer Theory . History: Ancient, World, and U.S. History; History of Art.
Government; Sociology, Anthropology, Economics, Philosophy, Psychology; Speech. Note:
Accelerated Programs; Independent study; College texts used in most classes.   Concurrent
enrollment with local universities- Faculty teach college majors only. Languages taught by native
speakers.

In connection with the International Language Institute, a year round program of English and
Academic Preparation for International Students who wish to enter U. S. High Schools is also
available; usually very small classes with a high degree of personal attention.

Athletics: Not req.; Intramural Tennis, Interscholastic Soccer, Basketball, Softball. **Clubs**:
National Honor Society, Drama, Camping.   **Publications**: Newsletter, Yearbook.
Community Involvement: Community Service Program

Plant: Language Lab, Science Lab at a local college; Computer Lab.

Admission: Interview, School Visit. Biographical sketch; $50 fee with Transcripts &
Standardized Tests.

Tuition: (1995-96) $6,800 **Books**: $150. *Dress Code*: Good taste.

Future Plans   To expand facilities

WASHINGTON CHRISTIAN SCHOOL......... (301) 649- 1070

1820 Franwall Avenue, Silver Spring, MD 20902
Protestant-Interdenominational 1960   **Head**: James Koan

Grades: N3- grade 8 **Enrollment**: 275 Co-ed **Faculty**: 12 full, 10 part-time
Average Class Size: 20; (Pre-school, 15)

Special Courses: Spanish 5-8; Art, Music; Bible; Science Lab, Computer..
Extended Day and Day Care: 6:30 a.m.-6 p.m.

Athletics : P. E. Req.; Intramurals. **Clubs**: Chorus, Band

Plant: Library, Playing Fields, Science Lab.

Admission: Principal Interview. Registration fee $150; Testing.

Tuition: (1995-96) $3,550 approx. discount for siblings   *Dress Code*: Appropriate and decent.
Financial Aid: Some, partial.

WASHINGTON EPISCOPAL SCHOOL..........(301) 652-7878   FAX (301) 652-7255

5161 River Road, Bethesda, MD 20816
Episcopal 1986 **Head**: Mrs. Isabelle Schuessler

Grades: N3-grade 8. **Enrollment**: 250 Co-ed **Average Class Size**: 16; Pupil/teacher ratio 1:8

Special Courses: French N4-8, Latin: grades 5-8. Computer skills taught & used in relation to all
curriculum areas. Music, Art, Chapel. **Note**: After school Enrichment Classes in Art, Sports,
Music, Crafts, etc. **Extended Day**: until 6 p.m.

Athletics; P.E. req., After school sports program offered

Admission: Applications accepted Sept.-Feb.1 (later if space available). Testing generally
scheduled Nov.- Jan.,; Transcript & Independent School Recommendation Form; school visit
by applicant req .

Tuition: (1995-96) N3, $5,450;   N4 -grade 8, $10,500. *Dress Code*: Uniform req. grades 1-8.
Financial Aid: Based solely on financial need.

Summer Program: Summer Camps, on and off campus, ages 4-12.

WASHINGTON ETHICAL HIGH SCHOOL..........(202) 829-0088

7750 16th Street, N.W., Washington, D.C. 20012
Founded 1964 (as Eberhard School). **Head**: David Mullen.

<u>Grades</u>: 9-12. <u>Enrollment</u>: 40 Co-ed. <u>Faculty</u>: 8 full-, 6 part-time. <u>Average Class Size</u>: 6

<u>Special Courses:</u> French I, II; <u>Math</u>: Algebra, Geometry, Trig, Pre-Calculus. <u>Science</u>: Biology, Chemistry, Physics, Ecology. <u>History</u>: Contemporary Issues in Science. History and Social Science- Becoming Equal: Studies in civil Rights & The Holocaust; World Culture through Literature (English and Social Studies), Shakespeare, British Literature; Leadership; Street Law, Ethics. Remedial Reading & Math (Independent Study) Art, Crafts, Music. Advanced studies in Genre; Writing Seminar. <u>Note</u>: Untimed SAT's given to qualifying students; On site tutoring; Small classes and individual attention.

<u>Athletics</u>: Not req.; Informal Basketball & Volleyball; Involved in Washington Small Schools Association League for Interscholastic Soccer, Basketball, Softball. <u>Clubs</u>: Student Government, Fairness Committee, Yearbook, Community Action Committee. <u>Publications</u>: Literary Magazine, Newsletter, Yearbook.   <u>Community Service</u>: All-school participation in social action project to be decided on by student committee. Students & Faculty work on such topics as hunger (working in soup kitchens and/or food banks, etc.) or the environment. Assemblies often have speakers who will address the topic.

<u>Plant</u>: Campus close to Silver Spring Metro, Rock Creek Park; Science Lab, Art Studio, Computer Lab, Auditorium, Volleyball & Basketball Court.

<u>Admission</u>: Parent/Child Interview with Director, Students generally visit school for one day. Application Fee $50.

<u>Tuition</u>: (1995-96) $9,700   <u>Books</u> $50 deposit   *Dress Code*: Appropriate dress is expected. <u>Financial Aid</u>: Some Available.

WASHINGTON INTERNATIONAL SCHOOL......(202) 364-1800

3100 Macomb Street N.W., Washington, D.C. 20008
Founded 1966   <u>Head</u>: Anne-Marie Pierce

<u>Grades</u>: N-12 <u>Enrollment</u> : 655 Co-ed   <u>Faculty</u> : 67 full-, 24 part-time. <u>Average Class Size</u>: 15/16

<u>Special Courses</u>: French & Spanish immersion in N & K. Bilingual curriculum req. in 1-3; offered in 4-8. In Intermediate and Upper Schools, History, Geography, & Literature are taught from a world perspective. All Upper School students take Biology, Chemistry, & Physics. In grades 11-12, all students follow the International Baccalaureate Diploma Program, which is recognized as comparable to, if not more advanced than Honors or <u>AP</u> classes. <u>Extended Day</u> : 8 am-6 p.m. through grade 6.

<u>Athletics</u>: PE Req. to grade 10. Intramural & Interscholastic. Track, Basketball, Soccer, Softball, Volleyball, & Tennis. <u>Publications</u>: Yearbook, Newspaper, Literary Magazine. <u>Community Involvement</u> 60 hrs. of community service req. in grade 11 & 12; some involvement at younger levels.

Plant: 2 campuses(8 buildings on 7 acres); 3 Libraries, 16,000 vol.; 7 Science Labs, 2 Art Studios, Darkroom, Auditorium, Basketball Court, Playing Field.

Admission : Applicant Visit, Interview, Recommendation, Transcript; Parent Interview. No standardized testing req. but achievement testing is done at time of interview. Apply before Feb. 1.

Tuition: (1995-96) $10,150-$11,650. Bring Lunch   Books $200-$350. **Transportation**: Limited. **Financial Aid**: Available

Future Plans: New Gym/ Arts Building complex within 6 yrs.

Summer Program: Academic review on a tutorial basis when needed.   Summer Camp: Bilingual, ages 3-12. General camp activities. Summer Language Institute: French, Spanish, and ESL intensive courses for 9-12 yrs. old.

WASHINGTON-MCLAUGHLIN CHRISTIAN SCHOOL..........(301) 270-2760

6500 Poplar Avenue, Takoma Park, MD. 20912
Interdenominational 1983   **Head**: Dr. Pauline P. Washington

Grades: N-8 **Enrollment**: 160 Co-ed   **Faculty:** 15 full-time.
Average Class Size: N-20; K-6, 27.

Special Courses: Art, Music. Computer grade 2-6. Religious Studies req.
Extended Day: 7 a.m.-6 p.m.

Athletics: P.E. req. **Clubs**: Glee, Ballet.

Plant: Library, Auditorium, Playing Fields, Computers.

Admission: Interview, Transcript; Grades 3-5, California Achievement Test.

Tuition : (1995-96) $2,600 in all grades including **Extended Day**.   Books: $27-$146. *Dress Code:* Uniform req.

WASHINGTON WALDORF SCHOOL....(301) 229-6107 (Lower School)
                                                      (301) 229-1040 (High School)

4800 Sangamore Road, Bethesda, MD. 20816
Founded 1969   Faculty Directed

Grades: N-12. **Enrollment**: 310 Co-ed. **Faculty**: 27 full-,13 part-time.
Average Class Size: 26 Lower, 16 High School.

Special Courses: An international educational movement with 600 Waldorf Schools worldwide. Waldorf Schools (Rudolph Steiner Education) offer a developmental approach balancing the academic, artistic, and practical to educate the whole child. Two foreign languages in Grades 1-12; Greek, 5; Latin, 6. History includes Ancient, Medieval, Renaissance, American, Modern. Social Studies and Geography. Art is an integral part of the curriculum, 1-12, and includes Painting, Drawing, Sculpture, Woodwork, Handwork. Music, Drama, and Eurythmy (movement to speech and music) throughout. Recorder and Strings, middle and high school Orchestra and Chorus. HS Math includes Trig, Calculus, and Computer. Four years of HS Science: Biology, Chemistry, Physics, and Earth Science. HS Typing, Driver's Ed.

Athletics: Full school program. Interscholastic: Member of Potomac Valley Athletic Conference. Interscholastic: Baseball, Soccer, Basketball, Cross Country, Softball, Track and Field, Volleyball.. Hiking and Camping in both Lower and Upper School. **Publications**: Yearbook, Literary Magazine. .**Community Involvement**: Class Service Projects.

Plant: Library 10,000 vol.; Computer Lab, 2 Science Labs, 2 Art Studios, Music Room, Multi-purpose Room, Music Room, Wood Working Shop, Sewing & Crafts room, Eurythmy Room. Tennis Courts, Playing Fields.

Admission: Lower School: Parent/child Interview with appropriate class teacher; Child visits class 2-3 days. High School: Parent /child Interview with class advisors; student visits HS for 2-3 days. $35 Application fee. Transcript ; Evaluation of Math and Language Skills.

Tuition: (1995-96) N (Half-day) $3,950; N (full day)- grade 8, $7,900; 9-12, $8,200 Lunch: Bring Supply Fees: $275-$400 *Dress Code*: Clean, neat & practical. **Financial Aid**: Some Availble.

Future Plans: Build an Auditorium/ Gym.

WAY OF FAITH CHRISTIAN ACADEMY..........(703) 573-7221

8800 Arlington Boulevard., Fairfax, VA. 22031
Founded 1975. **Head**: Rev. Ellen Blackwell.

Grades: K4-12. **Enrollment**: 125 Co-ed. **Faculty**: 12 full-, 6 part-time.
Average Class Size: 12-15.

Special Courses: Spanish 9-12. Computer, Word Processor. Science: General Science, Biology, Physics; History: U.S., World, U.S. Gov't.; Religious Studies req.; Music-Vocal & Instrumental. Typing, Bookkeeping.

Athletics: Req. 1-10. Basketball, Softball, Soccer, Parallel Bars, Volleyball, Tennis. **Clubs**: Spanish. **Publications**: Yearbook, Newsletter.

Plant: Library, Science Lab, Chapel, Recording Studio, Tennis Courts, Playing Fields, Auditorium.

Admission: Parent/child Interview, $50 Registration fee. Enrollment, April lst - August 25th.

Tuition: (1995-96) Half-day K $1,300;   K-12 $2,100   <u>Books</u> per semester: K4-3 $100; grade 4-12, $150. *Dress Code:* Uniform Req. for all grades.

WESTMINSTER SCHOOL..........(703) 256-3620   FAX (703)256-9621

3819 Gallows Road, Annandale, VA. 22003
Founded 1962. **Head**: Ellis H. Glover, Jr.

Grades: K-8. **Enrollment**: 296 Co-ed.(166 Boys, 133 Girls) **Faculty**: 25 full-, 1 part-time.
Average Class Size: 13-14.

Special Courses: French K-8, Latin 6-8, Art & Music K-8, Study Skills, Drama.
Teacher-centered instruction; <u>disciplined learning environment</u>; homework; early mastery of English grammar, spelling, etc.; strong History & Classical Studies program; frequent subject related field trips, all grades, including performing arts performances.

Athletics: Req. 1-8. Interscholastic: Basketball, Soccer, Track, Softball, 6-8. **Publications**: Newsletter, Literary Magazine, Yearbook.

Plant: Library 5,000 vol., Gym/Auditorium, Playing Fields, Outdoor Basketball Court.
Note: 23 classrooms, carpeted, paneled, air-conditioned.

Admission: Placement Testing K-8, Jan.-March; Parent & child Interview. Registration new families Feb. to August. Enrollment Contract.

Tuition: (1995-96) Full-day K -grade 8, $6,100- $7,300 **Transportation**: 9 bus routes, cost varies by zone. *Dress Code:* Uniform req.

Future Plans: Little Theater building by 1997; Camp site.

Summer Program: Academic Review (Reading, English, Math, etc.) for lateral entry grades 2-7; Enrichment Courses (Science, History, Drama; French Grammar, Conversation, Culture, and Cooking) Basketball Camp, "Summer Fun Camp".

WEST NOTTINGHAM ACADEMY............(410) 658-5556   FAX (410) 658-6790

1079 Firetower Road,   Colora, Maryland 21917
Non-Denominational 1744   **Head**: Edward Baker

Grades: 9-12, PG. **Enrollment**: 115 Co-ed, 65 Boarding. **Faculty**: 32 full-, 3 part-time.
Average Class Size: N, 9-10;   K/1, 12

Special Programs: Chesapeake Learning Program for above average IQ Learninng difference students. ESL, <u>AP</u> and Honors courses. Drama.

Athletics : Competitive. **Publications**: Newspaper **Community Involvement**: Community Service programs.

Admission: Interview, 3 letters of Recommendation; Testing

Tuition: (1995-96) $17,450- $22,450   **Financial Aid** : Available

Summer Program: Field Hockey & Lacrosse Camps; Enrichment camp for K-6. ESL summer program.

WILLOWBROOK MONTESSORI SCHOOL.......... (301) 445-1563

8151 15th Avenue, Hyattsville, MD. 20783
Head: Mrs. Harvey

Ungraded: Ages 2 -9. **Enrollment**: 82 Co-ed **Faculty**: 4 full-time, 4 aides, 2 part-time aides.

Special Courses: Montessori program, Spanish, French. Creative Movement.
Extended Day: 7 a.m.-6 p.m.

Admission: Interview parent/child. Registration fee $25.

Tuition: (1995-96) N, $360/mo.; K-3, $380/mo. including   **Extended Day**

Summer Program: Ages 2-9, Arts & Crafts, Sports. **Extended Day**: 7 a.m.-6 p.m.
Fees same as above Tuition.

THE WINCHESTER SCHOOL ....(301) 598-2266

3223 Bel Pre Road, Silver Spring, MD. 20906
Founded 1970   **Head**: Mary L. Rhim

Grades: N-1 **Enrollment**:   75 Co-ed **Faculty**: 6 full-, 3 part-time. **Average Class Size**: 8-10.

Special Courses: Art, Music, Cooking, Baking. **Extended Day**: 7:30 a.m-6 p.m.

Plant: Libraries 500-800 vol.; Playing Fields.

Admission: Parent Visit, Interview. $25 Application fee. No Testing. Open to all children who are not severely handicapped, emotionally disturbed, or retarded.

Tuition: (1995-96) Half-day $350/mo.; Full-day $560/mo., (reduction for less than 5 days) includes **Extended Day** Bring Lunch

Summer Program: Organized play program with art, music, stories, water play, field trips

WOODBERRY FOREST SCHOOL...........(703) 672-3900   FAX (703) 672-0928

Woodberry Forest, VA 22989
Founded 1889   **Head**: John S. Grinalds

Grades: 9-12   **Enrollment**: 365 Boys, All Boarding.   **Faculty**: 60 full-3 part-time.
Average Class Size: 12

Special Courses: Latin, French, German, Japanese, Spanish- all I-IV.   Science : Biology,
Marine Biology, Chemistry, Physics, Physical Science: various electives include Relativity,
Physiology, Microbiology, Human Genetics, Animal Behavior, Ecology. History- Ancient,
European, U.S.-also electives including The Eisenhower Presidency, Winston Churchill & 19th
Century Engineers (both studied through biographies)., Latin American Civilization. Principles of
Business Management   and Economics. Religious Studies req. for one semester-Sunday evening
Chapel. **Art**: Painting, Drawing, Sculpture, Architectural Drawing. Music, Typing, Driver's Ed,
Drama Speech. **AP**.:History, Biology, Chemistry, Physics, English, European History, Languages,
Math, Science, Computer Science.
Note: Each year 14 Seniors spend a trimester living in Cambridgeshire, England studying British
Literature, History, Contemporary Britain and the Fine Arts.

Athletics: Req.; Intramural & Interscholastic. Football, Soccer, & Cross-Country, Indoor
Track, Basketball, Wrestling, Swimming , Diving, Squash, Outdoor Track, Baseball, Lacrosse,
Golf, Tennis. Also Weight Training, and Rapidan: an outdoor program of Kayaking, Rock-
climbing, and Conditioning on a ropes/obstacle course. **Clubs**: Chapel Council, Civil War, Choir,
Math, Model U.N., Literary Society, Outing, Rod & Gun, Science. **Publications**: Literary
Magazine, Newspaper, Yearbook. **Community Involvement**: 60 hrs. of Community Service is
req. for graduation.

Plant: Library 55,000 vol. with Audio-visual center & 3 viewing rooms; 5 Science Labs, Shop,
Art Studio, Theater, 8 Dormitories, & Computer Lab., 3 Gyms, Auditorium, 11 Playing Fields,
Both Indoor & Outdoor Pool, 3 Indoor and 14 Outdoor Tennis Courts, 1 Racquetball Court, 4
Basketball Courts, 8 Dormitories, 9 hole Golf Course, Indoor Track, 3 Squash Courts, Computer
Lab.

Admission: SSAT, Interview at school. For consideration in first round acceptances,
complete Application by Feb. 15. School seeks boys with proven academic success, desire to
learn, good character, active involvement in extra curricular activities. $50 Application fee.

Tuition: (1995-96) Boarding, $17,800. Books & Supplies : $500   *Dress Code*: Neat
attire- Long pants, collared shirt. **Financial Aid**: Available, 28% of student body receives aid.

Future Plans: Renovation of Dormitories and Classroom facilities.

Summer Program: 6 week Co-ed (boarding) Enrichment or Remediation program in major
academic fields. Courses also in Art History, Computer, ESL; Language study programs abroad
in France, Japan, Spain. Summer Camp: 4 week all sports camp, Boys 10-13. Includes weekend
field trips to nearby activities, i.e. Baltimore Orioles baseball game.

WOODBRIDGE CHRISTIAN SCHOOL............(703) 670-0200

5023 Davis Ford Road, Woodbridge, VA 22192
Head: Rev. Dean Kennedy

Grades: K3-grade 10   **Enrollment**: 240 Co-ed **Faculty**: 10 full-, 4 part-time.
Average Class Size: 21

Special Programs: French 7-9; Algebra, Geometry, Computer. General Science, Biology.
Virginia, American, & World History. Religious Studies required. Remedial Reading & Math.
Art, Music. **Extended Day**: 6 a.m.-6:30 p.m.

Athletics: Not required. Girls Volleyball & Basketball; Boys: Volleyball, Basketball, Baseball,
and Track. **Publications**: Yearbook

Plant: Gym, Auditorium, Playground, Soccer Field..

Admission: Interview, Registration fee $65.

Tuition: (1995-96) $2,440; Books : Extra **Extended Day**: Extra   *Dress Code*: Described
in handbook. **Financial Aid**: Some available

Summer Program: Remedial and advanced academic program. General recreational activity
program.

Future Plans: To add grades 11 & 12.

THE WOODS ACADEMY..........(301) 365-3080 FAX (301) 469-6439

6801 Greentree Road; Bethesda, MD. 20817
Catholic 1977. **Head**: Paul V. Boman

Grades: Montessori Pre-school ages 3-5; Traditional class-room 1-8. **Enrollment** : 220 Co-ed.
Faculty: 19 full-, 7 part-time. **Average Class Size**: 18-20

Special Courses: French K-8; Computer K-8; Kumon Math; Hands on & Lab Science 4-8;.
Drama 7-8; Fine Art, Music, Religion. **Extended Day**: 7 a.m.-6 p.m.

Athletics: P.E. req. Intramural & Interscholastic. Basketball, Field Hockey, Softball, Soccer,
Track & Field. **Clubs**: Computer Club; Cooking. **Publications**: Yearbook, Newspaper.
Community Service: Committee on Caring works closely with Student Council to heighten
their awareness and encourage helping others throughout the community.

Plant: Computerized Library 7,800 vol.; Science Lab, Garden (ties in with Science program);
Computer Lab, Art Studio, Auditorium, Gym, Playing Fields, Tennis Courts.

Admission: School visit by applicant. Testing; Recommendations.

Tuition: (1995-96) $3,950-$5,990; Reduction of $1,000 for 3rd child. **Transportation**: Available. *Dress Code*: Uniform req. **Financial Aid**: Available

WORD OF LIFE ACADEMY..........(703) 354 4222

5225 Backlick Road, Springfield, VA.22151
Head; Ralph Southerland

Grades: N-12   **Enrollment**: 300 Co-ed

Special Courses: All academic courses; Spanish I & II. Computer, Typing, Introduction to Business; Home Economics, Family Living; Art. Religious Studies. **Extended Day** 6:30 a.m. -6 p.m.

Athletics: P.E. req. Competitive (for Boys and Girls) Basketball, Soccer, Volleyball, and Cross Country.

Admission: Registration Fee $65 Pre school; $100 grades 1-12

Tuition: (1995-96) Half-day N, $260/mo.; Grades K-6, $311/mo.; Grades 7-12, $333/mo. **Note**: Reduction for siblings.   **Books and Extended Day**: Extra.

Summer Program: Day camp, N-6; Day care available. **Academic** Enrichment program 6-12.

The YESHIVA OF GREATER WASHINGTON SCHOOL.......(301) 649-6996

1216 Arcola Avenue, Silver Spring, MD.20902 (Boys)
1910 University Boulevard, West, Silver Spring, MD. 20902 (Girls)
Jewish Orthodox 1963. **Head**: Rabbi Irving Merkin.

Grades: 7-12. **Enrollment**: 271 (117 Boys, 154 Girls) Note : 40 Boarding   **Faculty**: 20 full-, 26 part-time. **Average Class Size**: 15

Special Courses: Math through Calculus; Honors: Probability & Statistics. Chemistry, Physics. Religious studies req.; Talmud, Hebrew. Critical Thinking, Typing, Drama, Music; Family Living. **AP**: English, Biology, Chemistry, Physics, Calculus, European History, American Government, Computer Science, Psychology.

Athletics: P.E. req.; Basketball, Softball teams. **Clubs**: Dance, Drama, Chorus. **Publications**: Community Newsletter, Yearbook. **Community Involvement**: Work at Hebrew Home for Aged.

Plant: Library 5000 vol., Science Lab, Art Studio, Gym, Playing Fields, Tennis Court.

Admission: Students admitted on basis of previous academic record and interviews; must come ` from Jewish religious background.

Tuition: (1995-96) grades 7-8 $5,900; grades 9-12 $7,000. **Financial Aid**: Available

Future Plans: To build new facility for girls on Norwood Road in Silver Spring.

NOTES

EDUCATIONAL SPECIALISTS

CENTER FOR APPLIED MOTIVATION, INC..................(301) 468-1200; FAX (301) 468-0708

6208 Montrose Road
Rockville, MD 20852

Director: Peter A. Spevak, Ph.D

Services: Established in 1984, the Center for Applied Motivation specializes in motivating underachievers. We are a private organization whose professional staff are licensed psychologists who work full-time at the Center. Our success in treating underachievers is based on a developmental approach which addresses the problems of underachievement psychologically. Significant improvement in both attitude and performance can be achieved as a result of this approach. In addition to our Applied Motivation program for underachievers, we offer psychological assessment, career and vocational testing, and consultation and workshops to community, school, and parent groups.

As a public service, our newsletter, Issues in Development, Education, Achievement and Success (IDEAS), is available without charge.

Offices are conveniently located in Rockville, Maryland and Annandale, Virginia.

CERTIFIED LEARNING CENTERS, INC...................(301) 774-3700

3403 Olandwood Court, Suite 102
Olney, MD 20832 (additional locations in Bethesda and Silver Spring)

Director: Patricia Marie Felton, B.S., M. Ed.*

Services: CLC operates the largest centers in the Metro area offering complete educational and psychological testing, psychotherapy, one-on-one remediation in all subjects and Scholastic Aptitude Test (SAT-I) and (PSAT) Preparation, as well as most other prep courses (i.e. LSAT, GMAT, MCAT, GRE, GED, ASVAB, ACT, etc.) Career and College Counseling, Study Skills, reading, math workshops, speed reading, ESOL, and writing classes. Through an affiliation with Indiana University's Independent Study programs, high school and college credits can be awarded for make-up at our centers. Full support for home instruction is provided to parents educating their children at home.

CLC staff consists of certified teachers, with advanced degrees in subject specialties, including learning disabilities. Services are available in the student's home, at school or in our centers. Clientele served include pre-schoolers through adult learners. Contractual arrangements are available to private and public schools for applicant screening, resource support and all services provided at the centers.

The Centers are open from 9 a.m. to 9 p.m., seven days a week. The Director is State certified at the Advanced Professional level. She has been in practice for over fifteen years.

*Patricia Marie Felton Biography B.S. Elementary Education, West Chester University, West Chester, PA (cum laude); M.Ed., Special Education and Learning Disabilities, George Mason University. MD state certification at the Advanced Professional level. LD resource and self-contained classroom teacher for Fairfax County Public Schools. Elementary school teacher for Prince George's County Public Schools. Pre-school instructor at the Accotink Academy in Springfield, VA. Established the Certified Learning Centers, Inc. in 1981.

COLLEGE BOUND...................(301) 468-6668

>6809 Breezewoood Terrace
>Rockville, MD 20852

Educational Counselor: Shirley Levin, M.A.

Services: Comprehensive college and career counseling for high school students and adults. Evaluation of academic credentials and extracurricular activities, advice on high school curriculum, summer activities, scheduling of SAT, ACH, AP, GRE, MCAT tests, etc. Assistance with all aspects of undergraduate and graduate college selection and application procedures, including planning college visits, interview preparation, essay evaluation.

Biography: B.A. (Honours), M.A., University of Toronto, Psychology; President, College Bound, Inc. 13 years; career/educational counselor, 25 years; College Programs Coordinator, Jewish Community Center. Published books: Summer on Campus: College Programs for High School Students; What to do Until the Counselor Comes , Member: NACAC, IECA, PCACAC, ACCESS, WISER Listed in Who's Who in the East.

COLLEGE PLANNING SERVICE, INC................................(301) 320-5311

>6704 Pawtucket Road
>Bethesda, MD 20817

Director: Diane E. Epstein
Associates: Adah Rose Bitterbaum
>>Ellen Brewster Ward

Services : Since 1979, we have advised over 1800 students from 160 high schools who have matriculated at over 280 colleges nationwide. In addition, we have personally visited and assessed close to 300 college campuses. Our service helps students and their families with college and graduate school preparation, selection and admission. We include help with course selection, activities, testing, summer plans, interviews, early plans, applications and essays. Data from CPS's own extensive database aids in predicting admission to hundreds of colleges and graduate schools.

Biography : B.A., George Washington University, 1956; Certificate of Clinical Competence, American-Speech-Language-Hearing Association; PTSA President, Walt Whitman High School, Montgomery County, MD; Director, College Planning Service, Inc. since 1979. Member: IECA; PCACAC; WISER; ACCESS.

SUSAN SAMUELS DRANITZKE............(202) 544-5222

   124 12th Street, S. E.
   Washington, D. C. 20003

Educational Counselor and Psychotherapist: Susan Dranitzke, M. Ed., M.S.W.

Services Educational Counseling for parents and children, problem solving for children with social, emotional, or learning difficulties: school or grade placement consultations for students in independent or public schools, D.C., MD., and VA; ages served: nursery, elementary, high school, day or boarding, special education,-LD/ED offices in D.C. and McLean.

Biography: B.A. Sarah Lawrence College; M. Ed. University of Maryland; M.S.W. at Catholic University. Licensed Clinical Social Worker in D.C., MD, and VA. Twenty- five years experience as an educator and counselor. Director Resources For Children since 1980. Previously Special Education Counselor, Dominion Day School; teacher at Yale Child Study Center and Capitol Hill Day School. Past President (1984) of Parents Council of Washington; founding member ACCESS (Association of Counselors and Consultants for Educational Support and Services.

ELEANOR B. DUNLAP, M.Ed. ....(703) 528-3528

   740 N. Vermont Street,
   Arlington, VA 22203

Reading Specialist

Services: Diagnostic testing. Tutoring in language/reading skills (word recognition, comprehension and rate, composition, spelling and study skills). Students: all ability levels. Ages 5-adult. Emphasis on student's application of skills to school texts and to books of appropriate interest/reading levels. Consultations with parents and teachers when necessary.

Biography: B.A. University of North Carolina. M.Ed. in field of reading, The George Washington University. 13 years experience as classroom teacher. Previously part-time Reading Specialist at G.W.U. Reading Center. Private practice as a Reading Specialist since 1980

EDUCATIONAL AND GUARDIANSHIP SERVICES..................(301) 530-6944

   P.O. Box 2561
   Rockville, MD 20847

Founder: Jeanette Simpson, M.Ed., Ed. S.

Educational and Guardianship Services provide counseling by professionals who have extensive knowledge of the U. S. educational system and are experienced in working with foreign students and diplomate families. These professionals are committed to provide the best possible academic guidance and personal counseling to students of all ages and backgrounds.
E&GS is ably headed by Mrs. Jeanette Simpson. She has nearly twenty years of experience as an

Academic Counselor for private and public primary, secondary, and college level students. She has worked extensively with foreign students studying at U. S. institutions and has a comprehensive knowledge of the financial aid programs available for all age groups in the U. S. and abroad. Her other experiences include working for international organizations in the U. S., the United Kingdom, and the Middle East.

EDUCATIONAL GUIDANCE SERVICE...................(301) 469-6973

> 9213 Farnsworth Drive
> Potomac, MD 20854

Director: Virginia Vogel

Educational Guidance Service was founded to assist students and parents in their search for an appropriate school or college choice. Our counseling process begins with an evaluation of the student's developmental and academic needs, leading to a presentation of selected school or college programs. Assistance is given with interviewing skills, application materials, and curriculum decisions.

Virginia Vogel, Ed.S. presents a background of extensive graduate work in counseling with higher education administration. She is a former admissions counselor at the N.Y.U. Graduate Business School and was Director of Guidance and College Counseling at Georgetown Visitation Preparatory School for ten years. A member of National Association of College Admissions Counselors and the Independent Educational Consultants Association, Virginia Vogel was a board member and past treasurer of IECA.

JANE ERVIN, P.P.D., Ed.D. ....(202) 337-1132

> 3604 Fulton Street, N. W.
> Washington, D. C. 20007

Dr. Ervin has practiced in Washington, D. C. for over 20 years. She is particularly known for her concentrated programs for children with learning problems. As well as tutoring, she does educational testing and counseling for parents and children.

Jane Ervin also teaches study skills and reading comprehension courses to small groups based on her books published by Scholastic and Educators Publishing Service, which are used in schools throughout the nation.

Jane Ervin has authored over twenty educational books for children, parents, and teachers. She has appeared on television and radio and is a popular speaker at a wide variety of parent, teacher, librarian and volunteer groups. She received a post doctorate diploma and doctorate in education from U.C.L.A.

GERALDINE C. FRYER, I.E.C.A. ....(202) 333-3230

> Suite 42
> 5125 MacArthur Blvd.
> Washington, D. C. 20016-3300

Geraldine C. Fryer is an Educational Advisor, formerly associated with Ethna Hopper Associates. She is nationally recognized for her expertise in college and graduate school advising, especially in the field of Learning Differences. Her primary goal is to determine with the students and their families, what is in their best educational interests so that the proper criteria for selecting appropriate schools can be established. Mrs. Fryer has found over the years that if this selection is done thoughtfully and carefully the process becomes a pleasant and rewarding experience for all concerned.

Geraldine C. Fryer received her B.A. from Brown University in 1960; has graduate credits in History and Guidance and Counseling from New York University; and taught in New York City. She has been in private practice since 1982 and has successfully counseled more than 1,000 students.

RUTH C. HEITIN, Ph.D....................(703) 519-7181

> Educational Consulting Services of Northern Virginia
> 100 West Howell Avenue
> Alexandria, VA 22301

Dr. Heitin has more than 20 years experience as a teacher and/or administrator in educational settings ranging from the preschool to the university level. Her hands-on approach includes holding certification as a regular and special education teacher in elementary and middle schools and as an Elementary Principal in Virginia. Dr. Heitin is also proficient in sign language. (PSE)

Dr. Heitin is an enthusiastic and powerful advocate for the educational rights of all children. Her practice includes psychoeducational assessment, support for identification of Attention-Deficit Disorder, diagnosis of learning disabilities, support for the Gifted/Learning Disabled student, advocacy, and assistance in the special education process.

ETHNA HOPPER ASSOCIATES.....(202) 333-3530;   Fax (202) 333-3212
                                                           E-M ethna.hopper@his.com
> 4725 MacArthur Boulevard N.W.
> Washington, D.C. 20007-1904

<u>Director</u>: Ethna Hopper

Ethna Hopper has worked in the education field for thirty years, as a counselor, special education teacher and, since 1979, as an independent educational counselor. She has helped thousands of families through the maze of public and private school options by providing common-sense guidance on issues relating to learning and emotional needs.

Ethna Hopper Associates works with local families seeking a school change, and national or international families relocating to the area. Working with schools--academic, therapeutic, special--all over the country and around the world, our consultants simplify the admissions process; we act as the child's advocate to the school.

Our hourly fee structure allows clients to determine how much help they want. We find that this approach enables families to have access to the information and experience they feel they need, but lets them control the amount they wish to spend.

Ethna Hopper, a member of the Independent Educational Consultants Association, is one of the three co-founders of WISER (Washington Independent Services for Educational Resources). She is on the board of the Family Support Center.

GEORGIA K. IRVIN AND ASSOCIATES, INC...................(301) 951-0131 FAX (301)951-1024

4701 Willard Avenue, Suite 227
Chevy Chase, MD 20815

Director: Georgia K. Irvin

Georgia K. Irvin is nationally recognized for her personal knowledge of a broad range of schools that can meet unique needs of children entering nursery through post-graduate high school in day schools in the greater Washington area and boarding schools nationwide. Believing that understanding a child's strength interests and learning style is the key to selecting a school where the child will flourish, we meet with both the child and the parents before making specific recommendations. We work with local families, those moving into the area, and families from all over the country and abroad who are seeking boarding schools. Hallmarks of the firm are personal involvement with each child, commitment to each family and close personal contact with admissions officers.

Georgia Irvin was Director of Admissions and Financial Aid at the Sidwell Friends School for 15 years. She has served on the faculty of the National Association of Independent Schools Workshop for Admissions Officers, held membership on numerous local and national boards and committees, including the Secondary School Admission Test Board (SSATB). In 1988, she received the SSATB's prestigious Bretnall Award for her exemplary contributions to independent school admission. A brochure is available that describes the types of services, including a telephone consultation for those unable to travel to Washington. (see ad at back of book)

J. MICHAEL KIRCHBERG, M.A. ....(202) 244-4017

Tutorial Service
4545 42nd Street, N.W., Suite 212
Washington, D. C. 20016

Services: Diagnosis, remediation and routine instruction-particularly with long-term learning problems, including poor study skills, motivation problems and low self-esteem; English language and literature (reading and writing); math (through advanced algebra/pre-calculus), thinking skills and various learning skills; thesis/dissertation organization, writing and editing; consultation and evaluation regarding classroom instruction; SSAT, PSAT, SAT, GRE, GED, Achievement Test preparation for adolescents and adults.

Biography: B.S., U.S. Naval Academy; M.A., Oxford University (Rhodes Scholarship); M.A., University of Maryland. Teacher, Georgetown Day School, grades 7-12, 1971-1987, English, Social Studies, Learning Skills, Math. Private practice tutorial work: 1977 to present.

JANET S. LEE-THORP...........................(703) 893-9036

> Prospect Hill School
> 8546 Old Dominion Drive
> McLean, VA 22102

Janet Lee-Thorp is an academic therapist specializing in Learning Disabilities, Math and Science. She performs tutorial services in all these areas (math through calculus), K-adult, as well as in writing skills, handwriting, study skills, SAT and Achievement prep. She is available for school consultations upon request. She is trained as an Orton-Gillingham therapist and has been in private practice for 35 years.

PATRICIA S. LEMER...................(301) 654-0944

> 6701 Fairfax Road
> Chevy Chase, MD 20815

Educational Diagnostician: Patricia S. Lemer, M.Ed.

Patricia S. Lemer is an Educational Diagnostician who evaluates a child's aptitudes and achievement, and makes specific recommendations for instruction. Using a developmental, multi-disciplinary approach, she helps parents identify remediation most appropriate for a child experiencing academic difficulty. She also assists in locating appropriate educational alternatives if a school change is indicated.

As a consultant to many area independent schools, where she also does admissions testing, Ms. Lemer is familiar with the needs of students from nursery age through high school.

As a parent-child advocate, she also works with families who need assistance in obtaining special education services from their public schools.

PAUL K. PENNIMAN.....................(202) 364-4263

> 3522 Davenport Street, N. W.
> Washington, D.C. 20008

Mathematics Tutor : Paul K. Penniman

Paul K. Penniman is a mathematics tutor who has fifteen years of experience in mathematics instruction primarily at the secondary school level. A former chairman of the mathematics department at the Edmund Burke School, he is familiar with all kinds of mathematics curriculum and all kinds of styles of teaching and learning mathematics. His tutoring experience ranges from the severely disabled to the highly able, from elementary students to college students and adults. He is the author of the forthcoming Beyond Innumeracy: How to Solve the Problem in the Math Classroom.

Mr. Penniman received his B.A. in mathematical sciences and his B.A, in psychology from Johns Hopkins University in 1978. He is a member of the National Council of Teachers of Mathematics and the Independent Schools Mathematical Association of Washington. In 1983, he helped found the Computer Association of Independent Schools.

RIDLEY & FILL SPEECH & LANGUAGE ASSOCIATES, Chartered.....(301) 652-8997

4909 Hampden Lane, Suite 1
Bethesda, MD 20814

Ridley & Fill is a group practice of speech-language pathologists. Services are provided to children of all ages, and include diagnostic evaluation of speech-language problems, individual and group therapy, as well as other services. Ridley & Fill is known for its innovative treatment approaches, such as ultrasound for resistant articulation disorders, and classroom collaboration and intervention for the language learning disabled child.

Ridley & Fill has affiliations with a number of private schools, including Sidwell Friends School, The Lowell School, and Kingsbury Day School as well as with professionals in other disciplines.

JANE RONINGEN, M.A......................................(703) 920-6727

Educational Diagnostician and Tutor
4707 South 9th Street
Arlington, VA 22204

Services: Diagnostic Educational Evaluations including cognitive, perceptual, and academic testing for persons aged six through adult.

Tutoring: In reading, written language, keyboarding, and math for students (adults, too) working at first through sixth grade levels. Modified Orton-Gillingham method often used in language arts tutoring.

Biography: M.A. in Learning Disabilities from Columbia University Teachers College. Thirty-five hours beyond M.A. in educational assessment and the teaching of reading. Certified in Virginia as Reading Specialist and Learning Disability teacher. Educational Diagnostician in private practice for 9 years. Private tutor, 22 years.

LAURA SOLOMON, Ed. D......................(301) 495-0046

Metropolitan Building
8720 Georgia Avenue, 7th floor
Silver Spring, MD 20910

Special Education Consultant

Dr. Solomon has been working with children and families for over twenty years. She specializes in school placement and diagnostic evaluation for children birth through high school, development of individual education plans (IEP) , and consultation to parents and schools in the areas of social-emotional development, behavior management, curricular modifications, and instructional strategies.

SPECIFIC DIAGNOSTIC STUDIES, INC....(301) 468-6616

11600 Nebel Street, Suite 130
Rockville, MD. 20852

Director: Lynn O'Brien, Ph.D

Specific Diagnostics is a full educational service for pre-school through adult; testing, admission testing for area independent schools, tutoring, study skills, S.A.T. Prep. Founded in 1973 for the learning disabled, growth has expanded to assisting the under-achieving, different learning style-student. The nationally recognized SOS, Strengthening of Skills, study skills program teaches strategies in: listening, note taking, memory, time management, and test taking. SOS is given in the Rockville office throughout the school year as well as at numerous independent schools during the summer.

Specific Diagnostics has an experienced staff of 50 qualified educators and psychologists to meet the academic needs of all students.

RUTH SPODAK & ASSOCIATES....................(301) 770-7507   FAX (301) 770-3576

6155 Executive Boulevard
Rockville, MD 20852

Director: Ruth B. Spodak, Ph.D.

Services: A multidisciplinary team of professionals offering comprehensive psychological and educational evaluations to diagnose learning disabilities and Attention Deficit Disorder. Clients receive a full written report and consultation providing academic modifications, therapeutic intervention and/or recommendations for school placement. We also include referral to highly trained specialists and academic therapists for additional support as needed.

Counseling is available for individuals and families to help in understanding and addressing learning disabilities within the school and family. Particular specialization with Gifted/Learning Disabled individuals. Serving pre-school children through adults.

Our tutors have expertise in a variety of methods, including the Stevenson Language Skills Program, the Orton-Gillingham method and the University of Kansas Learning Strategies. Tutoring services include: reading, written language, math, study and organizational skills, cognitive strategy training and word processing skill. Tutoring is available at the client's home , school or our Silver Spring office.

TREATMENT and LEARNING CENTERS......................(301) 424-5200

9975 Medical Center Drive
Rockville, MD 20850

Contact: Patricia Ritter, Ph.D., CCC-SLP
Assistant Executive Director

<u>Services</u>: LTC offers comprehensive psychoeducational diagnostic evaluations and provides a variety of solutions for students with special learning needs. Working one-to-one with experienced tutors, students may improve reading, mathematics, written language and study skills. Speech and language therapy, counseling, and occupational therapy are also offered at TLC, using an interdisciplinary team approach to coordinate all services.

TRUST TUTORING.....................(301) 589-0733 or (703) 370-9392, in VA

    912 Thayer Avenue, # 205
    Silver Spring, MD 20910

<u>Director</u>: Lee Harvis

TRUST TUTORING was founded in 1992 to provide in-home tutoring instruction for any age or subject. We serve the entire Washington, D. C. metropolitan area with local evaluators, supervisors and tutors in each geographical area. We have a <u>structured, supervised</u> program which is individually designed for each student. Every student is initially evaluated for skill level ability and to find out the specific needs of the situation. A qualified tutor is then assigned to work under the direction of a supervisor- to implement the program determined at the evaluation.

Our primary concern in every tutoring assignment is long-term learning ability, so we emphasize <u>study skill</u> development and a <u>positive learning experience.</u> Tutors follow our routines to establish with the student a regular, daily study and learning in the specific subject area. In "reading" assignments, the tutors administer a special evaluation of "phonics" skills, and then re-tests periodically to measure progress. Special materials may be recommended to enhance the value of each program.

FRANCES TURNER LTD. ....(301) 299- 2012   FAX (301) 299-9404

    11137 Hurdle Hill Drive   35 Wisconsin Circle, Suite 560
    Potomac, MD 20854   Chevy Chase, MD 20815

<u>Director</u>: Frances Turner, M. Ed., Educational Consultant

<u>Services</u>: Frances Turner offers experienced, personalized, educational consulting services built around the philosophy that the student be thoroughly involved in the process and the primary focus of the school selection decision. She provides educational guidance to parents seeking advice about appropriate schools that meet the academic, emotional and social needs of their children in grades Pre-K through High school in public/private day or boarding schools. Educational services provide consultations with parents and schools, screening for readiness, achievement testing, presentations to parent groups, classroom observations and specific recommendations about suitable schools procedures for admissions.

<u>Biography</u> Frances Turner has a Masters Degree in Education and Reading and has dedicated over 25 years to educating young people in public and private schools in New York and Maryland. She was former Assistant Head/Director of Admissions, Dean of Students and Reading Specialist at McLean School, Potomac, Maryland for 10 years. Frances has served on AIMS admissions workshops and been guest speaker for numerous school/parent organizations. She is currently a member of the Advisory Board of the Bender-Dosik Parenting Center.

TUTORING FOR SUCCESS............(703) 242-8616

    3131 Valentino Court
    Oakton, VA 22124

Director: Cheryl Feuer

TUTORING FOR SUCCESS offers one-to-one tutoring for any age or subject at student's homes. All of the tutors are experienced and hold bachelors degrees, and many hold higher level degrees; several tutors teach students with special needs such as LD or ADD. We match every student with the most qualified tutor in that area. Tutoring is tailored to meet the needs of each student and adjust to the student's unique learning style. Monthly evaluations are furnished to track the student's progress. The director offers free consultations. We service the Washington metro area.

WAKE, KENDALL, SPRINGER, ISENMAN & ASSOCIATES......(202) 686-7699

    5247 Wisconsin Avenue N. W., Suite 4
    Washington, D. C. 20015

Wake, Kendall, Springer, Isenman, & Associates provides a full range of educational and psychological services to individuals and schools throughout the Washington Metropolitan area. These include assessment, counseling, school admissions testing, and school consultation for clients ranging from pre-school age to adult. All services are individualized to meet specific needs and are performed by licensed psychologists and experienced educational diagnosticians.

GAIL WISE, M.Ed...(301) 262-2868

    14300 Gallant Fox Lane, Suite 211
    Bowie, MD 20715

Educational Specialist: Gail Wise, M. Ed

Services: Educational assessments, remediation, parent counseling, school consultations, and treatment of learning disabled child, adolescent, and adult.

Biography: Gail Wise, M.Ed., is an educational specialist who received her undergraduate training at Adelphi University and completed her M.Ed. at Bowie State University. Mrs. Wise holds advanced professional certification from the Maryland State Department of Education.

Mrs. Wise has been a classroom teacher in Baltimore and Prince George's Counties. She served as a math demonstration teacher and as a reading specialist on the elementary and secondary levels in Prince George's County. Prior to entering private practice, she initiated and directed the Learning Disability Service for the Comprehensive Health Care Program at Children's Hospital National Medical Center in Washington, D.C.

INDEX

INDEX KEY For SCHOOLS

+..........Extended Day or Day Care
*..........Ungraded
b..........Boarding
&..........LD/ED
x..........Grades to be added

N.W. Washington, D.C.

	Name	Address	Grades	Sex	Page
+	Academic Enrichment Center	Georgia Avenue	N-8	C	1
+	Aidan Montessori	Military Rd.	N-6*	C	2
+	Annunciation School	Klingle Pl.	K-8	C	5
+	Beauvoir	Woodley Rd.	N-3	C	11
+	Blessed Sacrement	Chevy Chase Pkwy	K-8	C	17
+	Cadence Episcopal	Piney Branch Rd.	N-2	C	23
✗	Edmund Burke	Upton Street	6-12	C	43
	Emerson Prep	18th Street	9-PG	C	45
✗	Field School	Wyoming Ave.	7-12	C	52
+	Georgetown Day	MacArthur Blvd.	N-8	C	62
		✗ Davenport St	9-12	C	62
	Georgetown Visitation	✗ 35th Street	9-12	G	64
	Gonzaga	Eye Street	9-12	B	67
+	Holy Redeemer	New Jersey Ave.	K-8	C	84
+&	Holy Trinity	36th Street	N-8	C	86
+&	Ideal School of Washington	Gallatin St.	N-6	C	86
+	Immaculate Conception	N Street	N-6	C	87
+	Jewish Primary Day	Quebec St.	K-5	C	89
+&	Kingsbury Day	Bancroft Pl.	K-5	C	93
&	Lab School	✗ Reservoir Rd.	K-12*	C	93
+	Lowell School	16th & Kennedy	N-3	C	101
b&	MacArthur School	✗ MacArthur Blvd	1-12	C	101
+	Maret	✗ Cathedral Ave.	K-12	C	103
+	Mater Amoris	Ellicott St.	N-6*	C	105

N.W. Washington, D.C. (continued)

	Name	Address	Grades	Sex	Page
+	National Cathedral	Wisconsin Ave.	4-12	G	111
+	National Presbyterian	Nebraska Ave.	N-6	C	113
+	Nationhouse Watoto	Park Road	N-12	C	113
+	Nativity Catholic Academy	Georgia Ave.	N-8	C	114
	Oakcrest	Yuma St	7-12	G	119
+	Our Lady of Victory	Whitehaven Pkwy.	N-8	C	124
+	Owl Schools	16th Street	N-6	C	126
	Parkmont	16th Street	6-12*	C	126
+	Rock Creek Intern'l School	California St.	N-4x	C	134
+	Roots Activity	N. Capitol St	N-8	C	134
+	Sacred Heart	Park Road	N-8	C	135
+b	St.Albans	Wisc. & Mass Ave.	4-12	B	135
+	St. Ann's Academy	Wisconsin Ave	N-8	C	137
+	St. Augustine	V Street	N-8	C	139
+	St. Gabriel's	Webster St.	K-8	C	143
	St. John's College H.S.	Military Rd.	7-12	C	144
+	St. Patrick's Episcopal	Whitehaven Pkwy.	N-6	C	149
+	Sheridan	36th Street	K-8	C	155
	Sidwell Friends (Mid/Upper)	Wisconsin Ave	5-12	C	155
	Washington Academy	Connecticut Ave.	9-PG	C	168
✗	Washington Ethical Society	16th Street.	9-12	C	169
+	Washington International	Macomb St.	N-12	C	170

N.E. Washington, D. C.

	Archbishop Carroll	Harewood Rd.	9-12	C	6
+	Holy Name	West Virginia Ave.	N-8	C	84
+	Jewels of Ann	Bunker Hill Rd.	N-6	C	89
+	Nannie Helen Burroughs	50th Street	N-6	C	111
	St. Anselm's Abbey	S. Dakota Ave.	6-12	B	138
+	St. Anthony	12th & Lawrence	K-8	C	139
+	St. Benedict the Moor	21st. Street	K-8	C	140
+	St. Francis de Sales	Rhode Island Ave.	K-8	C	142

S.E. Washington, D.C.

	Name	Address	Grades	Sex	Page
+	Assumption School	High View Place	N-8	C	8
+	Capitol Hill Day	S. Carolina Ave.	N-8	C	26
+	Dupont Park School	Alabama Ave.	N-10	C	42
+	Holy Comforter-St. Cyprian's	E. Capitol St	N-8	C	83
+	Little People's Paradise	15th Street	N-6	C	99
+	Naylor Road School	Naylor Rd	N-6	C	114
+	Our Lady of Perpetual Help	V Street	K-4	C	124
		Morris Rd.	5-8	C	124
+&	Our Lady Queen of Peace	Ely Place	N-8	C	125
+	St. Francis Xavier	O Street	K-8	C	143
+	St. Peter's Interparish School	3d Street	N-8	C	150
+	St. Thomas Moor	4th Street	N-8	C	152
+	Sr. Clara Muhammed	M. Luth. King Jr.Ave.	N-9x	C	157

Montgomery County, Maryland

	Name	Address	Grades	Sex	Page
	Acad. of the Holy Cross	Kensington	9-12	G	1
+	Barnesville School	Barnesville	N-7x	C	9
+	Barrie Day School	Silver Spring	N-12	C	10
	Bullis School	Potomac	3-12	C	21
+	Butler School	Darnestown	N-8	C	22
+	Calvary Lutheran	Silver Spring	K-6	C	23
	Chas. E. Smith Jewish Day	Rockville	K-12	C	27
? &	Chelsea School	Silver Spring	1-12	C	29
+	Children's Learning Center	Rockville	N-5	C	32
+	Christ Episcopal	Rockville	N-8	C	33
	Concord Hill	Chevy Chase	N-3	C	37
?	Connelly School,Holy Child	Potomac	6-12	G	39
	Ets Chaiyim	Rockville	N-8	C	47
+	Evergreen Montessori	Kensington	N-6*	C	48
	Flower Hill Country Day	Gaithersburg	N-2	C	54
	Forcey Christian	Silver Spring	N-6	C	54
&	Foundation School	Rockville	K-12	C	55
	French International	Bethesda	N-13	C	58
&	Frost School	Rockville	7-12	C	59

	Name	Address	Grades	Sex	Page
+	Gaithersburg Int'l Montessori	Gaithersburg	N-1*	C	60
b	Georgetown Prep.	N. Bethesda	9-12	B	63
	German School	Potomac	K-13	C	64
	Good Counsel H.S.	Wheaton	9-12	C	67
+	Grace Episcopal Day	Silver Spring	N-K	C	70
		Kensington	1-6	C	70
	Green Acres	Rockville	N-8	C	71
+	Hadley Acres	Gaithersburg	K-8	C	73
+	Harbor School	Bethesda	N-2	C	74
+	Hebrew Academy	Silver Spring	N-12	C	76
+	Hebrew Day Institute	Rockville	N-6	C	76
+	Hebrew Day/Mtgy County	Silver Spring	K-6	C	77
	The Heights	Potomac	3-12	B	77
+	Hellenic American Acad.	Potomac	N-5	C	78
+	Holton Arms	Bethesda	3-12	G	82
+	Holy Cross Elementary	Garret Park	K-8	C	83
+	Holy Redeemer	Kensington	K-8	C	84
+	John N. Andrews	Takoma Park	N-8	C	90
+	Julia Brown Montessori	Silver Spring	N-3	C	91
	Landon	Bethesda	3-12	B	94
+	Lone Oak Montessori	Bethesda	N-6*	C	99
+	Maharishi School	Wheaton	N-6	C	102
+	Manor Montessori	Potomac/Rockville	N-3*	C	103
+	Mater Amoris	Ashton	N-6*	C	105
	Mater Dei	Bethesda	1-8	B	105
&	McLean School	Potomac	K-9	C	106
+	Montrose Christian	Rockville	K-12	C	110
	Muslim Community School	Potomac	N-9	C	110
+	Newport Preparatory	Kensington	N-12	C	116
+	Norwood	Bethesda	K-6	C	117
+	Oneness Family School	Chevy Chase	N-6	C	123
	Primary Day	Bethesda	N-2	C	130
	Puritan Christian	Laytonsville	N-12	C	131
	St. Andrew's Episcopal	Bethesda	6-12	C	136

Montgomery County, Maryland (continued)

	Name	Address	Grade	Sex	Page
+	St. Bartholomew's	Bethesda	K-8	C	140
+	St. Francis Episcopal	Potomac	N-5	C	142
+	St. John's Episcopal	Olney	K-8	C	145
+	St. Peter School	Olney	K-8	C	150
+b	Sandy Spring Friends	Sandy Spring	N-12	C	153
+	Sidwell Friends (Lower)	Bethesda	K-4	C	155
	Silver Spring Christian	Silver Spring	9-12	C	156
+	Sligo Adventist	Takoma Park	N-8	C	157
+	Spencerville Jr. Acad	Silver Spring	K-10	C	158
	Stone Ridge	Bethesda	N-12	G	159
&	Takoma Academy	Takoma Park	9-12	C	161
&	Thomas (Katherine G.)	Rockville	N-5	C	163
	Thornton Friends	Silver Spring	6-PG*	C	164
+	Torah	Silver Spring	K-6	C	165
+	Washington Christian	Silver Spring	N-8	C	169
+	Washington Episcopal	Bethesda	N-8	C	169
+	Wash. McLaughlin Christ.	Takoma Park	N-8	C	171
(k)	Washington Waldorf ? ?	Bethesda	N-12	C	171
+	Winchester School	Silver Spring	N-1	C	174
+	Woods Academy	Bethesda	N-8	C	176
b	Yeshiva High	Silver Spring	7-12	B/G	177

Prince Georges County, Maryland

+	Ascension Lutheran	Landover Hills	N-8	C	8
+	Beddow School	Ft. Washington	N-8*	C	11
+	Beltsville Adventist	Beltsville	K-8	C	12
	Berwyn Baptist	College Park	N-6	C	12
+	Bethel Bible Christian	Camp Springs	N-9x	C	12
	Bishop McNamara	Forestville	9-12	C	16
	Bowie Montessori	Bowie	N-6*	C	18
	Canterbury School	Accokeek	7-12	C	25
+&	Capitol Christian	Upper Marlboro	N-12	C	26
	Christian Family Montessori	Mt. Rainier	N-4*	C	35

Prince Georges County, Maryland (continued)

	Name	Address	Grades	Sex	Page
+	Clinton Christian	Upper Marlboro	N-12	C	35
+	Concordia Lutheran	Hyattsville	N-8	C	37
+	Cornerstone Christian Acad	Bowie	N-8	C	39.
	DeMatha High	Hyattsville	9-12	B	40
+	Divine Peace Lutheran	Largo	1-8	C	41
	Elizabeth Seton	Bladensburg	9-12	G	45
+	First Baptist School	Laurel	N-6	C	53
+	Freedom Christian	Forestville	N-12	C	58
+	Friends Community School	College Park	K-6	C	59
+&	Grace Brethern	Clinton	N-12	C	69
	Grace Christian	Bowie	K-8	C	69
+&	Henson Valley	Temple Hills	N-6*	C	78
+	Holy Family	Hillcrest Heights	N-8	C	83
+	Holy Trinity Episcopal	Bowie	K-8	C	85
+	Hope Christian Acad.	College Park	N-6	C	86
+	Independent Baptist	Clinton	K-12	C	88
+	Julia Brown Montessori	Laurel	N-3	C	91
+	Lanham Christian	Lanham	K-l2	C	96
+	Laurel Baptist	Laurel	K-12	C	96
+	Montessori Children's	Bowie	N-8*	C	107
+	Mount Calvary	Forestville	K-8	C	110
+	Nat'l Christian Acad.	Ft. Washington	N-12	C	112
+	New City Montessori	Hyattsville	N-5*	C	115
+	New Hope Acad.	Landover Hills	N-8	C	115
+	Our Lady of Sorrows	Takoma Park	N-8	C	124
	Our Saviors' School	Forestville	N-6	C	125
+	Paint Branch Montessori	Adelphi	N-6*	C	126
+	Potomac Heights Christian	Indian Head	N-8*	C	128
+	Queen Anne	Upper Marlboro	6-12	C	131
+	Riverdale Baptist	Upper Marlboro	N-12	C	133
+	St. Ambrose	Cheverly	K-8	C	136
+	St. Bernard's	Riverdale	K-8	C	140
	St. Hugh's	Greenbelt	K-8	C	143
+	St. Joseph's	Beltsville	K-8	C	146

Prince George's County, Maryland (continued)

	Name	Address	Grades	Sex	Page
+	St. Mary's Star of Sea	Indianhead	K-8	C	149
	St. Vincent Palloti	Laurel	9-12	C	152
	Silver Spring Christian	Hyattsville	9-12	C	156
+	Willowbrook Montessori	Hyattsville	N-4*	C	174

Anne Arundel & Howard Counties, Maryland

	Name	Address	Grades	Sex	Page
+	Aleph-Bet Jewish Day	Annapolis	K-5	C	3
+&	Annapolis Area Christian	Annapolis	K-12	C	4
+	Antioch Christian	Arnold	N-12	C	5
	Archbishop Spalding	Severn	9-12	C	7
+	Arnold Christian Acad.	Arnold	N-6	C	8
+	Atholton Adventist	Columbia	N-8	C	9
+	Bethel Christian Acad.	Savage	N-8x	C	13
+	Book of Life Academy	Annapolis	N-12	C	18
+	Calvary Baptist	Glen Burnie	N-12	C	23
+	Chesapeake Academy	Arnold	N-5	C	31
+	Chesapeake Montessori	Annapolis	N-5*	C	31
	Columbia Academy	Columbia	K-4x	C	37
+	Gibson Island School	Pasadena	K-5	C	65
	Glenelg School	Glenelg	K-12	C	66
+	Granite Baptist Church	Glen Burnie	K-12	C	71
&	Harbour School	Annapolis	N-12	C	74
	Holy Spirit Lutheran	Severn	6-8	C	85
+&	Indian Creek	Crownsville	N-8	C	88
+	Key School	Annapolis	N-12	C	92
	Lake Shore Christian	Pasadena	N-12	C	94
+	Love of Learning Montessori	Columbia	N-6*	C	100
	Martin Barr Adventist	Gambrills	K-8	C	104
+	Montess. Int. Children's House	Annapolis	N-5*	C	108
+	Odenton Christian	Odenton	N-12	C	121
	Old Mill Christian Acad.	Millersville	N-12	C	122
+	Open Door Christian	Hanover	N-7	C	123
+	St. Andrews Elementary	Edgewater	N-5	C	136

Anne Arundel & Howard Counties, Marylland (con't)

	Name	Address	Grades	Sex	Page
+	St. John Evangelist	Severna Park	N-8	C	146
+	St. Martin's Lutheran	Annapolis	N-6	C	148
+	St. Mary's School	Annapolis	K-12	C	149
	Severn School	Severna Park	6-12	C	154
+&	Summit School	Edgewater	1-8	C	160
	Tree of Life Christian Acad.	Glen Burnie	K-12	C	165

Frederick & Hagerstown, Maryland

+	Banner School	Frederick	K-8	C	9
+	Broadfording Christian	Hagerstown	N-12	C	19
	Frederick Acad. Visitation	Frederick	N-8	G	57
+	Frederick Christian	Frederick	N-12	C	57
+	Frederick Adventist	Frederick	K-8	C	58
+	Grace Academy	Hagerstown	K-12	C	68
&	Heritage Academy	Hagerstown	N-12	C	79
+b	Highland View	Hagerstown	9-12	C	80
	New Life Christian	Frederick	K-12	C	115
	St. John's Literary	Frederick	9-12	C	145
	St. Maria Goretti	Hagerstown	9-12	C	147
	Truth for Youth	Hagerstown	K-8	C	166

Alexandria, Virginia

+&	Alex. Country Day	Russell Rd.	K-8	C	4
+	Aquinas Montessori	Mt. Vernon Hwy.	N-6*	C	6
	Bishop Ireton	Cambridge Rd.	9-12	C	15
+	Brentwood Academy	Nalls Rd.	N-3	C	18
+	Browne Academy	Telegraph Rd.	N-8	C	20
+	Burgundy Farm	Burgundy Rd.	N-8	C	21
+	Calvary Road Christian	Beulah St.	N-8	C	24
+	Christian Center	Franconia Rd.	N-6	C	34
&	Different Drum	Telegraph Rd.	8-12*	C	41
+	Elfland School	Glenwood Dr.	N-1	C	44
+	Engleside Christian	Highland Ln.	K-12	C	46
b	Episcopal High	N. Quaker Ln.	9-12	C	46
	Grace Episcopal	Russell Rd.	N-5	C	70

Alexandria, Virginia (continued)

Name	Address	Grades	Sex	Page
+& Heritage Academy	May Blvd.	N-6	C	79
+ Immanuel Lutheran	Bellaire Rd.	K-6	C	87
⟋ Islamic Saudi Academy	Richmond Highway	K-12	C	89
& Leary School	Lincolnia Road	1-PG*	C	96
+ Montessori of Alex.	Florence Lane	N-6*	C	108
St. Stephen's/	St. Stephen's Rd.	9-12	C	150
St.Agnes	Fontain Street	K-8	C	150

Fairfax and Prince William Counties, Virginia

Name	Address	Grades	Sex	Page
& Accotink Academy	Springfield	K-PG*	C	2
+ Apple Tree School	Vienna/Fairfax	N-3	C	5
+& Bethleham Baptist	Fairfax	N-12	C	13
+ Brooksfield School	McLean	N-3*	C	19
Cardinal Montessori	Woodbridge	N-4	C	27
↯ Chesapeake Ability	Springfield	K-12*	C	30
Christian Assembly Acad	Vienna	K-8	C	34
+ Early Years Academy	Manassas	N-6	C	42
Edlin School	Oakton	K-8	C	43
+ Evangel Christian	Dale City	K-12	C	48
+ Fairfax Baptist Temple	Fairfax	K-12	C	49
+ Fairfax-Brewster	Baileys Crossrds.	N-6	C	49
+ Fairfax Christian	Vienna	N-12	C	50
+& Flint Hill	Oakton	K-12	C	53
+ Gesher Jewish Day	Fairfax	K-6	C	65
+ Green Hedges	Vienna	N-8	C	72
Immanuel Christian	Springfield	K-8	C	87
Islamic Saudi Academy	Fairfax	K-12	C	89
+ Kenwood/Grasshopper	Annandale	N-6	C	92
+ Langley School	McLean	N-8	C	95
+ Linton Hall	Bristow	K-8	C	99
b Madeira	McLean	9-12	G	101
Montessori of McLean	McLean	N-6*	C	109
+ Montessori of N. Va.	Annandale	N-4*	C	109
✦ New School of N. Va.	Fairfax	K-12*	C	116

for k 4 min page 55

Fairfax and Prince William Counties, Virginia (con't)

	Name	Address	Grades	Sex	Page
+	Nysmith School	Herndon	N-8	C	118
&	Oakwood School	Annandale	K-9*	C	120
&	Paul VI High School	Fairfax	9-12	C	127
	Pinecrest Primary	Annandale	N-3	C	128
	Potomac School	McLean	N-12	C	129
+	Reston Montessori	Reston	N-3*	C	132
+&	St. Luke's	McLean	K-8	C	147
	Seton Jr./Sr. High	Manassas	7-12	C	154
+	Springfield Academy	Springfield	N-3	C	158
+&	Sydenstricker	Springfield	N-2	C	161
+	Talent House	Fairfax	N-8	C	162
	Tara/Reston Christian	Reston	N-8	C	163
+	Town & Country Vienna	Vienna	N-3	C	165
	Trinity Christian	Fairfax	1-8	C	166
+	Vienna Jr. Academy	Vienna	K-11x	C	166
	Way of Faith Christian	Fairfax	N-12	C	172
	Westminster School	Annandale	K-8	C	173
+	Woodbridge Christian	Woodbridge	K-10x	C	176
+	Word of Life Academy	Springfield	N-12	C	177

Arlington & Falls Church, Virginia

	Name	Address	Grades	Sex	Page
	Bishop Denis O'Connell	Arlington	9-12	C	14
+	Cloverlawn Academy	Arlington	N-7	C	36
+	Congressional School	Falls Church	N-8	C	38
+	Early Years Montessori	Falls Church	N-3*	C	43
+	Fairfax Collegiate	Falls Church	5-8x	C	50
+	Falls Church Chldrn's House	Falls Church	N-2*	C	51
	Grace Lutheran	Falls Church	K-8	C	71
	Juniper Lane	Falls Church	N-3	C	91
	Montess. Sch. Holmes Run	Falls Church	N-6*	C	109
+	Our Savior Lutheran	Arlington	K-8	C	125
	Rivendell School	Arlington	K-8	C	132
+	St. Charles Elementary	Arlington	K-8	C	141
+	Teresa Home	Arlington	N-5	C	163

Loudon and Fauquier Counties, Virginia

	Name	Address	Grades	Sex	Page
	Blake Pre. School/Munger Acad.	Sterling	N-2x	C	16
+&	Faith Christian	Sterling	N-8	C	51
b	Foxcroft	Middleburg	9-PG	G	56
+	Highland School	Warrenton	K-8	C	79
	Hill School	Middleburg	K-8	C	81
	Leesburg Christian	Leesburg	N-12	C	97
+&	Loudoun Country Day	Leesburg	N-8	C	100
b	Notre Dame	Middleburg	9-12	C	118
b	Wakefield Country Day	The Plains	N-12	C	167

Other Area Schools

	Name	Address	Grades	Sex	Page
	Blue Ridge	Dyke, VA	9-12	B	17
+	Calverton	Huntingtown, MD.	N-12	C	24
b	Chatham Hall	Chatham, VA	9-12	G	28
b&	Christchurch	Christchurch, VA	9-PG	C	32
+	Christ Church Day School	La Plata, MD.	N-5	C	33
	Country Day School	Charles Town,W.VA	K-9	C	39
b	Fork Union Military Acad.	Fork Union, VA	6-PG	B	55
+b	Garrison Forest	Garrison, MD	N-12	G	61
b	George School	Newtown, PA	9-12	C	62
b	Grier School	Tyrone, PA	7-PG	G	73
b	Gunston School	Centerville, MD.	9-12	G	73
b	Hargrave Military Acad.	Chatham, VA	7-PG	C	75
b	Hill School	Pottstown, PA	8-PG	B	81
	Leonard Hall Jr. Naval Acad.	Leonardtown, MD	4-12x	C	97
	Lexington Park Christian	Lexington Park, MD	1-9	C	98
b&	Linden Hall School	Lititz, PA	6-PG	G	98
b	McDonogh	Pikesville, MD.	K-l2	C	105
b	Mercersburg	Mercersburg, PA.	9-PG	C	106
b&	Oakland	Boyd Tavern, VA.	3-10*	C	120
b	Oldfields	Glencoe, MD.	8-12	G	121
b	Phelps School	Malvern, PA	7-PG	B	127
+	Powhathan School	Boyce, VA.	K-8	C	129
b	Randolph Macon Acad.	Front Royal,VA	7-PG	C	132

Other Area Schools (continued)

	Name	Address	Grades	Sex	Page
b	St. Anne's Belfield	Charlottesville, VA	N-12	C	137
b+	St. Catherine's	Richmond, VA	N-12	G	141
b	St. James (near Hagerstown)	St. James, MD	7-12	C	143
b	St. Margaret's	Tappahanock, VA	8-12	G	147
	St. Mary's Ryken H.S.	Leonardtown, MD.	9-12	C	148
b	St. Timothy's	Stevenson, MD.	9-12	G	151
+	So. Maryland Christian Acad.	White Plains, MD	N-12	C	157
b	Stuart Hall	Staunton, VA.	6-12	G	160
	Waldorf Adventist	Waldoorf, MD	1-8	C	168
b&	West Nottingham	Colora, MD.	9-PG	C	173
b	Woodberry Forest	Woodberry, VA	9-12	B	175

Index to Educational Specialists

"How can I ensure that my child is getting the education he needs?"

The Certified Learning Centers can help your child achieve to his fullest potential. We provide educational services which supplement those provided by private and public educational systems. Our services are primarily directed toward remedial education, for regular students of all ages having difficulty in the educational mainstream, and toward serving students with special needs, such as the underachiever, the learning disabled and the gifted.

We offer many services including:

Educational Diagnostic and Psychological testing and counseling

Tutoring on all subjects (private and group)

Preparation courses for the SAT-I, PSAT, GMAT, NTE, LSAT, CAT, SSAT, GRE, MCAT, and many other popular achievement tests.

College counseling and assessments

Home-instruction support with High School or College credit awarded

Adult and ESOL education programs

Sessions are conveniently held in one of our three centers, at your home, or on campus at your school.

Certified Learning Centers, Inc.

Washington's Largest Full-Service Agency

301-774-3700

CENTERS IN SILVER SPRING, OLNEY AND BETHESDA

287 2700 Causley

Selecting The Right School For Your Child?

Our Experience Can Help You.

Georgia K. Irvin & Associates are independent educational consultants with over 20 years of experience in matching the individual needs of each child in the Washington, D.C., area and boarding schools nationwide. Our personal knowledge of the subtle differences between schools will help you identify programs that offer your child the greatest opportunities for success and happiness. Our experience will simplify the admissions process for you.

A nationally recognized educational consultant, Georgia Irvin is the former Director of Admissions of The Sidwell Friends School.

For a personal approach, sound advice and expert assistance, call (301) 951-0131 or gki@eworld•com.

GEORGIA K. IRVIN & ASSOCIATES
Educational Consultants - Nursery Through High School

4701 Willard Ave., Suite 227 • Chevy Chase MD 20815 • FAX 301-951-1024

Member Independent Educational Consultants Association.